An Act

Guide

# Getting Work

# An Actor's Guide to Getting Work

### Third Edition

## Simon Dunmore

A & C Black • London

Third edition published 2001
by A & C Black (Publishers) Limited
35 Bedford Row, London WC1R 4JH

ISBN 0-7136-5732-4

Second edition published 1996

First edition published 1991 by Macmillan Publishers Ltd

© 2001, 1996, 1991 Simon Dunmore

A CIP catalogue record for this book is available from the British Library.

Typeset in 10 on 11.5pt Sabon
Printed and bound in Great Britain by
Creative Print and Design (Wales), Ebbw Vale

'More than a practical guide through the terrors of the audition minefield, Mr Dunmore's book is so positive and encouraging in its approach that it must be essential reading for any young actor setting out on this perilous career.

If it's true that "Luck gets you there; talent keeps you there", then Mr Dunmore goes a long way towards explaining the mystery of "luck".'

Maggie Smith

# Contents

# Preface to the Third Edition

Several actors, agents and directors read early drafts of this book and made numerous helpful suggestions, most of which I incorporated into the final draft. There was one major criticism which I finally decided to reject: 'Directors do not seem to come out of this terribly well.' I do not exempt myself from what charitably might be called 'eccentric' behaviour in the casting process. I have made mistakes — some examples are cited in what follows — and I have watched other directors do likewise. To some extent this 'eccentricity' can be excused by the pressures on time that dominate our working lives. But not entirely. Like all human beings, directors have their prejudices. Much of the advice given in this book is how to avoid such prejudices being exercised so that you can get closer to the ideal — to be judged on the basis of your talent as an actor and not rejected on apparently unfair or irrational grounds.

I don't think it's just directors who 'do not come out of this terribly well'. Those who read the manuscript were amazed at how stupid some actors seem to have been. You, the actor, can be responsible for your failures through lack of attention to minor but important details which can colour our whole perception of you. Consider the following analogy. Once a production is designed and cast and the essential ideas behind it have been communicated properly to everyone involved, the creative part of the director's job is well on the way to being completed. What remain are the details. Those time-consuming details can make or break a production in the eyes of its audience. The same is true for an actor in quest of work in the eyes of the employment-brokers. You can help yourself by attention to peripheral details (for example, spelling and grammar in your letters) as well as to the central art of acting.

I've learned a lot more practical realities in the ten years since I wrote the first edition of this book. The intervening years have considerably sharpened my awareness of good (and bad) 'sales technique' — especially through my work with students. I've also had the chance to 'experiment' and refine my ideas. This third edition has also benefited from the facility to ask questions and debate issues over the Internet. I've made many new friends, with similar concerns, all over the UK and in North America — a number of whom have been extremely helpful.

There are numerous people whom I would like to thank for their contributions and comments. First, I must thank all the students, teachers, actors, directors, casting directors, agents and all the other 'professionals' I've ever met; you have each given something to this book. Second, a special thanks to the following who cheerfully allowed me to pick their brains: John Ainslie, Mark Allen, Pat Armitage, Iain Armstrong, Adele Bailey, Laurie Bates, Sophy Boreham, John Bowler, Carole Boyd, Chris Bramwell, Tracey Briggs, Robin Browne, Alex Caan, Amanda Caswell-Robinson, Jacquie Charlesworth, Mary Churchward, Roy Civil, Martin Cochrane, John Colclough, Ruth Cooper, Tim Crouch, Angus Deuchar, Alan Dunnett, Richard Evans, Nicky Furre, Marsha Gorbett, Louise Grainger, Tina Gray, Bob Hamlin, Vicky Hasted, Chris Hocking, Phillip Hoffman, Ed Hooks, Bill Hughes, Cameron Jack, Anna Koutelieri, Beccy Lamb, Sarah de Larrinaga, Iain Lauchlan, Steve Lawrence, Maggie Lloyd-Williams, Nichola McAuliffe, Peter McCarthy, Elizabeth McKechnie, Sally Marshall, Mike Maynard, Terry Meech, Peter Messaline, Richard Moore, Alex Nash, Tom Nordon, Pilar Orti, Mark Pitt, Fiona Power, Rachael Rena, Hannah Rothman, Denni Sayers, Nigel Seale, Andrew Sharp, Nik Simmonds, Guy Slater, Sharon Small, Amy Stoller, Alison Taffs, Barbara Thompson, Jude Tisdall, Chris Wallis, Malcolm Ward, Eric Watson, Liz Whiting, Tana Wolf, Peter Yapp and Lesley Young. Third, similar thanks to those who contributed but preferred their input to remain confidential. Fourth, enormous thanks to the following who not only gave me insights but whose especial contribution deserves separate mention: Tim Bentinck, Don Gilét, Wyn Jones, Stephanie Pack and Michael Tucker. Fifth, apologies and many thanks to anybody I've inadvertently missed out of these credits. Sixth, many thanks to my original editor, Susanna Wadeson, for the wonderful final coat of clarity she gave to my first manuscript and to Dame Maggie Smith for her generous endorsement.

I'd also like to remember two actors especially, who not only helped me, but also cared deeply about the profession: Bert Parnaby and Nicholas Geake. Bert, in his guise as a senior inspector of education, was a towering support to the Theatre-in-Education movement in the 1970s and latterly (in his retirement job as an actor) gave me useful insights for this book. Nick read the final draft of the first edition; his only comment was 'This is what has taken me nearly twenty years to learn.'

Finally, I am indebted to my wife, Maev Alexander, who not only contributed to the content but also read every draft and told me when I wasn't being clear and gave me 'house-room' for my many hours at the computer.

# Introduction

I have spent over thirty years directing all kinds of productions. In the course of this career I have met many thousands of actors, read tens of thousands of letters and CVs, looked at a similar number of photographs, and my right ear is permanently flattened by all those telephone calls. I have deposited a forest load of paper into the bin and felt guilty about the time wasted and money spent by the people I didn't even interview, let alone employ.

There are so many letters from individual actors and suggestions from agents to consider for each production that there simply isn't time to give each one much more than a cursory skim in the initial weeding-out process. Anybody attempting to read each and every letter and CV and looked at each photo with the full care and attention that its creator deserves would not have enough time left to interview any actors at all. I do not exaggerate.

Directors could probably cast most of their productions from actors they already know, so why should we use up valuable time in the highly inexact process of auditions? Isn't there a better way of doing it? Some directors do cast almost entirely from people they know; it saves time, stress and money. I often cast from people I already know, but believe that the best and most creative chemistry is achieved by a company made up of a vital mixture of those I've worked with before and those new to me. And, yes, there is a better way of casting the unknown actor than just on the basis of a speech or reading. It is by looking at every observable aspect of that actor: the letter and CV, how I get on with them in the interview, and what results if I choose to work on their speech or reading. Mine is a kind of overall-assessment approach to casting. Colleagues have similar approaches, and there are also those who unconsciously (sometimes consciously) make instant judgements — positive and negative — on the basis of one audition speech or reading, even a single photograph or the impression created in the first ten seconds of meeting — the 'Wham! Bam! Thank you, ma'am!' method. Every detail of every aspect in your search for work can be vital. You have to think about every area and be prepared for anything.

Not every director likes every actor, and vice versa. Everyone perceives things differently. Everyone has blind spots and seemingly irrational prejudices; that's only human. There are all kinds of peculiar reasons for liking or not liking people or thinking they have or haven't any talent. There is no absolute measure of talent. In fact talent is beyond any explanation or measurement, and an actor's talent, or lack of it, can vary considerably in the eyes of different beholders. Of course there will often be a consensus of opinion, but rarely, if ever, is that judgement unanimous. This may seem obvious, but many actors do not seem to realise how incredibly widely directors' opinions vary. Each of us has to draw up our own personal parameters in order to make our own judgements and, crucially, we have very little information on which to do it. A letter, a CV, a photograph and a short interview/audition: it's not much evidence on which to commit yourself to several weeks of close — even intimate — working relations. But that's the way we have to do it because of lack of time and money.

No other profession requires individuals to write so many letters and go to so many interviews to sell themselves so much and so often. Nobody else suffers rejection as frequently as actors; it is part of an actor's life to be continually let down. Too many of you complain about how unfair it all is, the difficulty in writing a good letter, interview nerves, the artificiality of audition speeches and readings. Yes, there is something inherently unsatisfactory about the whole process, but it is all we have, so you have got to find ways of working through it. You didn't train as an actor just to perform. You learnt an awful lot of personal presentation skills along the way. Use them! Why should it be so much more difficult when you are not on stage? Your life and soul will go into the creation of a part. You have to do the same thing to create the opportunities to get the job of playing that part. You have to develop the skills of selling yourself on paper and in person — and, some time in the future, via the Internet.

Careful consideration of every element is an investment in your future. With so many actors available and so few jobs going any little thing can count against (or for) you. I am constantly amazed at how careless so many actors are with the details of their selling processes. A perfect analogy would be actors only learning the lines that they like. You will have to work even harder at getting the work than at doing it. Only the famous few can sit back and wait for the offers to come pouring in, and most of them had to work hard at getting jobs to start with. Talent is only part of what's necessary to be an actor; self-discipline and sales technique are also vital to success.

You have to recognise that as an actor you are not master of your own fate, you are at the end of the creative chain; almost everything else has been worked out before you're even thought about. I'll never forget overhearing a man on a mobile phone say, 'All we have to do now is find some actors.'

You have to be a survivor. You have to recognise the fickle nature of the whole business of casting — its short-term memory (long for miscreants) and its frequent ability to seem almost inhuman. You must keep up the need to work and believe in yourself or you won't survive.

On the outside you have to acquire a durable veneer of resilient rubber to cope with the constant rejections and bounce back every time. You will be knocked down many, many more times than you are picked up. On the inside you must keep all the sensitivity that is fundamental to the job of acting. No other profession relies so much on its practitioners' ability to use the painful and difficult parts of their personalities to work in it. As an actor you need to be vulnerable; as a salesman for yourself you need to be invulnerable. You also have to be organised — ready for the unexpected at any time. 'Chance favours the prepared mind' (Louis Pasteur). And you have to be mentally prepared for the 'unexpected' not to happen for some time.

In the ten years since this book was first published I have received letters (and more recently, e-mails) and verbal comments from many, varied people — largely, favourable. Mark Pitt (an actor then totally unknown to me) — made a very interesting point for which I am extremely grateful:

> 'I think it would be worthwhile pointing out the "taste" factor. What I have established in my short time as an actor is that there is no accounting for it...'

I think that Mark is right, a lot does come down to 'taste', but I believe that this is inherent to the subtext of the book — I simply don't use the word. Why do I find the need to comment on it? It's a very useful concept to carry around in your sub-consciousness as you graft through all the processes of getting work. There's no way that you can be 'all things to all men' (you'd end up a complete spiritless creep) but you should develop the art of encompassing as many 'tastes' as possible along the way. Surely, this is at the centre of the art of acting: getting inside the skins of people different from yourself.

The extensive research I did for this book made me look very hard into the ways I made my professional decisions. Many people have asked me how I now 'feel' when reading letters and interviewing people, and so on — armed with this far deeper understanding of the 'psychology' of my own decision-making processes? Sadly, too many actors still make the kind of mistakes I point out. I think I have become better at seeing the real person behind them, but the very fact that mistakes are still being made inevitably biases me in the process of offering the little work I have. I feel sorry for these erring actors — I'm sorely tempted to offer them advice, even recommend they buy the book, but my professional discipline insists that I do neither. My job in these contexts is to judge whether these actors are right for what I'm doing, not to give them career advice. I do that when friends ask and when I'm employed to do it. The other thing I find is that the whole process is even harder for me, just as many experienced actors maintain that acting gets harder the longer they do it. However, I am certainly proud of one piece of casting that started with a terrible letter, a nigh-on unreadable CV and an incredibly toffee-nosed looking photograph. That actor very nearly got removed from the interview process in the first weed-through of the paperwork, but he turned out to be wonderful.

Finally, the advice that follows is not a 'philosopher's stone' for success. You should take what you need, use your instincts and use it in your own way.

# Chapter One

## *For Aspiring Actors*

People who aspire to become professional actors are of all ages and backgrounds, ranging from those still in primary education to those who have held steady jobs for decades but still have yearnings for the profession. Each group of people has different things to consider, so I will deal with them in chronological order.

### Those of school age
The performer is in most young children. (The onset of puberty, and the awful consciousness of self that this brings, eliminates many.) For those wedded to the idea, remember that it is one thing to perform in front of people you know, very much another to do it before those you don't.

So what is the best course for the child who won't let go of the idea of being a professional actor? There are numerous stage schools for children which provide not just training but also the minimum education required by the State. However, these are expensive and it is virtually impossible to get a grant for one. Such schools are often allied to agencies which provide children for television series, films and major theatre productions, but it is a fact that many child stars do not succeed as adult actors. There are notable exceptions — Nicholas Lyndhurst, Dennis Waterman and Jenny Agutter, for instance — but they are the exceptions that prove the rule. I also wonder whether a childhood devoted to performing is entirely healthy — what about learning about life?

Generally the best thing for the stage-struck child is to send him or her to one of the numerous youth theatre groups and drama workshops that exist in almost every town and city. Play production is often the last priority of such groups — especially for the younger ages — but a terrific amount can be learnt by the young from what seem like simple make-believe games. Children in such groups won't learn many of the technical skills necessary to acting but they will learn a lot of important social skills and the fundamental business of 'interacting' that is so important to an acting ensemble: that it's not just what you can create that matters, it's what you can create with other people.

Many managements choose to use the freshness and spontaneity of untrained talent for their productions. They will audition hopefuls but not always through public advertisement; usually they directly approach appropriate youth theatres or conventional schools with strong drama departments.

**Drama/Theatre Studies exams** Whilst success in these can lead on to a university course they are not necessarily a good idea for a genuinely aspiring actor. Although they contain some practical content, they are predominately theoretical — and this concentration on looking from the outside can be very confusing for someone going on to 'do' acting with its concentration on working from the inside. (They also don't teach important acting techniques like how to breathe properly.) The study of alternative subjects can be more beneficial in the long term because they can broaden the student's horizons in finding alternative work when not acting. (Also see 'University drama and theatre studies degree courses', page 17.)

**Other early training** Elocution lessons may enable someone to speak 'beautifully' but they can be damaging to a future actor as their method is directed towards recitation of words with little account of the feelings behind them. Correction of a speech defect is better done by a qualified therapist. The well-established 'Speech and Drama' examinations tend to have very little to do with modern acting. These, as one drama school maintains in its prospectus, are 'judged on entirely different criteria' from those for entry to full-time training.

## School-leavers

It is essential to get a proper training! It used to be possible to become an actor without formal training — and why not? An awful lot of what is fundamental to acting is that indefinable instinctive something which you either have or have not. In the past, doing menial tasks and watching the professionals at work could teach aspirants all they needed. But nowadays getting started without formal training is virtually impossible for the school-leaver. That is not to say that it is not worth getting work experience in order to observe and learn from others; that experience can be very valuable for the future. (See 'It's different in the real world', page 25.)

## The mature entrant to the profession

If you are one of these, you have far more going for you than your younger counterpart, whether you trained in your youth or not. (If you did, then see 'Returning to the profession', page 7.) This is principally because professionals of your age, if you are over thirty, are fewer on the ground (many drop out in their first decade for financial and domestic reasons) and those that are around tend to become more choosy about what work they will accept. Therefore, there is not quite as much competition and it is easier to find those small parts that are the essential first step in an acting career. Also, there is great value in having life experience before training, which brings me to the primary question:

**To train or not to train?** Most of the actors I know who have successfully made the transition from a 'conventional' career to one in acting have been to drama school. Often they've found it difficult to adjust to the 'school' disciplines after so long. Many have also found the immaturity of their fellow-students hard to cope with for the first few months. However, through patience and by standing back from the herd and ignoring any 'ageist' attitudes, they have found their respective niches and have often got a lot more out of the training than the younger students. As a mature student you should have a much better idea of how to learn, how to organise your life and how to sell yourself.

Incidentally, I've met several people who've gone to drama school in their 40s and even one who started her training at the age of 59. It's never too late, but some drama schools do have upper age limits — I think they're wrong. If you're not sure that full-time student life would suit you then try a part-time course, but you'll find it much harder to crack the nut of gaining a toe-hold in the profession as it is generally the full-time schools where agents and casting directors search out new talents.

**Former dancers** It is a common phenomenon for 'maturing' dancers — as their bodies decrease in flexibility — to wish to continue performing, albeit less athletically. It is essential to get proper acting-training — you have got to unlearn those bodily positions which 'people do not use in real life', let alone learn how to use your voice properly.

**The amateur theatre as a training ground** Some people think they know it all through amateur work. This is almost invariably untrue. I am not saying that all amateur theatre is bad (or that all professional theatre is good), but there are numerous techniques and professional practices which amateur theatre cannot teach you. For example, rehearsing a play for three evenings a week for three months requires a completely different discipline from rehearsing five or six days a week for three weeks before opening. Performing the same role for three weeks or more (even for several years) requires much more stamina and technical skill than the four or five performances which are the norm of amateur theatre. Amateur actors must find out what further training they need — and can get — and do the drama-school round just like the school-leaver.

**Returning to the profession** Many people trained in their youth but had to give it up when domestic obligations took priority. After years, suddenly these obligations disappear: children have grown up, a spouse or an aged parent who needed care has died... Going back into the profession becomes a real possibility.

If this is your position, you should still have the basic technical equipment that your drama school taught you. But times and fashions change. No, Stanislavski has not been discredited — the fundamentals have not changed — but he has been significantly refined. Some revitalising classes are a good idea.

## Training courses

If you want to be a professional actor you have to have proper training at a drama school. (Most won't admit you until you are eighteen.) You should obtain prospectuses and see which ones you think might suit you best. Audition procedures vary and you will have to pay for the privilege — around £30 for each school as of Autumn 2000. The chief things to remember are that it costs money to attend auditions — travel and fees — and that competition is extremely fierce. Figures vary, but only a tiny percentage of applicants actually get accepted into the principal drama schools.

**The drama schools** At the moment, there is a core of established schools who belong to an organisation called The Conference of Drama Schools (CDS). Most of these run courses that are 'accredited' by The National Council for Drama Training (NCDT), which was established in the mid 1970s to monitor standards. This organisation assesses courses every few years and decides whether each is up to a sufficient standard — a process called 'accreditation'. (The schools themselves are not 'accredited', it's their individual courses: there are schools outside the CDS which have courses with 'accreditation' and there are courses in CDS schools that are not 'accredited'.) Essentially, it is better to get on to an 'accredited' course. There are two reasons for this (apart from the obvious one of checks being made): (a) you will stand a much better chance of getting funding than you would for a 'non-accredited' one and (b) directors, agents and casting directors are far more inclined to look at graduates of 'accredited' courses.

A complete list of CDS courses, called *The UK Guide to Drama Training*, is available from Westlake Publishing Ltd., 17 Sturton Street, Cambridge, CB1 2SN; (01223) 566763; e-mail: info@datalake.com. You can also access all the CDS's member schools websites via <www.drama.ac.uk>; other schools advertise in *The Stage* and can be found via the NCDT's website at <www.ncdt.co.uk>.

**Length of training** For the school-leaver there's no question that three years is essential. (I would advocate a year out before starting training — simply to gain some 'life-experience' away from educational institutions.) Most mature students seem to go for a one-year training, but from my observations that is usually not sufficient. Of course, most will be funding themselves and one year is significantly cheaper than three, but I would like to see more 'accredited' two-year courses for mature students. (There are currently only three to my knowledge.) While these are still lacking I don't think that there's any question that three years is much, much better than one for the vast majority.

**Degrees** The other complication nowadays is that some 'accredited' courses have 'degree' status. This used to mean that if you got a place you could be entitled to a 'mandatory' grant from your local education authority; non-degree courses were only eligible for 'discretionary' grants. The way that students are funded was completely changed in the Autumn of 1999 (See 'Funding your training', page 14), but over half the 'accredited' courses maintained their degree status. Degree status means very little in the profession and courses with degree status are not necessarily better than those without it. A number of schools have been quite vociferous about not wishing to become embroiled in the whole philosophy and bureaucracy that is fundamental to 'degree' education — believing that joining with a university would compromise the purely vocational character of their courses. (One such adds: 'Universities are academic institutions and the intelligence required of an academic is different to that required of an actor. Whilst some are blessed with both kinds, many talented and intelligent actors are of indifferent academic ability. We would not wish to exclude them.') However degree status will enable you to go on to a higher degree and enhance your employment prospects outside the profession.

**Where to apply?** It is well worth obtaining the prospectuses of as many drama schools as possible to see which ones might suit you. Seek advice from drama teachers, youth theatre leaders, drama advisers and anybody you can find who knows about the profession. (The 'theatre' and 'acting' newsgroups on the Internet can also be useful places to ask for opinion on specific schools.) But never rely on the word of just one person — get a consensus of opinion. It has become very clear to me that standards have dropped considerably in one CDS school over the past few years and risen dramatically in another over a similar period. I am not going to name names, because the position could easily reverse itself over a similar period in the future. The only way to find out is to talk to a number of people. The best advice will come from those with recent contact with drama schools, not from those who trained decades ago and have no idea of current trends in those establishments. A drama school is only as good as its current teachers. A list of famous graduates (and/or patrons) or a glossy prospectus with smart graphics doesn't tell you what it's really like now. It is also wise to be cautious if you encounter an overuse of names like Stanislavski and terms like 'The Method' — both have been considerably refined for today's actors. There is no one absolute 'system' of good acting; 'You act how *you* act.' as a friend expressed it.

NB Largely ignore public statements made by famous actors about their training (positive and negative) — things will have invariably changed since they left.

**Don't apply to just one school!** Unlike almost every other form of further or higher education there are almost always no recognised qualifications for an applicant trying to gain entry to drama school. The decision on whether to accept you or not is based on what you can do in audition, not on what you've done before. (Although some 'degree' drama school courses also require certain exam passes.) Of course, someone who has had good tuition from school, Youth Theatre, and so on, stands a better chance; but that 'good tuition' is not nationally regulated and is available only randomly around the country. Also, you may well never have auditioned before in your life and all the practical experience of auditioning you can get will help. Apply to as many schools that you feel 'suit you' as you can afford.

**Application deadlines** You need to check these for each school. Some — generally the more prestigious one — have application deadlines of around March 31st each year; at least one only sees the first seven hundred applicants and others see people all year round. It is also important to check with each school if there's a deadline for application for funding (see 'Funding your training', page 14). Check the deadlines of every school you intend to apply for about a year before you'd like to start your course.

Once you've sent off your applications you can be called to audition at any time — have your speeches (and, if necessary, songs) prepared in advance of sending off those forms.
NB Some 'accredited' courses with degree status require applications via UCAS; some don't seem to be on UCAS lists — I don't know why.

**Audition requirements and formats** These vary from school to school, and you will be told beforehand what they want you to do — in varying degrees of detail. You may have to do movement and voice classes, do some improvisations, sing a song you've prepared; you may be auditioning with a number of other people or you could be on your own. What you will definitely be asked is to prepare at least two audition speeches — often one 'classical' and one 'modern' (see 'Modern' and 'Classical' (and 'Period'), page 127). However, check the audition requirements carefully. A few schools ask for three speeches, some give you a set list of 'classical' speeches to choose from, some ask for just two 'moderns' and one used to have a list of speeches (and complete plays) not to use — they'd become fed up with hearing them.

Most schools specify a maximum length of speech, whether the classical should be in verse, and so on — check each school's specifications very carefully.

**Preparing your speeches** You'll find plenty of advice on this in chapter 13, but one fault I have too often observed in drama school auditions is an over-concentration on getting the lines right so that they come out parrot fashion — with no sense of a 'real' person saying them. I suspect this is because they've focused on learning those lines off by heart — with only scant attention to the details of what the character is thinking and feeling. You should think of characters in plays as real people, and that people say things because they have a 'need' to do so. You should study each speech (and the play it's from) and work on the character's thoughts and feelings without learning a line. If you do this over a period of time, you'll gradually find that you learn the lines naturally, by absorption — even with a Shakespeare speech.

**Somebody to help** Several schools counsel against this and I have seen numerous circumstances when the outside help was downright misleading. There seems to be a cottage industry out there of people happy to take your money for their guidance. How do you know if you're being helped properly? In general, it is best to find someone who has close contact with the profession (and/or drama schools) and not someone whose experience is concentrated in speech and drama exams. If you can't find anybody whom you feel is suitable, then at least try your speeches out in front of somebody you trust, first. They may not be able to give you detailed constructive criticism but at least you'll get a gut reaction and doing a speech in front of even just one person is very different from doing it by yourself.

**'Drying'** It doesn't matter if you forget your lines — 'dry'. Drama school auditions are not memory tests. If the words temporarily disappear from your mind, just stop and go inside yourself (perhaps by lowering your eyes) and calmly think back to what your character has just said. If this fails, simply say something like, 'I'll start again,' and do just that after a suitable recovery period and proper re-immersion into your character. Full immersion inside your character and his or her situation is far more important than remembering the lines properly.

**Arrangements** It is important to be relaxed for your audition. Apart from proper preparation of your speeches, it is essential that you are organised — appropriate clothes, travel arrangements and over-night accommodation (if necessary). If the date and time offered is awkward, then contact the school to change it as soon as possible — most schools are flexible if you give them sufficient notice. Don't leave it until the last moment except in extreme circumstances. If you are perceived to be disorganised — even at this early stage — it could well count against you in the highly competitive audition system.

**Nerves** There is one extra factor that is important to bear in mind: nerves! After all, auditioning is a very strange idea to those not used to it. In my experience the most overtly nervous people are those auditioning for drama school. Too often desperation takes over and all that careful preparation flies out the window, leaving a shuddering wreck trying to spit out lines that seem meaningless. Audition speeches are harder because you are all on your own with no support from anyone else. Added to that, you will be in a strange place with strange people who won't smile very much and will spend a lot of time writing notes and not looking at you — apparently not a very sympathetic audience. In fact they are concentrating on you very hard and wanting you to succeed.

It is not wrong to be nervous. A calm actor will often give a boring performance. However, when your nerves become too disordered and chaotic your whole concentration goes and your limbs become numb. You have to find a way of focusing your nervous energy on your speech and not on the fact that the tension is growing. Tension, once you are aware of it, can escalate out of control very quickly. Don't even begin to contemplate it. Do something else! For instance, actors, whilst waiting in the wings on a first night, will often jump around and wave their arms about to get the blood circulating and counteract the terrible numbing effect that nervous tension can bring.

Other 'tricks' are to imagine that you are doing your speech at home in front of your friends or that the whole audition panel is sitting there stark naked. You have to discover what suits you and your nervous system. Remember also that you know something that your auditioners do not in your individual interpretation of your speeches. Focus your nerves on that advantage and don't let your 'need' to become an actor turn into a numbing chaos of nervous desperation. Above all, aim to enjoy performing your speeches (whether comic or tragic) and try not to think of it all as an examination.

If these ideas aren't good enough for you try some 'Alexander Technique' classes — these should do the trick.

**Recalls** Most schools operate recall systems, that is at least one extra session in which you will have to display your speech(es) again — and possibly a variety of other aspects of your talents. Different schools have different methodologies, but the one thing they have in common is that you will be seen by many more people than in the first round. You should aim to communicate to them all in spite of the fact that some of them don't speak to you.

The other factor to bear in mind is that the gap between first audition and final acceptance can vary between a few hours and six months.

**The interview** What has an interview to do with your acting ability? It gives your auditioners a chance to assess your attitude. They have got to feel sure that you can make a positive contribution to the school. I've seen a significant minority of applicants fail because they are persistently negative in interviews. However well your speeches go, negativity can knock you out of the running, because nobody wants negative influences round a close-knit community like a drama school.

There are certain standard questions which are worth thinking about beforehand. They are variations on: 'Why do you want to be an actor', 'Who's your favourite actor — and why?', 'What productions have you seen recently?', 'What other drama schools are you applying to?', and so on. Don't prepare scripted answers, just think about how you might respond to these kinds of questions.

NB Sometimes interviews don't take place until a recall stage, sometimes it'll be someone other than your auditioner(s) who'll interview you and sometimes you'll be interviewed more than once.

**'Any place is better than no place at all' or 'spoilt for choice'** In spite of the 'accreditation' system some schools are quite frankly a waste of time and money. The libel laws prevent me from naming such schools and the standards in all schools will vary as teachers and other circumstances change. (See 'Where to apply?', page 9.) Before accepting a place find out what you can about a school — ask around. And if you find too much inauspicious information about the school's current state, then consider auditioning elsewhere.

If you are lucky enough to be offered several places, consider carefully which will be the best school for you. Again, you have to ask around. Go and see productions, hover in the bar to pick up vibes, try to talk with current students, even ask if you can watch classes at each school. Look again at what each says about its training methods: is their entire focus on theatre, do they have radio and television classes, and so on? You should also balance up the relative prestige of each school. Those higher up the scale will attract more prestigious professionals to final productions and showcases.

## If you don't get a place

No drama school, to my knowledge, will tell you why they rejected you. If they did it for one person, they would have to do it for everybody and that would take more time than they can afford. Specific explanations are usually far too complex to be communicated briefly.

For those who don't succeed the first time round in getting a place there are several things to consider:

**Rejection** This is a fundamental part of an actor's life, and the worst thing you can do is to feel that this is the end of any possibility of being an actor. If you are determined, then you must go on and try again, and again, and... I've known lots of aspirants who have had to spend two or three years auditioning before gaining places — and one who took seven years.

Each drama school, like each professional employer, has different views on what it looks for in a student. If one doesn't think you have potential, another may disagree. Principally, try to learn from each experience without drowning yourself in a sea of regret at what you might or should have done. Try to learn from your rejection(s). Discuss them with someone you trust; it is all useful for the next occasion. Determination and persistence are prerequisites for being a professional actor.

**Do something else first** This has two advantages: (1) You can gain some valuable 'life experience' essential to the actor's craft, (I was not sympathetic to the third-year acting student who explained his failure over a particular part with 'I've no real emotional experience to take from'). (2) You could start to gain insights into the other job you are going to do to earn a living in those inevitable periods of being out of work. (That dreadful euphemism 'resting' is completely misplaced; I would personally like to strangle whoever invented it.)

## Funding your training

As soon as you start applying for drama school, also start looking into this. Fees vary, but as of Autumn 2000 they are up to £3,000 a term — that's £27,000 for a three-year course. (Some schools are cheaper than this because they have other funding or because their fixed costs are lower.) On top of that you've got to find the money for accommodation, food, transport, equipment, books, and so on — all of which could come to another £20,000 over three years.

**Dance and Drama Awards (DaDA)** The introduction of this scheme has dramatically improved the funding situation. The old 'discretionary' grant system meant that it depended upon where you lived as to whether you had a chance of getting a Local Authority grant. This inequity has now largely disappeared. However, because of the ways individual schools sought to get round these problems in the 'discretionary' grant days (by acquiring degree status, for instance) the DaDA scheme works differently in different schools. Also, currently some schools are not included and some students are funded like those on conventional degree courses. The scheme is in its infancy and it has been recognised that it does not yet 'allow the maximum number of the most talented students to attend the best schools'. However, these awards do mean that there is some more money for training and a recognition (from government) that the performing arts are a vital part of the UK economy and our image abroad. It will continue to be tough to get funding, because there persists (in some minds) a belief that acting and the other arts do not constitute 'proper' work.

In the long term, it is hoped that further improvements will be made. In the short term, it is essential that you ask each school to which you are applying about their particular funding arrangements (including whether, or not, you would be eligible for a student loan to cover maintenance costs) — and study them carefully to see what action you might need to take. Check the NCDT's website for developments in the scheme (<www.ncdt.co.uk>).

NB A curious phenomenon of the current DaDA scheme is that you can still be eligible for funding even if you have already done a degree course — and vice versa.

**Other funding** Even if you do get a place and a DaDA (for instance), it is almost certain that you will have to find some of the money for yourself. In the first instance it is important to talk to the administrator or registrar of that drama school; if anybody can help, they can. Some have acquired a great deal of expertise in helping students find some of their funding. In addition some drama schools have scholarships to be won, there are a few nationally awarded bursaries for drama students and there are charities which can be tapped. (It is important to note that almost none of these will cover the full costs of an entire course.) The other obvious thing to do is to write to famous actors — and many have been very generous over the years. However, this area of support seems to be becoming saturated and it can be a better idea to look for local individuals and businesses who might be persuaded to support a future 'star'. In short, guided by your drama school you need to explore every possible funding avenue — in good time before you start your course. (Given the column-inches devoted to actors in the 'small' papers, I suggest that they should give scholarships to generate future front-page material. I also think that the television companies should contribute to actor training.)

The other possibility is to find part-time work to pay your way through. However, you must ensure that that work is flexible enough to fit in with the school's long and varying hours, and that you will not be so exhausted from work or training that you are unable to do either properly.

Getting funding still has its anomalies and unfairnesses, and talent is only part of the requirements. You have to be determined; don't be put off at this early 'fence'.

**Preparations** It is important to prepare the ground for your fund-raising tactics early — it's a time-consuming process.

1 Make lists of everybody who might be sympathetic (school-friends, family-friends and any other good contact you may have made) — even if they can't help financially, they might be able to put you onto someone who could.

2  Make lists of charities who might help — your local library will have directories that list thousands of them. It is important to check (a) whether each charity will fund a vocational acting training and (b) that there are no restrictions (where you live, for instance) that would rule you out.

3  Prepare the letters you are going to send. These could contain your connection to the recipient, a brief explanation of what you want to do (and why) and what they might get in return — a quarterly newsletter, for instance.

4  Prepare the material that you are going to send out with your letters. For instance, a printed leaflet with photos, reviews, character references, messages of support, fees, living expenses — anything that could further your cause. It should all be clearly expressed and well laid-out, and the end result should not look too glossy (you're short of money, remember) — also see chapter 9 for further thoughts on promoting yourself on paper.

5  Open a separate bank account for the money you receive and keep accurate records.

*Notes*

a  Don't treat 3 and 4 above as a mathematical formula. There are many variations and if any potential donor starts receiving similar format appeals, he or she might start looking elsewhere to spread their generosity.

b  Always say 'Thank you' — even for a small donation. Not only is this a common courtesy, but neglecting to do so could 'queer your pitch' (and that of others) on a wider field than you might imagine — you'd be surprised at who knows who, who knows who, who...

c  It is essential that you are not seen to 'fritter' any money you receive — the consequences could be far worse than the above. I know of a student who gambled the thousands from one funder in an attempt to improve his situation further. He lost — his place and his school's reputation with that particular funder.

If you prepare all this in parallel with doing the audition-round, you'll be up and running with your mail-out immediately you're offered your place.

**Tactics**  Some of the most successful fund-raisers that I've known have helped their causes through activities using their acting skills for the benefit of others. For instance, I know someone who set up and organised her own youth company as a public relations exercise (touring old folks' homes and hospitals). It was so successful that she got financial support from several local businesses and a significant (and unexpected) bequest from someone in one of her audiences. Previously she'd written lots of letters asking for help and received very few replies, let alone any money. So she deferred her place for a year (not all drama schools will allow you to do this; some insist that you audition all over again) and worked at doing something positive rather than write 'yet more whinging letters'.

## Other training

Nowadays, it's increasingly difficult to progress without doing at least a year at drama school. However, there are courses which can help you on your way.

**Part-time courses** There are numerous part-time courses, a few of which are run by CDS drama schools. They cannot be seen as a complete training, they can only really touch the tip of the iceberg — however, they are a good grounding for those who want to go on to a full-time training.

There are also 'non-accredited' drama schools that are completely geared to part-time training whilst you continue to earn a living at a non-acting job. These are a viable, but much more difficult way into the profession. You'll be working during the day and training for much of the rest of the time — you've got to be extremely fit, disciplined, organised and be prepared to all-but give up your social life for a while. At the moment, they don't have very much credibility within the profession, but there are a couple that are gradually gathering reputations; with continuing funding problems, more may come along and the whole idea receive the validation of the profession.

Unfortunately, the vast majority of these courses are concentrated in London.

**University drama and theatre studies degree courses** If you've got the exam results there is always the possibility of one of these. However, a university drama degree is no longer a passport into the profession. It used to be the case that any degree from some of the more prestigious universities made potential employers look several times at a CV, but this is generally no longer true. Nowadays a degree, even one in drama, is largely not regarded as any kind of qualification for an actor, because the actual acting training is only part of the course and, generally, is inadequate. (Some of them specifically state that they are not training you for the profession. One senior university lecturer told me that his department wouldn't even interview anybody who said that they 'wanted to be an actor' in their personal statement.) Today's graduate should try to get a place on an 'accredited' postgraduate course (preferably a two-year one). These tend to be extremely hard work as they usually embrace much of what is contained in the full three-year courses.

## Some fundamental considerations

If you enjoy acting and feel the need to take it up professionally, there are several other crucial things, apart from training, to consider.

1 Will you be able to cope with having a fluctuating income which, unless you are extremely lucky, will probably be less than the 'average industrial wage'? A recent survey revealed that only 10% of actors earned more than that statistical average and two-thirds earned less than £5000 a year from acting, that is, roughly 25% of the current 'average industrial wage'.

2 Are you prepared to work unsociable hours and stay away from home for much of your working life?

3 Are you prepared to pay higher insurance premiums, be refused credit, and generally be regarded as unreliable and disorganised? I know that this is grotesquely unfair — actors have to adhere to the most incredible disciplines in their work — but that attitude is a fact of our working lives.

4 Are you able to keep sufficiently fit in mind and body in order to work? Essentially there is no time available for you to miss any rehearsals except under extreme circumstances, and only the bigger productions can afford the luxury of understudies during performance. In television, film and radio the days for recording are set far in advance, and any absenteeism will cause an earthquake of disorganisation. A reputation for absenteeism, however reasonable the causes, will count significantly against you in the jobs market.

5 Do you have the personality to go out and sell yourself to other people — possibly several times a week?

6 Can you organise the funds to pay for all the 'equipment' necessary to start out on an acting career? (See 'An actor's start-up kit', page 29.) I estimate that you'll need at the very least £500 for these essential items before you start earning any money from acting. This figure can easily double, if not quadruple, if you have to spend money on 'basics' like having a telephone line installed, for instance.

7 Are you aware that being an actor can seriously change your life? That perhaps should have read: 'As an actor it is difficult to be a normal human being.' But perhaps that's part of the reason you want to be an actor — because you don't want to be 'Mr/Ms/Mrs Normal'. It is a gypsy life — and like that minority you will be persecuted with lack of understanding from non-actors and by constant rejections. Being an actor puts a terrific mental and physical strain on you and your family and friends with its extremes of ups and downs. Your life will never be regular and ordered. Sometimes you will be on 'Cloud Nine', at others you will be deeply frightened and lonely as the months of unemployment seem to drag on for ever. If you really feel that you will be able to cope with such extremes of emotional temperature then perhaps you have the chemistry that can make you a professional actor.

## Early preparations

If you are thinking about becoming an actor, read plays and read about acting (I have listed a number of suitable books in the Bibliography). Don't just read books; they can't give you up-to-date trends and happenings. Read *The Stage* (published every Thursday) for information, and publications like *Theatre Record* for critical comment. Compare what they say with your own views. Ask other people what they think and, above all, watch acting critically. Examine television, theatre and films — don't just sit back and watch them mindlessly. Constructively criticise what you see. It is no use just saying you didn't like a production or an individual performance — work out why for your own future use.

If you want to be an actor in order 'to get up late and do funny walks in the evening' (Dan Leno) and lead a glamorous life, forget it. It's much, much harder work than is generally realised. On the positive side actors are usually amongst the kindest, warmest and most helpful of people. Cheap fiction (including the tabloid newspapers) will have you believe that the profession is riddled with vice and back-stabbing. This may be true amongst a small band of publicity-seekers, but it is not true of over 99% of this profession. You may be 'down' and out of work, but you will always find a friend.

# Chapter Two

# *For Acting Students*

You've got over the first big hurdle — getting a place (and funding it). Your focus will be on classes and productions (initially internal ones), but there are many other things you should start thinking about and preparing for.

## Being at drama school

Drama school training is incredibly demanding — physically, mentally and emotionally. The hours you spend in classes and rehearsals are much, much longer than those of your contemporaries studying other disciplines. You won't have nearly the same amount of written work to do, but you'll still need to do a huge amount of 'homework' if you're to make the most of your hard-won training. (There is more written work attached to the degree-based courses.) An acting training is not simply 'learning different walks and changing your voice' (a very honest first-year student), it is an immensely complex (and punishing) emotional and physical re-examination and re-working of your self. It isn't easy and cannot be approached in a casual fashion — it's a serious business. You cannot borrow someone else's notes in order to catch up on classes you've missed. As in the profession itself, there isn't time to be ill or absent for any but the most catastrophic of reasons. It is essential that you arrive, and stay, mentally and physically fit.

**'Chaos theory'** Contrary to its popular image acting has to be highly organised in order for it to seem spontaneous or chaotic.

*Self-motivation* One of the principal problems I have found in drama schools is that many students who have come straight from a conventional school lack self-discipline, initiative and the ability to use their own imagination. This enhances my argument for doing something else first, to begin to learn some 'life skills' before taking up your place. Fundamentally: (a) the more you put into learning the more you will get out of your teachers and (b) drama schools get asked for recommendations from agents, directors, casting directors and managements. If you 'queer your pitch' too often, you will not only get less than full value from your training but you could also prejudice early career chances.

*Self-organisation* Given the above-mentioned assault on your body and psyche it is very important to ensure a good base. Boring things like budgeting, tidiness, eating and sleeping properly are very important. Too often (especially early on) students tend to neglect these essentials and their work suffers — sometimes irretrievably.

*Self-discipline* It is essential that you go along with the basic disciplines of your school and the individual teachers. Acting is a group activity and it is incredibly destructive to have a class or rehearsal disrupted by late-comers, mobile phones going off and irrelevant private conversations. Losing scripts, rooms littered with festering food and drink remains, and so on, are all destructive to your group as a whole. Good schools are quite specific in their required disciplines — they're not being petty-minded; those rules are there for very good reasons.

**Bitchery** Drama school is where you will make your first professional contacts: teachers, directors and fellow students. Some you'll get on with famously; others you'll find intensely annoying (even, apparently incompetent); some you may take months even to notice because they are so unforthcoming. It is very important to keep negative personal opinions to yourself and work at getting on with everyone — not only because harmony is very important to a close-knit community like a drama school, but also because you never know who might 'go places' in the future. In the last production I directed at university was a shy, young first year who, thirty years on, has one of the top theatre jobs in the country.

**The disciplines** There are numerous aspects to an acting training (movement, voice, and so on) — don't treat them as entirely separate entities. They're all fundamental to good acting. You should look to bring things learned in your movement classes, say, into your acting classes.

Different teachers in the same discipline might well work in different ways and use different 'languages'. Don't think that only one is right and the others are wrong. Think of them as different perspectives and try to make connections.

**Ask questions!** The majority of the teachers who work in drama schools are not 'tired old has-beens' as some students seem to think. ('Only those who can should teach.' Uta Hagen.) In them I find more passion about the art and craft of acting than in any theatre. Many teachers will go out of their way to give extra help — with acting and career advice — to those who ask good questions. And remember that in acting instinct often counts as much as (and periodically more than) intellect.

**Fully exploiting your acting skills** Explore fully all of the possibilities for employment as an actor. (Or 'Look to broadening your work-base' as a friend put it.) Actors' skills are being deployed in more and more areas — and there are probably some that haven't even been thought of yet. Some are very technical, and 'art' is irrelevant, but at least they pay. Too many students only think of a repertory theatre company as the first stop in their career. This used to be true; it isn't any longer. ('Repertory' theatres are now called 'Regional' and they rarely have ongoing 'repertory' companies any more.)

Imagination is the 'engine' of acting. Use yours to drive on into creating new projects (often with contemporaries) that might benefit you later on — at the very least, they'll be a welcome addition to your CV.

**Get organised early on** Get the 'business' side of your career organised early on. Don't leave it to the last minute as too many people do. Practise writing work letters, learn keyboard skills, work out a budget, and so on. (See 'An actor's start-up kit', page 29.) Also start to learn about tax (too many people leave this too late and get into terrible trouble) and the ways the DSS has with actors. If you start early — during the summer holidays before your final year at the latest — it will help you be more on top of things at the moment when you do finally graduate.

**The helpful secretary** Many students don't have immediate access to the means of typing up their letters and CVs and there might be a helpful secretary who might do the job for you. The danger is that every such letter and CV will seem the same — in content and layout. I know your details are different, but one person typing up a number of these items will inevitably work to a formula — it's quicker. If you do find yourself having to rely on a secretary, at least get yourself some well-designed headed paper.

There are similarly helpful people in 'conventional' businesses. Be wary! The problem is that the approach to a CV's contents in the business world is very different. If such a person is performing this service for you, then refer to chapter 9 and work with them on its contents.

**Drama school jargon** Like any institution drama schools have their own jargon. For instance, I've come across the terms 'modules', 'workshops' and 'showings' to describe internal assessment productions. Such terms are all but irrelevant to a potential employer. Find straightforward ways of expressing your abilities and achievements on your CV and in interview. Also, if you are fortunate enough to win one of the prizes that drama schools give, bear in mind that, however prestigious, they generally mean very little to the majority of employers. (The exception to this is the Carleton Hobbs Award for radio.)

**Your professional name** It is vital to decide upon this before your first public performance and it is vital to get it right. Your professional name represents you and your public image and must suit your personality. (If you do have to invent one, start from names within your own family.) Once you've made your decision (it is well worth discussing this with teachers and others) you must check with Equity — whether it is real or assumed — that there is nobody else registered under that name. You should also make sure that everybody (parents, flatmates, drama-school switchboard operator, and so on) knows who is being referred to when the phone rings 'professionally' for you. Changing it later can cause damaging complications. (Also see 'Student membership' on page 32.) NB Remember that you will have to give your real name (if different) to any employer for use on your pay-cheque and your national insurance contributions.

**Your first public productions** The best advertisements you will have early in your career are the public productions at the end of your time at drama school. It is essential to get your letters, CVs and photographs organised before the first one of these — say, a month before opening night — ready to be popped into the post as opportunities arise. A greater concentration of professionals with influence will come to these productions than to anything else you do for quite a while — it's a fertile hunting-ground for saleable new talent. Even if you are playing a small part or way beyond your own age, such 'cognoscenti' will be able to pick you out if you are of interest to them — I've seen this happen so often. ('There are no small parts; there are only small actors.' Stanislavski.)

**'They didn't turn up'** It so often happens that after all the effort put into letter-writing (and so on), let alone that put into your performance, you find that very few (even none) of those levers into the profession has seen you. Don't despair! You simply have to keep up the propaganda campaign. Somehow, somewhere... something will happen — if you keep on steadily trying.

Non-appearance can even occur if you managed to extract a promise of attendance — something more pressing has prevented them. In this circumstance — without embarrassing them — try to carry forward that 'promise' for the future.

**Your directors** Final productions will probably be directed by outside directors. Use what they have to give you. You may be deeply frustrated by aspects of the school and its teachers, but don't take those frustrations out on the outsider. It's nothing to do with them, and it is very important for you to come over well in those final productions. An outside director also provides an opportunity for a fresh start; for you not to feel weighed down by previous criticisms. (I'm not advocating ignoring those 'criticisms'; simply, putting them in better perspective.) Also, these directors are links with the profession, and good contacts are very important to your career. You should keep in touch with the ones you get on with (see 'Keep in touch', page 199) and you should see those you find difficult as positive learning experiences — there's no mileage in blaming someone else for a failure.

**Showcases** All drama schools now stage showcases where all the graduating students are given opportunities briefly to show off their talents to a concentration of directors, agents and casting directors. Different schools have different ways of approaching these, but generally the onus will be on you to find the material to show yourself off with. Start thinking about this early and find something 'original'! However, don't choose something with the idea of it being a 'challenge'. Find potential material that will show you off well — as you appear to be. A good choice of 'original' material, well executed, will definitely help you stand out from the crowd. (See chapter 13.)

**An agent's approach** I have so often stood in theatre bars after show-cases and seen groups of students who don't quite know where to put themselves, indulging in almost farcical non-conversations. Throughout the rest of the crowd are unfamiliar faces, amongst whom are agents and others with casting clout. Eyes flick everywhere for the approach of someone new... It is a horrible situation — horrible, because there is no consistency of approach. A few agents like to stay on and approach people directly, others much prefer to rush off anonymously — then phone or write to those they find interesting. Some fear monopolisation and many know they can't afford to be away from their offices for too long. In these circumstances, try and wipe any thought of any possible 'approach' out of your mind. I know it's difficult, but try to focus on my guesstimate that only 10% of 'consummated' approaches occur in person immediately after a showcase.
NB It is generally better not to accept any offer of representation until the end of your training — there may be someone better 'waiting in the wings'.

**A professional job offer whilst training** If you're one of the lucky few to whom this happens think carefully about (and discuss with the school's 'powers that be') the pros and cons. Is it the best thing for you to do, given the training and production/showcase opportunities you'll miss? (See 'Turning down an offer', page 99.)

**Leaving early** Dissatisfaction with casting, a rock band 'taking off' and a girlfriend in New York are just a few of the reasons I've encoun-tered for students leaving early. (Running out of money is another, but that's another problem.) If you still intend to become a professional actor it is invariably stupid to leave early unless the reason is an extremely positive 'professional' one.

(NB You may be asked to pay some of your funding back in this circumstance — wherever you got it from.)

**It's different in the real world** Students of any subject emerging into their chosen professions — even if they are going into the profession for which they were trained — will find a welter of new technical terms and unspoken rules that they were never taught in college. In the fierce competition for acting work nothing is more likely to mark you down than the precious time an employer has to spend on teaching what has become as fundamental as breathing to him or her. If you can get as much practical experience as possible, where you can observe the pros at work — as a dresser, a follow-spot operator or an usher, for example — before leaving, you will have given yourself a head start. And if you can find a way to learn more about the workings of television and radio — maybe simply as an observer — that can be extremely useful. Don't simply rely on those television and radio courses.

**Contacts** 'It's not what you know, but who you know' is often true. Anybody could be a 'contact' for future work. (See 'Professional public relations', page 197.)

## Your first professional steps...

**Advice** You'll get plenty of career advice, both formal and informal, and some of it will be contradictory: for example, different people will like different photographs on your contact sheet. Finally you have to make up your own mind by using your own instincts — often by going back to your first gut reaction.

**Directors** You may already know a few professional directors from shows you've done at drama school — you may even be given your first break by one of them — but don't think that all directors are like the ones employed by your school. Most of these are not only experienced directors but they usually also have the patience to help you overcome the acting problems you encounter along the way. In the profession there isn't the time to do this, and some directors just don't have this facility for patience in their emotional make-up. (This is a piece of tact on my part.)

**Don't let your technique show** Of course there is a wide variety of directors and a wide variety of methodologies, but most directors do have a common denominator: they don't really know how the techniques of acting actually work. This may be galling to you after all the sweat to get your breathing right, your received pronunciation correct, and so on, but it's generally true. 99.9% of an audience won't have the faintest idea, so why should the director? I have seen too many actors, especially those recently out of drama school, concentrating on these techniques to the detriment of the final product — making it look like a series of mechanical operations. You have to climb beyond the essential mechanics and 'fly'.

**Early interviews** Some people fall into the trap of just talking about their drama school and its whole philosophy. That simply exaggerates your lack of experience. Some even go as far as to claim that they have 'learnt nothing' from their training. That sounds very arrogant and doesn't say much for your loyalty. If you came straight from school into training, you may feel that you've not done anything else worth talking about; but you must have done something that could help illustrate more of yourself. Think about it! (See chapter 12 for much more detailed discussions.)

## Early work (and the lack of it)

In your first few years it is very important to carry on acting and not lose all the momentum you built up in your final months at drama school. Also, drama-school audiences are dominated by other students and friends — they can give a misleading impression. Your teachers will tell you what they think, but nobody but a real audience drawn at random from the general public can really tell you whether you're communicating or not. And 'communication' to those you don't know is at the heart of acting.

**Outside productions** A student (in between her second and third years) recently returned from a moderately successful sojourn at the Edinburgh Festival Fringe, said to me: 'It's so good to perform somewhere else.' I believe that doing a production outside your school environment, whilst training, can be a very valuable learning experience. However, you must make sure that your school is happy for you to do this — a few aren't.

**Your first proper job** Don't feel you have to take work for work's sake — even if it is your all important first properly-paid acting job. In the early stages career enhancement should be your chief objective. For example, a tempting long tour in the chorus line will probably do very little for you; don't take it unless you're really sure there is nothing else. There is a limit to how much you can learn working with the same group of people and you could be missing out on other opportunities by being away too long. It is important that early jobs have reasonable publicity value for your career and provide good opportunities to start learning about how the profession works. (A good agent will guide you in this.) Aim to get something positive from each one.

**Ideals** On the other hand, don't be too 'purist' about what you would like to do. There is no point in crossing musicals off your list because you prefer straight theatre (or vice versa). You have to look carefully at each job-opportunity and see what it might do for you. It may not advance you — indeed you may feel you could be sliding back down the ladder — but don't forget your bills. Ideals are not wrong, but you mustn't let them blind you to immediate realities. Keep them in perspective — for the long-term. In spite of what media coverage of individual actors' lives may suggest, virtually nobody always gets the kind of work they most want.

**Jaded professionals** I'm afraid that a minority of experienced professionals waste time and/or mess around whilst working. I'm not talking about those bits of harmless (but responsible) fun that we all need periodically when working hard; it's those silly attempts to catch others out — by trying to make you 'corpse' on stage, for instance. Do your damnedest not to join in these futilities; if you do, you — with less experience — will probably be the first to get caught out.

An actor's job is to communicate the story to the audience; messing about is not only unprofessional, but it is also alienating to that audience.

**Career structure** An actor's career is very like a life-long game of 'snakes and ladders' — with far more (and longer) snakes than ladders — for the vast majority of the profession.

**Good intentions and broken promises** One of the hardest things for newcomers are promises that come to nothing. I'm afraid the profession is rife with these — you simply have to face the fact that, because there are too many actors to choose from, you will often be let down. How-ever, most people who break such promises do feel at least a little bit guilty and your aim should be to find ways of letting them 'off the hook' and utilising that 'promise' in the future.

**Kicks in the teeth** In spite of all my (and many others') warnings most students seem to avoid taking on board what the profession is really like. (The same is more and more true for graduates in other disciplines — the rest of the working world is beginning to catch up with what the 'jobbing' actor has known throughout history.) For a (very) few it is a comparatively simple process of being spotted by an agent in a final year production and the agent pointing the student in the correct direction towards their first job. But, in the cattle-market of final year productions and showcases, it is impossible for any agent to cover everything. And even if one does see you and like you they won't necessarily leap onto the phone with an instant offer of representation — let alone have a job waiting for you. Looking for new talent is only a part of an agent's working life. Their main focus has to be on their current clients and not so much on future investment — there aren't enough hours in the week. An agent may have liked you in something, but his/her attention can easily be distracted and you disappear from the memory. It is a fact that if you are male, have a strong singing voice and a saleable regional accent (Scouse, Geordie or Glasgwegian, for instance) you stand a much better chance of being snapped up than if you're female, wouldn't claim to be a strong singer and have an 'ordinary' natural accent.

I know of two contemporaries fitting the above descriptions: he got over twenty offers of representation; she got none. She, with encouragement, sat down, gritted her teeth and phoned agents who had seen their West End showcase. She got varying degrees of 'short shrift' from most, but after much hard graft is now ensconced very happily with a good co-operative agency. Many of their contemporaries are still wandering around wondering what's not happening to them — and not doing anything about it.

I'm not trying to frighten; I'm trying to give you a realistic outlook so that you are able to cope better with the kicks in the teeth that you will undoubtedly receive — and have to recover from.

**'Extra' work** If you can get 'extra' work (a 'non-speaking crowd artiste') it can be a very valuable learning experience. (You can find specialist agents listed in *Contacts*.) But if you become known as an 'extra', you'll find it difficult to move into the conventional acting sphere. People still do 'come out of the chorus line' and make a career for themselves in theatre, but it's more difficult to come out of a television crowd to do likewise. (Being part of a crowd that is intended to be seen as a group and not as readily identifiable individuals is a different discipline from playing a part which needs specifically to shine through the screen.) It is a fact that many television directors and casting directors are prejudiced against people who do 'extra' work, thinking they can do nothing else.

**Soaps, series and sitcoms** One of the most common questions I get from students is 'Should I take a part in one of the "soaps"?' My gut reaction is 'Take what you can get. There's little enough work going as there is.' However, for the lucky few, here are a few thoughts. Such an offer will invariably arrive via an agent who will be able to advise you in more immediate detail, but the crucial thing is to try to sign for a limited period with an option, if possible, for further work. Unlike the long tour in a chorus line, it's not as though you won't be seen, but you could find yourself stuck in a typecasting situation which is hard to get out of. The other crucial element is that you may learn a lot about television but the development of your stage experience will be zero and that will not help you in the long run. The stage is where you find out what works (and doesn't) and learn about audiences.

For a television 'sitcom' you may have a studio audience, but its reaction is not always 'real' because of the constant breaks in recording and because that audience can see everything else that's going on — cameras moving about, floor-managers talking intensely into headsets, actors waiting in the 'wings' picking their noses, and so on. The audience has also been warmed up beforehand by a professional warm-up artiste, and audience reactions during the takes are cleverly amplified in the final editing stage after everybody has gone home.

Soaps and series which are not meant to have a comedic element do not have studio audiences. You might think that this doesn't matter, that it'll make no difference to your acting. You are wrong! A performance does not finally exist until it is placed in front of an audience, and that audience will change it if the actor is responding properly. A silence speaks just as loudly as laughter. In short, get theatre experience early on, and if a soap, series or sitcom comes along consider carefully how it might affect your future saleability and your development as an actor.

**A deafening silence** Of course you'll be looking to create chances wherever possible, but that first job just does not appear — and no agent seems interested in you. Extra classes will keep you in trim, but there is no substitute for actually doing productions to consummate all that training. If you can't get a 'legitimate' job, try the Fringe — with all the caveats listed in chapter 7. It can also be fulfilling to look for other ways of exploiting your training — by setting up a drama group, for instance.

## An actor's start-up kit

You need the following essential items before you even get your first interview, let alone an agent and/or your first job. You should start getting organised as you approach your first public productions:

1 a good, strong professional name,
2 well-designed headed paper,
3 a secure telephone number with answerphone and/or a reliable human message-taker,
4 a current copy of *Contacts*,
5 a good set of photographs and sufficient copies,
6 a well laid out CV,
7 a word processor/computer with printer,
8 a good standard letter,
9 a dozen (or more) varied audition speeches,
10 half-a-dozen (or more) varied audition songs,
11 a check-list to help respond to the inevitable 'What have you been doing recently?'/'Tell me a bit about yourself?',
12 an entry in *Spotlight*,
13 a reasonable selection of clothes for interviews,

14 the funds to pay for the above and the many other minor things not listed: postage, Equity entry fee and annual subscription, subscriptions to *The Stage* and other professional publications, travel costs to interviews, and so on. All the above items can easily add up to much more money than you might think — you need to calculate your potential professional expenses and budget for them,

15 a permanent temporary job that is flexible enough for you to drop at 24 hours' notice — only about 10% of the profession earn a living solely from acting. And, even for those, incomes can be incredibly variable — £200 one year to over £20,000 the next to quote just one example,

16 a great deal of patience, persistence, determination, cunning and resourcefulness,

17 a stoical source of solace for the bad times,

18 a copy of this book for reading on the loo.

## Slog

The odd person leaps straight out of drama school into persistent work. It can take most who stick at it at least a year to get their first properly paid job; it probably takes most at least five years to find any credibility within the profession. Even then it's an incredibly up and down life. It is a lifetime's 'slog', but with a lot of hard work in selling yourself you will find work, learn, and within three to five years — maybe sooner — be at one with those who've been forty years in the profession. Their only advantage over you will be that they have more stories to tell in the coffee-breaks and in the pub.

And I'll end this chapter with one of my favourite quotes:

> 'If life doesn't have that little bit of danger about it, you'd better create it. If life hands you that danger, accept it gratefully.'
>
> Anthony Quayle.

# Chapter Three

# *Equity*

Once upon a time there were stars and there were other actors. On stage the stars would dominate and the others would have to fit in around them. The stars could command high fees, the others would take what they could get. (Young actors would even pay West End managements to play small parts in order to be 'seen'.) At the end of the nineteenth century when naturalism began to take hold, the job of director evolved to sort out the stylistic mess on stage. It took several more decades to begin to sort out the grotesque imbalances in remuneration.

In 1929, with the support of some famous names, the actors' trade union Equity was established in the UK. Although the stars, with their considerable ticket-selling power, can still command high fees, at least the 'others' are being paid much better and work many fewer hours than their pre-Equity counterparts.

**The Union** Equity is an organisation surrounded by misleading myth and legend. Essentially, it exists to look after the interests of not just actors, but also performers in many other fields — from opera singers to stunt people, from ballet dancers to ventriloquists and many more. It also represents production staff like stage managers, directors, designers, and so on — indeed a recent survey showed that actors only constituted 50% of the Union's membership.

Its principal function is to negotiate minimum pay and conditions agreements in all areas of work — and there are far, far more of those than you might imagine, and new ones are being invented all the time. Under current employment legislation a management cannot refuse to employ somebody who is not a member of the Union, but there are Equity/Management agreements which state that the latter will endeavour to employ people with previous professional experience, that is Equity members. (NB This includes newcomers who have completed an 'accredited' course.) And it generally makes more sense for managements to employ those with 'previous professional experience' rather than someone with none at all. Equity is not an all-powerful monolith, obstructing aspiring actors: entry is not tightly restricted as so many seem to think. All the Union requires is some evidence of professionalism to be eligible for membership.

**The Equity card** There are various ways of acquiring your Equity card. For example, if you complete an 'accredited' drama-school course then you are entitled to join and obtain your card. There are numerous other routes to joining and eligibility has eased significantly in the past few years. The details of the whole system are too complex to go into here; it is best to contact the Union for up-to-the-minute details. Guides to entry are available from their offices; there is also a list of membership criteria on their website (see p. 34).

(NB With the recent reforms of membership criteria the concepts of 'provisional' and 'full' cards have thankfully disappeared.)

An Equity card is only a passport for, and not a guarantee of, getting work, but it will give you a better chance of getting interviews and auditions. It's not that employers (and agents) won't see non-members, but they are generally disinclined to do so. It is possible to get non-Equity work; there are numerous companies (with no agreement with the Union) who employ non-members, but they commonly pay under the negotiated rate for the job and some have been known to vanish without paying at all — Equity has a very long list of miscreants. Sometimes it can be worth working with such a company to gain experience, but it might not be 'quality' work and after paying your expenses you will certainly not make much money. (There are Fringe venues that are very good shop windows but currently outside any agreement.) More importantly, most legitimate acting work is indifferently paid already and managements who exploit actors' 'need' to work and the actors who work for them are undermining the profession as a whole. Acting is a profession that desperately needs to be together in order to fight for fair treatment in pay and conditions.

**Student membership** If you are on a full-time higher education course lasting for a year or more, which is preparing you for work in many areas of the performing arts, you can become a student member. For a small annual fee (currently £10) you get regular information on what's happening in the industry and the Union, the option to reserve your professional name (as long as it is not already in use by an existing member), opportunities to meet experienced performers, special discounts on insurance and other concessions, and eligibility to join the Actors' Centres around the UK. On graduation you can move up — subject to other qualifying rules — to full membership, and the amounts you have paid as a student member are deducted from the costs of joining. If you aren't immediately eligible for full membership (you've done an 'non-accredited' course, for instance) you can continue at the student rate for up to two years after graduating.

**Equity's other doings** Apart from negotiating (and re-negotiating) a whole range of contracts, the Union provides numerous other services: a job information hotline, specialist legal aid, insurance services, an advice service on tax and benefits, and so on. It is also highly pro-active — campaigning for better theatre funding, for instance — all for one of the lowest subscription rates of any trade union in the country: see the website for current rates. Equity now not only has informative leaflets covering all aspects of its work, it also has an excellent (and easily navigable) website where you can find an enormous amount.

**Who runs Equity?** The Union is run by a Council of (currently 46) volunteer members who are elected by the membership. There are also elected committees representing specialisms and geographical areas who focus on the problems and needs of their particular remits. Backing all this up are the full-time staff who do the day-to-day work and who advise the Council and committees. Unfortunately, Equity elections tend to excite about as much interest as those for MEPs — largely because members don't understand the ins and outs of it all. In spite of a vocal minority, the performing arts and their Union haven't seemed to have mixed well. (On top of this the restrictive government legislation of the 80s and early 90s has made it even more complicated to operate on a completely legal basis — and make those operations clear for the membership.) However, Equity is rising to the challenge.

**Equity's 'image'** Equity, in the UK, is too often seen as 'doing nothing for me', 'weak', and so on. This is fundamentally not true. It is true that dealing with all the problems that blitz that organisation every day badly over-stretches the existing staff — many of whom willingly work over their contractual hours in order to get their jobs done. Combined with this is the fact that there are too many individuals willing to under-cut agreements simply in order to work, thus undermining those hard-won agreements. It can sometimes seem like a very uphill struggle. However, if you are a member with a problem that no-one else can solve you can be sure of the best advice and support from Equity. Even better, get involved with your local branch, constructively express your opinions and things can be made to happen.

**How to use Equity** In general an actor with a contractual or legal problem should first contact his or her agent — there are clear-cut agreements over nudity and broadcasting extracts from productions, for example, which a good agent should know. Beyond this, your next recourse is the Equity Deputy (often known as the 'Equity Dep' — under the agreements every theatre company should elect one of these) — he or she should then contact the Union for advice. If you do find it necessary to contact Equity directly (a) don't leave it until the last minute and (b) try to avoid Monday mornings and Friday afternoons. You the actor have to try to solve your own problems as far as you can — often with the help of your agent and/or your fellow actors, but when you do have a genuine problem that is beyond you, you will receive very good support, expert advice and positive action — I know.

**Non-Equity work** There are some areas of work where Equity has no management body with which to negotiate (training films and corporate videos for example). However, Equity has evolved (and continues to do so) many sets of guidelines and forms of engagement which are well worth asking for when such work arises. Equity often has no real power in these areas but can offer expert advice and considerable clout. They will even try to assist where the work is unpaid (or expenses only) if a significant problem arises.

**Address** Equity, Guild House, Upper St. Martin's Lane, London WC2H 9EG; (020) 7379 6000; website <www.equity.org.uk>.

# Chapter Four

# *The Spotlight*

The Spotlight is a small organisation with a massive output. It is 'the hub of the industry' (Clive Swift) — it is where you advertise yourself, whether you have an agent or not. The organisation's two major annual publications are *The Spotlight Directory* and *Contacts*. (It also publishes specialist directories of Children, Graduates, Presenters, Afro-Asian Artists, Stunt Performers, North American Artists and Performers with Disabilities — the latter four on behalf of Equity.) Although it was founded in 1927, it is no extinct dinosaur. It moves very much with the times and has a massive, constantly updated computer database of not only actor's addresses and agents but also personal skills, physical attributes, languages, accents and abilities, which can be accessed in seconds if someone has a casting problem. If you subscribe you also have free access to their experienced and confidential advisory service.

### The Spotlight Directory
This is commonly known simply as *Spotlight* and it is essential that you are in it — virtually every director and casting director will give it at least a skim for each production. Some actors get interviews simply on the basis of what they look like in their *Spotlight* photograph, but more often than not that image of you serves as a reminder of your existence if you've already met or they've seen you in something.

It is published annually in both book and CD-ROM forms (the latter is also available on the Internet), in separate 'Actors' and 'Actresses' editions. They contain photographs, contact details and other information for some 20,000 actors and actresses. For the price of an entry (costing about the same as an annual colour television licence) you'll have 5000 adverts on employers' and casting directors' desks all around the country — and, crucially, all around the world via the Internet with *Spotlight Casting Live*.

On application you are sent a form to fill in. It is important to fill in everything that you can (clearly) — too many blanks will lessen your chances of being found when a reader is doing a search on the CD-ROM or Internet versions. Some sections are self-evident, others are worth thinking about more carefully.

*Height and weight* Most people fill these in, so if you don't the reader will start to wonder how much out of the ordinary you actually are —

especially height. If you feel that you need to bend the truth a little don't go overboard into telling an outright lie; it will count against you.

*Hair and eye colour* These are important, especially if the black and white photograph cannot convey them properly: for example, red hair or green eyes.

*Playing range* See my thoughts on this, page 71.

*Skills* It is important that you can actually accomplish everything you list — essential if you claim to be 'highly skilled'.

*Your credits* A number of people don't list dates in this section — I think that this is a mistake as the omission(s) serve to imply that you are trying to conceal something. Also, it is very important to make sure that all spellings are correct (see 'Fundamentals' on page 61).

*How to contact you* If you're represented by an agency then you should list them. If you aren't, it is better to put The Spotlight's number rather than your home telephone number as yours may change but theirs doesn't. (NB They will vet any enquiry for you before passing on your contact number.)

*The date of your photograph* Omission of this can make the reader wonder what you might be trying to conceal. 'How long ago was this picture taken and what is he or she trying to hide from me now?'

*Your photographer* Don't forget that your photographer owns the copyright of your photograph and must be credited (see 'Copyright' on page 82).

*Very important* If you miss the deadline for an entry, you will have to wait nearly eighteen months before your new one will be published in the book and CD-ROM which (in spite of the Internet version) are still used by a lot of people.

> Actors' deadline:    1 November (published in the following April).
> Actresses' deadline:  1 May (published in the following October).

NB You can enter *Spotlight Casting Live* at any time of the year. Your details will immediately appear on the Internet and will automatically be published in the next editions of the book and CD-ROM.

## The CD-ROM and *Spotlight Casting Live*

These contain a great deal more of the above information than the printed version. Users can access lists of actors using their chosen parameters — in any combination they like. For instance, they can click 'French' in the 'Language' box and get a complete list of those who filled in the fact that they speak the language — all within a few seconds. The user can also do a search specifying 'native' next to the language (or an accent). Further refinements could involve finding French-speaking actors in a particular age range, hair colour and height — whatever combination might be desired. It's all quite mind-boggling. What's important from your point of view is that you list everything on the application form that you genuinely can. Remember that it is essential that you provide them with good quality photographs, accurate credits and other details.

The Spotlight provides each subscriber with a PIN number so that you can update your Internet entry at any time.

The Spotlight has long been at the cutting edge of the use of computer technology in the actor-information arena. They will continue to keep abreast as the technology develops.

**Clones** There have been periodic attempts by other companies to offer similar advertising services for actors. The turn of the millennium saw a sudden rise in Internet casting directories. Most are cheaper than *Spotlight*, but none has yet come anywhere near it in the ease of use, search facilities and number of entries — and crucially number of users. Also, most that I have found are very sloppily designed and hard to search. The expertise and contacts that The Spotlight has built up over the decades will take anybody else a very long time to catch up with — if they ever do. Go for entry in *Spotlight* first and anything else, if you can afford it, after your other essential outlays (see 'An actor's start-up kit' on page 29). (Also see 'Internet casting directories', page 92.)

**Contacts** This is The Spotlight's other major annual publication and is consistently the most accurate (and most frequently updated) list of 'contact' names and addresses available. It is inexpensive, costing £9.99 for the 2001 edition. The profession has a highly mobile population of people you need to contact, so some details are quickly out of date. You should update your copy annually. It is available in some bookshops, via the 'sales hotline' ((020) 7440 5026) and through their website.
NB Some of this information should also be available on The Spotlight's website by the time this book is in print.

**Address** The Spotlight, 7 Leicester Place, London WC2H 7BP; (020) 7437 7631; website <www.spotlightcd.com>.

**Final note** It is essential that you keep the Records Department up to date with changes of permanent address and/or agency.

**Stop press!** At the time of writing they are adding short sound-clips (at no extra cost, beyond that for recording) and have plans for video-clips in the future. Check their website for future developments.

# Chapter Five

# *For Experienced Actors*

You will probably know a lot of the advice given in this book; you've probably given some of it to less experienced actors in your time. You may well disagree with some of my thoughts. That's fine. Nobody is right all of the time, and I'm no exception to that rule. I learnt very early on that a good, experienced actor knows much more than I do when it comes down to the essentials of communicating a text to an audience — the centre of any good production. So why are so many actors, at best, indifferent at communicating on paper and in the interview-room? And why, oh, why, do so many experienced actors, when asked to read, literally do just that — with apparently no attempt at showing any of their undoubted talents? Under-acting in readings is just one fault I often find with the more experienced actor, and there are many more. In fact, generally the only basic difference between most young and most experienced actors is that the former are generally clumsier than the latter, but through that clumsiness manage to give more of themselves. As another director said to me: 'Why do so many experienced actors think it admirable to be so cool, withdrawn and blasé?' Being neutral — perhaps to defend yourself — will get you nowhere. Sales technique doesn't need to be a phoney or calculated business. You have to show something of the energy and ideas you could give to the rehearsal process as well as what you could do on stage or screen.

Maybe it gets harder to go through the same old routine, week in and week out, as the years go by and as the directors get younger ('There's a new bunch of schoolboys running the networks each week.' Joan Collins) and all that waiting in dirty and cramped corridors has lost its excitement. I have met a number of actors fresh from drama school full of that 'brass neck of youth' and then several years later met them again only to find pale shadows of their former selves — 'all passion' apparently 'spent'. This is a common and saddening phenomenon; it is also unnecessary. I know that being placed in almost impossible, and sometimes humiliating, situations by 'us over the table' must get harder and harder to bear but it is fundamentally still part of your job as an actor.

You have to exploit your most precious asset — your acting skills — to continue to get you through the painful processes of job-finding. 'Doctor Theatre' has got you through many a performance you physically or mentally thought you couldn't do, so why not find a way to use him (or her) to help you get work? All you need is a well-prepared scenario that will cope with most problems. A performance doesn't stop, or go permanently downhill, if somebody says a wrong line or dries stone dead (the potential hazards are endless); you instantly find a way out of the problem, and its energy is renewed.

Continually think about and update your sales technique. Even if you have a considerable track record and your agent is regularly putting you up for parts, try writing some letters for yourself. Approached in the right way, you will not be humbling yourself, and you never know what new opportunities you might open up.

# Chapter Six

# *Agents*

Some people do survive quite well without an agent — especially in those specialist areas like Theatre-In-Education where jobs are regularly advertised — but getting work without one is harder in theatre and extremely difficult in the recorded media. Actors without agents tend to lack credibility in the eyes of potential employers. It's not fair, but it's a fact. However hard you work at getting to know potential employers, most agents have their fingers closer to the pulse, know what's coming up, and simply have far more contacts than you can ever have. That's their job. Directors and casting directors rely on agents they trust to help in the filtering process of whom to interview. A good agent also understands contracts, knows the 'going rates' and has more clout to get money that's owing.

Being an agent is, most of the time, as disheartening and unglamorous as being an actor — and it's hard work, easily running into sixty or seventy hours a week. Agents putting clients up for things are putting themselves on the line. All directors and casting directors have blacklists of agents whose clients have messed them around too often, so good agents are very careful about how they select those they are going to represent. They have to feel that they can work with you at selling you effectively, just as directors have to feel that they can work with, and benefit from, you in a company.

There are all kinds of agency and agent. There are the ever increasing co-operative agencies (see page 50). There are conventional agents who seem to rely on sheer numbers of clients to produce an income and whose sales technique seems to be to send out a great wadge of CVs and photographs randomly in the hope that one will land on the right desk. There are the big, prestigious agencies whose focus can tend to be on their stars sometimes ignoring their less well known clients. There are those who are more like 'personal managers' who have only twenty or thirty clients, know each one extremely well and work very hard on behalf of each individual; I do not know how some of these make a living. There are those who actively discourage more experienced clients from doing lower-paid theatre — even to the extent of not passing on an offer. (I discovered such an agent when my offer was turned down for someone whom I knew was available and wanted to do the production (she and I had a mutual friend). I broke the rules and phoned her directly, and she sorted her agent out.) There are also those who are 'here today and gone tomorrow' — it's a very mobile population.

The important thing is that a good agent works hard at making contacts and makes sure that they are respected by those contacts. Just as the agent represents you, you represent your agent.

## Finding an agent

**Contacting agents** Check with teachers and friends for recommendations and write to these with your CV and photograph telling them when and where they can see your work. It doesn't have to be a leading role; agents are not necessarily blinded by who had the most lines. Don't phone (or e-mail) an agent who doesn't know you and don't turn up on spec on the doorstep.

Don't expect an agent to come whom you've tried to invite at the last minute. They are very busy people, out on business seeing clients in productions and so on almost every night of the week, and will be booked up well in advance.

When writing use all the parameters that are set out in chapter 9 — except that it is better to send an agent a 10x8in (25x20cm) photograph. (Don't forget to enclose a suitably-sized s.a.e. if you'd like your photograph returned.)

NB Many agents won't take you on unless you are in *Spotlight* — if you're not it makes it much harder for them to market you.

**Meeting an agent** If an agent invites you to come and see him or her, approach the interview in exactly the same way you would an interview with a director: dress comfortably and well, and don't be late. The major differences will be that: (a) you almost certainly won't have to do a speech or reading (but I have known agents ask for a speech, so be prepared) and (b) you could be constantly interrupted by the phone (see 'Interruptions', page 119).

**What to ask?** When meeting a potential agent, don't be afraid to ask questions. You are hoping to be 'represented'; you're not suing for work. Ask about how long they've been in operation (unless they're obviously established), the fields of work they operate in, number of clients, rates of commission, their attitude to Fringe work, and so on. In short, try to build an overall working-picture of the agency and their 'clout'.

**An offer** Don't feel rushed into signing up at the first offer of representation. Get advice from other actors and directors, but principally from The Spotlight, who have a much more objective view than the former — but even they can't know everything about such a 'mobile population'. Advice from others will be offered very freely but can be coloured by past experiences which may well have nothing to do with that agency's current situation.

Also, can you work well with that agent/agency? I don't mean is there a good 'shoulder to cry on' (see 'The actor-agent personal relationship', page 49), but do you feel that they would be good at working well with you — a bit like the ideal director-actor relationship? Don't sign up unless you feel at least fairly sure.

There are bigger, prestigious agencies who have access to more casting information than the others, but although you may acquire some of their prestige, will you get sufficient attention?

Don't be beguiled by special offers like 'no commission for the first year'. It'll probably take at least a year before you start earning enough money to make the commission worth having.

Be warned that no legitimate agency charges a registration fee; back off quickly if that is part of an offer of representation. The exception to this is the co-operative agencies who have joining fees which are perfectly legitimate — see pages 50–1 for more details.

**Signing up** So, you've selected who you wish to represent you; what next? The deal may simply be sealed with a handshake — or you may be offered a contract to sign. Read this carefully! It may simply consist of the rates of commission, but it may contain a period of notice clause, that is, the length of time, after you've given notice, that you will continue to have to pay commission on the work you do. (Not just to any new agent, but also to your old one — double commission.) Three months is common, but I've known it to be a year, which can be extremely awkward. Check any contract offered very carefully before signing — check it with Equity and/or The Spotlight if in any doubt.
NB Most agents will insist that you agree to 'sole-representation' for all your acting work. An exception to this is in the world of voice-overs, which has its own specialist agents (see pages 176–7).

**Selecting an agent** If you are one of the lucky few who suddenly gets offers of representation from more than one agent, take time to think and carefully weigh up the pros and cons of each one. It is possible to change if you choose wrongly, but it can be quite a hassle and the others may not be interested any longer.

A third-year student, who was on the verge of signing with one agent, was phoned up by another who had seen her in a production. The second agent, on learning the imminence of the signing with the first said: 'Well, I know a theatre who is looking for someone just like you.' 'Which one?' she asked. 'We'll get to that when you've signed with me.' She phoned the first agent, who had no idea which theatre it was and said: 'There's nothing I can do about it, I'm afraid.' Confused, she asked people what she should do — she chose the first; he had been straightforward with her. On the other hand, one of her contemporaries is very happy with the second.

**Not quite** Unless you are a well-established actor, an agent won't take you on until they see you in a production (sometimes on screen). I know of several instances where agents have said they are interested in an individual but haven't formally taken them on until the required showcase. This can take time, so be patient. And, of course, they have to like what they see before making the commitment. Being invited to go and meet agents who have seen your work doesn't mean that they are certain to take you on. It often happens that they will say: 'Not at the moment, but keep in touch.' It could be they have someone very like you on their books, that one more person will just tip the agency into being too big to handle or some other good reason that is finally not your fault. You just have to go along with this decision. Don't get frustrated, and do 'keep in touch'. If you are in this position, you can always consult them about the suitability of a particular job offer. You might also be able to ask them to negotiate an offer for you; they'll normally take commission on it, even if you don't finally get taken on.

## Working with an agent

**You can't relax now** When you have an agent to represent you, don't expect him or her to do all the work of selling you. (There are occasional exceptions, when an agent feels so confident in a client's saleability, that he or she says: 'Leave it all to me.') You will still have to write lots of letters on your own behalf (especially in the first few years of your career). Keep up your own contacts and make sure that your agent knows who you are writing to so that recipients don't get the impression that there's no communication between you both.

**The complete you** Tell your new agent everything that might help to sell you. Be prepared to give them a very full biography — you never know what might be useful. Go through your CV together so that all the possibilities and pitfalls are clear. If you claim horse-riding, for instance, your agent needs to know how good you actually are at it. An agent making a false or exaggerated claim can be as damaging as an actor doing likewise. (See 'Exaggerated claims', page 73.)

Let your agent have all those little details that don't go on your CV (measurements, for example) for the files — just in case. You never know what peculiarity or apparently unrelated physical quirk or skill some director might need all of a sudden. Make sure that he or she is clear about any kind of work you really don't want to do. It will be embarrassing and time-wasting if your agent gets you an interview for such a job and subsequently has to phone back to cancel on those grounds.

**Your availability** You must keep your agency in touch with your availability for interviews let alone for work. For instance, if you have a regular non-acting job, how much notice do you need to give to get time off? Make sure that anything that could affect arrangements for interviews is clear; it'll save a lot of extra phone calls and hassle. Some interviews — for commercials, for example — tend to be arranged at very short notice and only take place through a single morning or afternoon. It will not always be possible to fit in with your requirements.

Make sure your agent knows your holiday plans as far in advance as possible, and if you are going to be unavailable for any other reason.

**The keeper of your CV** It's quite common for agents to get details on CVs wrong — play titles, parts, writers, and so on. It's not necessarily their fault. After all, it was you who played the part. Did you give them the correct details? Errors can creep in very easily, especially when there are unfamiliar names. Periodically check up on the CV your agent has on file. I once came across a CV sent by an agent on which it was claimed that the client concerned had played a part in a particular production which in fact my own wife had played. I don't know whose fault it was, but agents do deal with lots of CVs.

It is common in interview for actors to complain in some way about the CV the agent has sent to the director — it omits recent and/or important work, for instance. A periodic check should avoid this potentially downbeat moment in an interview.

NB A note to agents: Why do most of you still lay out your clients' CVs so badly? (See chapter 9.)

**Stay in touch** Don't use the requirements of the preceding paragraphs as an excuse to keep phoning up with new fiddly little details. You should keep in regular not persistent contact with your agent. Agents vary as to how often they like you to phone; ask yours. Don't keep asking 'What am I up for?' That is extremely irritating as it takes precious time to comb through all the various lists. (Agents deal with an enormous amount of information.) Sometimes your agent will volunteer this information. Leave it at that.

Your general aim should be to keep your presence felt. You should do this subtly but consistently, especially if you are part of a large client-list and/or are in a long period of employment or unemployment. An agent's life is an extremely busy one, and there are never enough hours in the day or days in the week. Even if it's a slack time for interviews there are always general promotions to be done, charities phoning up asking for the services of the agency's stars, and so on. It can be easy for your presence to get lost amongst everything else that needs doing. I don't mean that it's a deliberate callousness on their part. The fact is that to earn a living an agency has to neglect some of its clients some of the time.

**The non-stop phone** Often the office will be frantic when you phone. Be quick to recognise the fevered voice and don't take offence at an apparently brusque manner. Make your point and ring off with decent speed. Remember all the time they spend on the phone already; don't add to that burden. On the other hand, don't become too remote.

**Times to phone** Most agencies don't start until 10.00 or 10.30 am, and work through until about 6.00 pm. It's best to avoid phoning on a Monday or a Friday except on pressing business; especially don't phone at 5.55 pm on a Friday unless it's mega-important, and don't try to phone outside normal hours. Many agents work from home. Others are in their offices early — I know one who's in at eight o'clock in the morning — but this is their quiet time in which to sort out their desks and their minds. I know they could put the answering machine on, but there could be an urgent call from a producer or casting director that just fits you.

(NB Don't forget that agents have lunch hours too.)

**Social calls** You should go and see your agent periodically. Phone calls are not as good as meeting in the flesh. Suggest meeting for lunch every so often — perhaps every couple of months.

**Your agent seeing your work** Hopefully your agent will come and see you in productions, but don't feel let down if you are so far away that he or she simply cannot make it. In these circumstances send copies of the good reviews you have received.

You may not be able to get complimentary tickets — you may have used up your allocation or your agent can only come on a 'no comp. night'. Unless your agent offers, you should pay for the ticket(s) your-self — without comment. However much agents may enjoy a prod-uction it is still 'work' as far as they are concerned. It is therefore common courtesy not to add to that burden.

Also, don't feel let down if they miss television performances even with the time-shift facility of video; they may simply not have time to watch. NB Be tactful in finding out what they thought of a production. (See 'What did you think?' on page 198.)

**Always be contactable** Make sure your agent knows how to contact you quickly all the time. A young, and phoneless, actor didn't phone in on the day an interview came through for a filming job for which he was perfect. The interview was the next day, but by the time he did phone it was too late to get there; several hundred pounds and a few precious ounces of goodwill went down the drain.

The same applies to checking e-mails, answerphone and pager mess-ages and any other means that the technology revolution comes up with.

**Get to know everybody in the agency** Get to know all the staff in the office and what jobs they do. Don't dismiss a secretary because you think she's in a lowly position. (See 'Secretaries and personal assistants', page 189.)

**Commission** You will have to pay your agent commission even if it was you who made the contact that led to your getting the job. You will often hear other actors complain that they get all their own work so why should they pay commission? The reasons are because your agent negotiated the contract for you and even if it is no better than anybody else's in the company your agency is also spending its time making phone calls, writing letters and generally looking for work for you all the time. They don't give up because you've got six weeks' work coming up. Don't even think of querying it! If you do, it could well sour relations with them and make it more difficult for you to work together in the future.

There are some variations in commission charges, for example different rates for the different media. There is no statutory set of rates, but, generally you'll pay a higher rate the better the work is paid. You should also establish clearly when your commission is due: weekly or at the end of a contract. Make sure it is all clear at the start of your relationship, so that there are no grounds for destructive disagreement later on. It is also very important to pay your commission promptly.

Sometimes an employer will pay your money directly to your agent and he or she will deduct the commission before sending the remainder on to you.

If you change agents then the commission due on any residual payments (a repeated television appearance, for instance) is owing to the agent who negotiated the original contract. (Also see 'Signing up', page 43.)

Most agents' turnovers are high enough for them to have to register for VAT. This means that they will have to add the appropriate percentage to your commission charge.

**Your new image** If you are radically changing your hairstyle or hair-colour or growing a beard, let everybody in the agency know immediately. They will be made to look very silly if you turn up at an interview having been advertised as having long hair and you now have a crew-cut. I know time can reverse such changes, but your agent will have lost some credibility points with whoever is casting, and it could sour future relations — for the agency and for you.

**The direct approach** Sometimes a director will approach an actor directly about an interview or even an offer. This usually happens when the director knows you or perhaps doesn't realise you've got an agent. Ask the director to do all the business through your agent. This might seem like taking the long way round, but it may be that your agent has you up for another job that clashes, and it is their job to negotiate not just money, but billings, and so on.

Even if it's a Fringe production, where there are no financial negotiations to go through, check with your agent first — too many actors don't. If your agent doesn't know your real availability you could put him or her in an embarrassing situation.

**Reporting back** Report back to your agent on how an interview went. This helps him or her get to know you better at that vital nerve-point of the whole profession. On the other hand if you are lucky enough to be doing a lot of interviews then it's not necessary to phone about all of them.

If one goes badly, work out what was your fault and discuss it with your agent with assurances that you can put it right next time. This maintains their confidence in you. If it was a difficult interviewer do mention it as the information can be useful for other clients.

**'You're up for...'** Your agent may well tell you that you've been put up for a particular part or that there has been an availability check on you — and then nothing happens. You don't even get an interview! Don't immediately blame your agent. It could easily have been down to the fickle nature of this profession.

**'My agent cocked it up'** In fact you shouldn't take your insecurities out on your agent at all. Yes, agents can make mistakes, but in my experience any 'cock-up' is much more likely to have been the actor's fault. You have to work together; it should be a professional relationship based on mutual trust. Inefficient agents don't survive for very long.

If you do discover that a serious error has been committed — you weren't even put up for a well-advertised part you were perfect for, for instance — check it out with your agent. The same applies if he or she hasn't seen your work for a significant amount of time. If you have a legitimate complaint, express it directly. Don't let it fester as gossip amongst other actors.

**'My agent's doing nothing for me'** Another common cry. Don't immediately blame your agent if nothing is happening. A few agents are lazy and/or inefficient, but remember that they only earn money from you if you are working and therefore it is in their interest to try to find work for you. The only thing to do if you genuinely believe this is to put it, simply and positively, to your agent. I have heard of several incidents of people doing this, and their luck changed.

**The actor-agent working relationship** Your agent is not your slave, but not your master either. Ultimately, you employ your agent — not vice versa. Ideally, your relationship is that of a partnership with each side having different but overlapping responsibilities. Your agent probably works harder for you than you ever realise, just as he or she may not fully understand what you go through in rehearsing a play, for instance. Trust and respect are essential, and a little appreciation from you in the form of home-made jam, shelves erected or a simple 'Thank You' card can only enhance that relationship and ultimately make it more profitable.

**Your responsibility towards your agent** It is important never put your agent/agency into an embarrassing situation — not only will it reflect on them, it could also reflect on other clients. A recent example was an actor who phoned his agent to say that he couldn't go to an interview because he had a hangover. Not only was all the work the agent had put into getting the appointment wasted, but it also made me wonder about that particular agency.

**Clarity** If your agent is discussing an offer made to you, make sure your feelings about the matter are made absolutely clear; agents have been known to accept offers when the actors have said that they 'think' they'll do the job, when what they meant was that they would probably accept but they weren't sure yet.

**The actor-agent personal relationship** If this becomes too close, the working relationship can often go wrong. If you have personal problems, find someone else to help you. Your agent should only know about them if they affect your ability to work and then you only need to give the essential facts and not the nitty-gritty detail.

Your depressions about rejections and bouts of unemployment are common to all actors and therefore tacitly understood. It is positively destructive to take those depressions out on your agent as it takes valuable time and will almost certainly depress them and reduce their ability to work well for you. It could all become a vicious downward spiral.

**Your other half** Most agents won't take on both halves of a couple because of possible knock-on effects if there are problems and/or the relationship splits up. However secure your domestic relationship seems to you both, don't even suggest the idea of your other half 'coming on to' your agent's books. On the other hand, your other half should get to know your agent; after all, he or she could be taking messages for you, and the agent wants to feel sure that they will be safely delivered.

**Babies** I've heard many stories of agents not being too pleased about their clients becoming pregnant. (I've also heard of instances of wonderful support.) Of course this can knock a new parent out of work in the final weeks and can restrict mobility of work after the baby is born. (I believe that any actor's work can be distinctly enhanced by direct experience of children.) The essential point is that you should tell your agent as soon as you know, and when the baby is born you must ensure cover is always available at short notice to let you go off to interviews.

An expectant father should also tell his agent. He will need to be around, so only very important jobs can be considered. And arrangements for the next eighteen years or so will have to be thought through.

**Leaving your agent** Like any relationship the actor-agent one can get 'tired'. If this is the case make a clean break. I have heard of too many messy 'divorces' which harmed the actor more than the agent. It's a small world and agents do talk to each other. Be especially careful if you are looking for a new agent whilst still with another one. The agents you talk with will be discreet; so should you be.

**Your agent asking you to leave** This happens occasionally when an agency feels that the relationship has gone sour in some way or other. I've never known it to be done indiscreetly, so don't create waves that might reach other agents' ears. There is no point in asking for a reprieve. Try to find out why it happened and make sure it doesn't happen with your next agent.

## Co-operative agencies

This idea started in the 1970s and there are now more than fifty co-operative agencies each representing about twenty clients ('members') — many more than this makes the important internal communications a nightmare. Essentially these are run by the actors on their books — everybody 'representing' everybody else. Often there are no salaried staff and all the work is done on a voluntary basis as and when individuals are available. The only costs are administrative (rent of offices, phones, photocopying, and so on) with no profit going to any individual. It's a great idea that's hard to put into practice as the pioneers discovered — in fact, some are taking on administrators to co-ordinate everything. The best are as efficient as the very best of conventional agents; a few as unprofessional as the very worst. In general, they probably don't have as much status as the more well established conventional agencies but are certainly not to be dismissed.

The crucial thing a co-operative has to do is to ensure excellent communications between its individual members as they take turns in the office. It is essential that each member has a good working knowledge of every other member. Smooth running of a co-op takes a great deal of detailed organisation and precise passing-on of information between the members is vital. For example, an offer will often take several days to discuss, and the employer won't want to have to go back over the previously discussed details when someone else takes over the manning of the phone. Indeed, some managements will have nothing to do with co-operatives because they feel they never know to whom they are talking. It has also been known for managements to approach individual co-operative members direct — mistakenly thinking that an agency staffed by actors cannot 'know what it's doing'. (Some managements feel uncomfortable about discussing money with a third party who also happens to be an actor.) However, co-operatives have learned these lessons the hard way and have adapted their democratic working processes to surmount these and other communication problems. Their credibility with managements continues to grow.

Commission is often lower than a conventional agency, but there is generally a joining fee and/or regular monthly/annual payments which are used to meet the costs of running the agency in which the member is a partner.

Before you are asked to join a co-operative the members will want to be sure that you will fit well into their team and are willing to and capable of learning the necessary office skills. Therefore there is usually a probationary period of membership after which you and the agency can decide whether or not to continue the partnership. You will also have to be sure that you'll be happy to commit time to taking your turns in manning the office, and the regular meetings that are necessary to the efficient running of these agencies — democracy can be a very slow form of management.

A friend who joined one found a new lease of life, a lot more work and said, 'It's a wonderful family atmosphere.' Another who works a fair amount and had been with a co-operative for a long time finally left and found a conventional agent. She said: 'I'm right with "All for one and one for all", but you must remember the dark side of human nature. What actually happens is "All for me".' You have to decide if 'co-operative' life is really for you if offered the chance to join one. It can be a very good way for a newcomer to learn about the insides of the mechanics of casting — however, some co-ops are wary of taking on newcomers as they don't feel they have time to train them properly.

Finally, a comment from a friend with long experience of co-ops: 'In my experience the people who flourish in co-ops are independent-minded and experienced (though not starry) actors who have grown dissatisfied with the performance of their undistinguished conventional agent. The bane of their lives is omniscient and over-confident recent-graduate members!'

## 'Casting agents'

These serve a different function. They are usually walk-on agents who take the responsibility for casting walk-ons/extras in television and film. They have client bases of lots of different types and on request can supply a suitable crowd for any occasion. Thus they fulfil the roles of both agent and casting director for non-speaking parts that don't need to be auditioned.

## Final thought

Agents come a close second to directors in actors' complaints sessions. I have several times been privy to agents' complaints sessions and some of their clients figure quite highly, though the problems are certainly more discreetly aired. There have to be faults on both sides — that's human nature. In the majority of cases I suspect that a lack of professional understanding is the root cause of most disenchantment.

# Chapter Seven

# *The Fringe*

The Fringe has grown considerably over recent years and for many graduates it is their first taste of so-called professional work. However, it is not just the preserve of the newcomer. Many experienced actors are willing to commit time and money to get themselves seen by casting directors and agents. There are also writers and directors anxious to get their work noticed, and there are those who do it simply because they believe in it. From your point of view it is important to assess whether despite the personal costs involved it could have real value for you.

**What is it?** In broad terms 'The Fringe' is smaller-scale theatre that operates on the 'fringes' of 'legitimate' activity. Essentially, the idea began at the Edinburgh Festival over half-a-century ago. It really started taking off (especially in London) in the late 1960s as an arena for 'alternative' and 'experimental' theatre. The 1990s saw a huge expansion in the number of venues being used and a downturn in the exploration of theatre forms — it became more commercial, much more competitive and not just in London (and Edinburgh).

The really confusing thing is that there are several theatres, regarded as part of the London Fringe, who offer Equity contracts — *The Almeida* and *The Tricycle*, for instance. There are also those who are non-Equity, but have huge reputations — *The Gate* and *The King's Head*, for instance. There are also several very reputable companies working on the Fringe who don't pay Equity rates.

**What does it pay?** The simple answer to this is that (apart from a few venues) you will effectively pay to perform rather than get paid. You should think of participating in a Fringe production as a possible investment in your future. Some companies will pay travelling expenses; others will offer you a share of the profits — a 'profit-share' production. You'll almost certainly be worse off with the latter deal as virtually none of them make profits. (A friend once earned just £10, for eight weeks' work, as his share of the profits on a prize-winning production.) The only reasons for being in a Fringe production are that (a) you might be 'seen', (b) you fundamentally believe in the production's potential and (c) it could help keep your acting-juices flowing.

**Will I get seen?** Agents and casting directors do scout for new talent on the Fringe. However, many are resistant to travelling too far outside

Central London unless the venue happens to be close to their homes. The other problem is that there are probably over a hundred Fringe productions on at any one time — plus many more 'legitimate' ones. (The Edinburgh Festival has even more productions packed into a few weeks — 1,700 in 2000, with an average audience of 11.) The agent or casting director has got to be given very good reasons to come and see yours — especially as the quality of Fringe productions is highly variable.

**Might it transfer?** In the past unpaid Fringe productions have been known to transfer into paid venues — even into the West End. In recent years, this has become a rarer phenomenon.

**Is it regarded as professional work?** In general terms it is. However, there is a tendency in Fringe productions for professional standards (and facilities) to be somewhat lacking — that is sometimes an understatement. Poor technical backup, indifferent front-of-house arrangements and general unreliability (for instance) are too often the case — almost inevitably damaging the quality of the final product.

**Problems to watch out for**
*The ego trip* A number of productions are set up by individuals wanting a starring vehicle for themselves — much like the old actor-managers. It is generally better to avoid such enterprises unless you can be fairly sure that the central 'ego' will not be damaging to your contribution. Ask around for objective advice before accepting a part in such a production.

*What else will you have to do?* Will you have to do other things — like paint the set, distribute posters, help with the get-in, and so on? You may think that you can make time to do things like this, but are you sure you want to be thus distracted in the last few days before opening night?

*Is the script good enough?* There really is no point in doing a production that's flawed before it leaves the page.

*Can you work well with the director?* This is a highly subjective judgement, but since you are not being properly paid, it is important that you feel as sure as you can be that it'll be a worthwhile experience.

*Can you actually afford to do it?* There really is no point in taking time out from paid work in order to do a Fringe production unless you really think that you'll get something out of the experience. (It can be worth asking if your rehearsal-calls can be arranged round your work commitments.) Also, check whether your participation will affect your benefits in any way.

*Your agent* If you have one will he or she be happy for you to do the production?

*Contracts* Whilst there is no standard Equity contract for this kind of work the Union does have a free set of guidelines which are very useful. Some companies issue their own contracts — it is important to read these carefully and check with Equity if you have any doubts.

*Will the production get reviews?* A good review equals good publicity — important for any production. Some productions in the most prestigious venues get reviewed in national newspapers. However, because there are so many productions at any one time, the press has strict rules (length of run, for instance) about what they will send reviewers to. It is important to note that the perceptiveness of some of the latter is somewhat shallow — that's not sour grapes, it's a fact.

*Is the publicity and marketing going to be sufficient?* After the cost of hiring the venue, publicity and marketing are the next major cost of a Fringe production — and too many productions try to skimp on these. In such a competitive environment these are very, very important.

*Does the venue have a good reputation?* It is much, much harder to get people into less prestigious ones.

*Promises* Whilst enthusiasm for a project is wonderful, beware of promises when they seem over-the-top — too much optimism can blind people to important practical realities.

*Is it going to be properly organised?* There is far more to putting on a production than most actors realise (see below). Ask questions based on the above and if you don't feel sufficiently satisfied politely back away — there's no point in being miserable, as well as unpaid, for several weeks.

## Setting up your own production

Too many people think that mounting a production is just a matter of getting a few friends together, borrowing some props and costumes, and getting on with it. What about the costs of hiring a venue, a rehearsal space, the publicity and marketing, the author's royalties (if still in copyright), and so on? You may be lucky enough to get some — even all — of these for free, or you might find a rich auntie. However you fund the above essentials, you have got to do a lot of careful planning before rehearsals start. Will the playwright (and/or translator) allow you to do a production of the play in the first place? Just because a play is in print, it doesn't mean that anyone can perform it. Is the rehearsal room available enough of the time? What is the deadline for getting the poster design to the printers, so that they can get the result back to you in time for the distributors to get them displayed in good time before opening night? And so on, and so on, and so on.... Oh, and it is essential to plan and budget with contingency in both time and money — there are always several things that take more time than you'd thought and several things that cost more than you'd thought, or forgotten to budget for in the first place.

Doing it yourself is far more complex than most people realise, but can be incredibly satisfying if you succeed. For a technically-simple production you probably need to find at least £5,000 — and that's without paying any of the participants. The chances of recouping this through the box office are very low. (The average audience on the Fringe is about 30%.) A recent report stated that, 'theatres are among the most over-regulated businesses in the UK' — legal requirements like Health and Safety, VAT and performance rights cannot be neglected.

## The Edinburgh Fringe Festival

I think that there is a real sense that every actor should try this 'Carnival of theatre' experience at least once. ('The biggest theatrical lottery in the world.') You'll meet lots of new people, make contacts and it's a great three weeks even if your own production doesn't hit the heights.

Advice on mounting a production on the Edinburgh Fringe is available from: Edinburgh Festival Fringe, 180 High Street, Edinburgh, EH1 1QS; (0131) 226 5257; <www.edfringe.com>.

## Setting up your own company

If you are dreaming of doing more, there is an incredibly helpful organisation who can guide you — for very reasonable fees. It is the Independent Theatre Council (ITC), 12 The Leathermarket, Weston Street, London, SE1 3ER; (020) 7403 1727. It has a website at <www.itc-arts.org> which contains a comprehensive list of courses covering fundraising, contracts, marketing and everything else associated with this complex business. You should also get advice from others who've done it before — particularly with regard to publicity and funding applications. (Your local Regional Arts Board, listed in *Contacts*, can supply lists of sources of funding.) There is a language called 'application-speak' which you will need help to decipher, and translate your responses back into.

I believe that the most important aspect of setting up your own company is being very clear about and committed to why you are doing it — simply wanting to act is not enough.

## Showcases

The drama schools have been doing these for years, and recently several organisations have been set up to provide the same for non-students. For a fee you get to perform your audition speech(es) to an audience (largely) of casting directors. (I know of one company that will record your performance on video for distribution.) Some casting directors (and agents) like these because viewing them takes up less time than a full production. There are others who firmly believe that they need to see more than just two minutes worth. Once again you should check out any such organisation thoroughly before committing your money.

NB Sometimes participants are selected by audition to ensure 'quality control' — essentially the company is working like an agent but charging an up-front fee rather than commission.

## Summary

I have seen many high hopes dashed — sometimes accompanied by considerable debt. I've also seen a few significant successes — through considerable persistence, enthusiasm, and careful thought and planning. If you follow the guidelines above, and do your research properly, you too can succeed.

# Chapter Eight

# *A Director's Life*

'I suppose you'll be having a bit of a rest now,' says the solicitous actor after the triumphant opening night. Kindly meant, but somewhat insensitive to the relieved but tired director. Apart from keeping an eye on the production during its run there are (lurking on his or her desk, beside it and under it) piles of paper demanding attention — amongst which is your precious letter, CV and photograph along with those of your peers. If the desk has been neglected for a week, there may well be several hundred letters from actors. There will probably be a dozen from other professionals (freelance directors, designers, and so on) seeking work, and several fat unsolicited scripts from aspiring writers demanding to be read. However, this 'art' section is only a small proportion of the new information to be digested and dealt with — and your package is most certainly not a priority. There are the messages insisting on urgent action, details of yet another complex funding scheme to absorb and act upon before Monday, letters of complaint from the public about the four-letter words in the last production or poor service in the restaurant or smells in the loo... The list is endless. Apart from all this there are the papers to prepare for the monthly Board of Management meeting, internal planning and policy meetings, the eternal energy-sapping battles with external bureaucracies — yet another long list of things to do, often to ensure the very survival of the theatre. I do not exaggerate. Who on earth would want to run a theatre? Well, some people do — probably for similar crazy reasons to those that made you want to be an actor. (Max Stafford-Clark, when Artistic Director of the Royal Court, said: 'I now run a business that occasionally puts on plays.') In some theatres the Administrator (or General Manager or Chief Executive) is senior to the Artistic Director, but even in these cases a lot of the director's time will still be taken up with urgent matters of administration and public relations which will have much greater priority than your sales package.

I have tried to give you a perspective on a theatre director's life not for sympathy, but so that you have a better idea of whom you are trying to reach. They may vary as individuals but they all have the above in common. And this kind of pressure governs the life of every kind of director — television and film directors coping with the mind-boggling, minutely detailed organisation that is necessary, and freelance directors looking out for their own next jobs let alone yours. Actors are obviously important to directors, but because you are not in short supply other matters take a much greater priority. That is an unchanging fact.

Casting directors and agents are obviously more actor-focused, however they are no less busy. The power-brokers of the acting profession all work very long hours, have constant demands made on them and find it impossible to focus properly on each and every actor who communicates with them.

# Chapter Nine

# *Letters, CVs and Photographs*

Writing a letter, with CV and photograph, is the primary means towards getting work (or an agent) for your first few years unless you are very, very lucky. Even if you are fortunate enough to have a good agent you will probably need to do some writing yourself. When you have some experience under your belt as well as a good agent it is amazing how a well-timed and well-presented 'sales package' can open up new directions for you. Considering how crucial these are, the lack of effort, care and attention the majority of actors seem to put into them is amazing.

Each director receives thousands of submissions per year — I reckon I received about a thousand for a recent production with a cast of four, for which I hadn't even circulated agents for suggestions. It takes time to read each letter and CV and absorb the photograph, and it takes more time to select the roughly 5% there is time to interview. In my last full-time job I reckon that the total time I spent in organising auditions and auditioning, reading and responding to actors' letters amounted to roughly three months a year — even with secretarial help.

So what do you do in your letter (and CV and photograph) to attract attention if a director doesn't know you? There is no single answer to this fundamental question, and the best submission in the world can pass in front of blind eyes if the recipient has weightier matters immediately to the fore the moment your carefully thought out piece of advertising lands on the desk. On a bad day there can be a real sense that they are just more junk mail to be thrown straight in the bin. I don't think many actually do this, but all look for ways of reducing the fast-growing pile as it threatens to overwhelm them. Some of this reduction will be done on the basis of appropriateness to forthcoming productions, some will occur for more trivial reasons — minor details which consciously or unconsciously irritate the reader — or sometimes because of the crude attention-seeking nature of the contents. Remember, we in the UK react strongly against the 'obvious' advert which bludgeons. Study an evening's commercial breaks for marvellous examples of the subtle sell.

Don't get the impression that receiving submissions is tedious in itself. It only becomes a chore when so many have contents churned out with the same old formulae, make the usual mistakes and rely on blatant gimmickry. Also, many of us would privately admit to feeling guilty at not being able to see everyone — and guilt can make people irrational.

The crucial thing to remember is that your letter, CV and photograph is your first point of contact with the recipient and will be flipped through along with a pile of others. The amount of time spent 'flipping through' your particular 'sales package' will probably be between ten and twenty seconds at the initial sort through to decide who appears interesting and who doesn't.

NB I shall refer to 'directors' throughout, but similar thoughts pertain when writing to agents, casting directors and other managements unless otherwise stated.

## Some pitfalls to watch out for in your letters

**Fundamentals** Bad spelling and handwriting and a disregard for accepted grammar and punctuation are immediately alienating to a literate reader. Remember, a lot of directors are language graduates and, even if not, they are used to working with — and care about — the written word.

**Exclamation marks!** Some people go overboard with exclamation marks and other visual emphases. The eye is instantly drawn to these, and they can easily undermine the impact of the actual words. The sense should be in those words — without any props.

**Alan who?** Equally off-putting are misspelt character-names, play-titles, playwrights' names. (You'd have thought Alan Ayckbourn was so famous that people would know how to spell his name, but probably a third of correspondents add an 'e' at the end.)

**The look of your letter** There is no doubt about how much the initial impact of the letter — before a word is read — counts. Unless your handwriting is pleasing to the eye and legible, use a computer or word-processor. Whatever sort of machine you use make sure that the print-out looks crisp and clear. Poor line-spacing, splodgy or faded print and extraneous 'crud' (often added by poorly-maintained photocopiers and printers) are common faults and make your letter — and consequently you — look amateur.

The overall look of your letter should be easy on the eye and easy to read. A page that is laid out with a line-spacing of $1\frac{1}{2}$ or 2 is much easier to read than one which has a line-spacing of 1. This can tend to look like a black 'splodge' of words which will need some concentration, and extra time, to read properly. (Think of how difficult those tightly printed classic playscripts are to work from.)

**'Dear...'** Mass-produced letters that have the recipient's name clumsily inserted after the 'Dear' look awful. I know it takes time, but insert people's names neatly into your general letter. I've also seen the 'Dear' and the director's name both written in; this can look very good if you've got good strong handwriting and not a childish scrawl like mine.

**'Dear Sir/Madam'** Over-formal letters which could just as well be requesting a consignment of bananas won't get you far. (Does this actor have any imagination?) Never write to 'Sir/Madam' and end with 'Yours faithfully'. Get a name and end with a warm greeting. However, don't get too familiar and address somebody only by their first name unless you know them.

It is accepted convention to use the recipient's full name rather than addressing him or her as Mr/Miss/Ms So-and-So. But be careful about using common abbreviations of first names — not everybody likes them and some prefer to reserve them for close friends.

Also, get their title right. As an Associate Director I used to get quite irritated if a letter was addressed to me as 'Simon Dunmore, Assistant Director...' Don't write to the Administrator/General Manager, either. They may have power but they won't have much, if any, influence over casting. They will usually pass your letter on to the director (or casting director), but he or she could be slightly alienated by its second-hand nature.

**'I'd like to introduce myself...'** Letters starting with this or 'My name is...' come over as being completely banal — the former is at the heart of the purpose behind your letter and the latter should be in your letterhead.

**Other banalities** A phrase like 'In my capacity as an actor' is also obvious. As are facts like 'I am an actor...' or 'I would like to audition...' or even 'I am writing...' Yet, an amazing number of people use these phrases (and similar ones) in order to bridge gaps or as a method of building up to a particular point. Don't do it!

**Attention-seeking gambits** It is a big mistake to resort to attention-seeking gambits like silly jokes, phrases like 'Gissa job' and vulgarity in general. Another popular but puerile trick is to send out spoof questionnaires for the director to fill in: for example, a list of potential reasons for not being seen, with boxes to put appropriate ticks in. This kind of stunt is incredibly annoying. I've known people resort to writing indifferent poems, appealing for the charity of an interview on the basis that it's their birthday or it's near Christmas. A friend once went as far as to disguise himself as a motorcycle messenger and deliver an oar to an impresario with a letter saying: 'I just wanted to get my oar in.' He got no reply whatsoever.

What follows is possibly the worst piece of 'attention-seeking' I've ever come across:

Hi Simon!
   Here's something that might interest you:
WHAT THE ACTRESS REALLY SAID TO THE BISHOP

MARIA, 24, Fresh out of [*Name of drama school*]. Young, confident and bursting with enthusiasm.

BISHOP, 93, Wise beyond his years.

*Maria enters open confessional box centre stage:*

Bishop: How long is it since you have been to confession, my child?

Maria: About eight years, your grace, but I do have an excuse. I ran away to Hong Kong to pursue a life on the stage.

Bishop: A life on the stage? But they don't have any stages out there, only stock markets and refugees. I'm afraid you'll have to do better than that.

Maria: But it's true! I worked in television there for six years; writing, directing and performing in my own series of children's dramas.

Bishop: Ah, television, that's not quite the thing is it? No, no. One must appear in, ah, the flesh. Although one must not be tempted by the flesh, indeed no. (*Coughs*) Tell me, my dear, have you had temptation put in, ah, your way?

Maria: Yes it has, your grace, many, many times.

Bishop: Good lord, my dear, can you, ah, describe them?

Maria: Well, I started off with groups, you know, five or six of us — just for fun — and then it started getting quite serious...

Bishop: (*Pause*) Yes, yes go on my dear go on.

Maria: Recently it's been on my own...

Bishop: (*Splutter*)

Maria: Although I still really enjoy doing it in schools...

Bishop: (*Suffers massive coronary from overdose of double entendres*)

\* \* \* \* \* \* \* \* \* \* \* \* \* \*

Get the whole story on the attached CV. I'd be happy to audition for any forthcoming productions or simply come in for a chat.

Yours devotedly,

However, a neat and clever gambit at the right moment, particularly if it's for film or television, can help. Mike Newall (director of *An Awfully Big Adventure*) told the story of how he met the girl who eventually played the lead in the film. She initially hand-wrote a letter on lined-paper that was 'very characterful'. She went on to appear at the interview in 'knee-socks' and clothes akin to the period — and 'all but played the part' in the interview. This all sounds very clever, but see 'Role-playing' (page 105) and 'What shall I wear?' (page 106).

I suspect this kind of strategy is only applicable to film, where it is generally the case that directors want the 'real thing' plonked under their noses. (See chapter 16.)

**The appeal** Frustration with your 'lot' is a fundamental part of almost every actor's working life. Don't let it creep into your letters. Too many people try to use it as grounds for appeal to the recipient's better nature.

An approach like 'I've done my stint in children's theatre, so give me a chance' is not only condescending toward a fundamental part of the profession but also reads like 'whinge' (that sound children make when they're working overtime to get what they want). Logic goes out of the window. The attack is based on those notes in the audio spectrum calculated to go right through me.

**'Brevity is the soul of wit'** As for letters that go on for several pages, nobody has the time. Especially those that go on about your whole philosophy of life, acting and the universe. Don't laugh; people do it. Two or three hundred words — at most — is perfectly sufficient, and fewer is better. That's not much — the next three sections combined contain just about two-hundred and fifty words.

However, don't take 'brevity' too far. 'I'm writing to you with regard to your auditions for [*name of production*], and I would like to be considered for an audition.' This tells me nothing about you.

**Flattery** Don't resort to base flattery about a director's productions. Compliments are good to receive, but some correspondents seem to think that going a little further can help their cause — that is not necessarily true. People often try the more general gambit of 'I've heard about the good work you are doing' or variations on this theme; this comes over as ingratiating and patronising. The other popular tack is the 'double' flattery approach: 'The wonderful work of your theatre would suit my talents precisely.' This is incredibly alienating. Your letter should be about you, not about me, but don't overtly flatter yourself by making statements like 'I am brilliant; you cannot do without me.' That just comes over as arrogance.

**Undermining yourself** The more modest correspondents go for statements like 'I'm a hard worker', 'I'd fit in well with your company' or 'I'll do anything, even work backstage'. Acting is hard work, so the ability to shoulder it is a prerequisite for the job and therefore doesn't need mentioning. Likewise the ability to work well with other people. As for implying that working backstage is the lowliest job — you are insulting very important people.

**'But' and other 'qualifying' words** 'But' is a very useful little word, but it can tend to bring a negative feel to your prose. Try to avoid using it and similar 'qualifying' words. 'I have been working on the Fringe. My main aim now is to work in Rep.' reads more positively than 'I have been working on the Fringe, but my main aim now is to work in Rep'.

**'I'd be so right for...'** Don't start going over the top about how right you'd be for a specific part. You may well be perfect but you don't know the approach to the play and, anyway, it's hardly up to you to make the decision. And don't suggest yourself for a part for which you're blatantly unsuitable — that is incredibly annoying.

**'Who are all these people?'** If you write as a group the recipient will get no real impression of each separate individual. This is not to say you shouldn't write as a group to invite someone to a production, but by not writing an individual letter you are missing out an important part of the communication.

Couples often write jointly; this is a big mistake (a) for the reason above and (b) because most directors are extremely wary of casting couples in the same production for fear of domestic dispute colouring things in the wrong way. I know that in writing together you are not necessarily expecting to be cast together, but the fear will be that if only one is seen there will be a barrage of complaints from the other half. It happens. If your basic purpose is to save on postage, then put the two submissions into separate envelopes and put them into a larger one. But don't use exactly the same or even similar letters and CV formats (see 'I've read this before', page 72); you may be together in spirit but you still have your own individual personalities.

**'How often should I write?'** If you've had some kind of positive response you think worth following up, never hassle but do gently remind. Always write to follow up; never ever phone unless specifically requested to do so. And don't keep on writing every month as some people do — you are only adding to the director's guilt complex, and you are even less likely to be seen. A gentle hint in about six months is probably the best approach, unless you feel that you can genuinely suggest yourself for a specific piece of casting.

**'How about your place?'** A way of sticking pins under people's fingernails is to suggest that you could 'come and see them in their office'. This does not make life simpler. An office is a sanctuary in which to concentrate on other matters.

On the other hand, I have known several actors successfully using the tactic of travelling the country staying with friends and writing to all the theatres within range of their ports of call saying 'I will be staying in your area on —. Could I come and see you?' This can sound like a more legitimate reason for inviting an actor into the 'sanctuary'. After all, if the actor knows someone in the area, that someone is a potential member of the theatre's audience. But this is an expensive way of getting to meet directors and there are much greater priorities for your meagre funds.

**Pretty paper** Rainbows, teddy bears and pretty flowers are just some of the items I have encountered adorning actors' note-paper (from men as well as women). These decorations tend to suggest that you haven't quite grown up yet. Of course in some ways not having 'quite grown up yet' is part of the essence of being an actor, but you have also got to appear as a responsible professional.

**Colours** Various ink and paper colour combinations are adopted by some to add extra impact. Yes, silver ink on black paper will make your letter stand out in the pile of conventional black on white, but what does this, or any other striking combination, say about you? More important, the effect of such a visual impact can be so great that the all-important contents may not be properly digested. (This also applies to CVs.)

**'You must remember me'** Too many people write in follow-up presuming that the recipient remembers the details of the original letter. Yes, the original letter can be dug out of the files, but be warned that most organisations gut those files periodically because of the sheer volume of paper.

Also, direct statements like 'You will remember I wrote...' can easily embarrass because you are one of hundreds who write each month and it is impossible to remember each and every one. Changing the word 'will' to 'may' takes the curse off this approach, and you should reiterate the salient facts of your previous letter. Don't use exactly the same format and phraseology; if your original letter does come to light, your lack of imagination could count against you.

**'I look forward to hearing from you'** This may seem polite but it is another inadvisable example of conscience-pricking. As one director said to me: 'It's nice when someone gives you permission not to reply.' However, don't end with, 'Please don't bother to reply' as this has a negative feel. It is best to omit the subject of replying entirely.

**Theatre-In-Education and children's theatre** Too many young actors write to such companies talking about work for children being an 'apprenticeship' — or similar word or phrase — for them. Various glowing adjectives may precede this crucial word but they cannot detract from the essential calumny. Working with and for children is a special skill in its own right. The 'legitimate' companies have considerable expertise and cannot 'carry' an apprentice.

**Dull letters** The following letter (a very typical example) does nothing specifically wrong, but gave me no idea of the writer as a person and did not inspire me to see her, when there are so many to choose from.

> [*Name, address and date*]
> Dear Simon Dunmore,
> I am writing to introduce myself. I am, at present, in my final year at

[*name of drama school*]. As I will be graduating in July, I am enclosing my CV and photograph for your reference.

I would like to take this opportunity to invite you to the 'Audition Show', which the students are organising on April 18th at the DONMAR WAREHOUSE in London or on April 20th at [*drama-school address*]. This would give you a chance to view my work.

In the 'Summer Season' at college, I am appearing in *Danton's Death* from 24th to 27th May. I am also playing Mrs Temptwell in *The Grace of Mary Traverse* which runs from June 21st to the 24th. I would be more than happy to arrange tickets for you. However, if it is not possible for you to attend, but you are interested in seeing my work, I would, of course, be very pleased to audition for you personally.

I look forward very much to meeting you in the future.

Yours sincerely,

[*signature*]

## Writing good letters

The preceding litany of what not to do may have left you feeling, 'But what can I do to attract attention in amongst all this intense competition?' An actor's job is to communicate another's personality through the spoken word. In order to help get that job you have to work hard at communicating your own personality through the written word. If you find that difficult (and most people do) then take time to experiment and evolve a good basic format. Try out drafts of your letters on other people — preferably someone who is used to reading such letters. As to content, more detailed suggestions follow, but basically you should use your actor's imagination to communicate yourself to the unseen and unknown recipient. Aim to surprise: to make the task of reading all those letters suddenly enjoyable with a delicious piece of humour, for instance. (However, see 'Make 'em laugh', page 118.) You can use the fact that the recipient doesn't know you to 'develop' or 'colour' the truth provided that you are sure you won't have to backtrack later.

You should write a brief introductory letter that puts over your personality with, maybe, the odd witty remark or brief personal anecdote thrown in. For instance, mention briefly the mad selling job you've just done or the curious phrasing in the local paper's review of your last production. (Be careful about using up your best stories too soon — you should also have something that might be useful in the hoped-for interview.) You should imply a confidence in your abilities without in any way actually saying 'I am brilliant'.

Every letter from an actor is making the same statement: 'I want work!' We know this, so you don't need specifically to say so. However, don't go too far the other way and be so bland as almost to deny that fact.

**Headed note-paper** It is a good idea to get your own headed note-paper; it makes you look organised. However, if your particular brand of note-paper is of a particularly strong colour, be careful. All children have their 'favourite' colour; most adults have their 'colour prejudices' — in the legitimate sense. If you are going for colour, be subtle about it. NB A good 'bonded' paper can add a bit of 'class'.

**Contact details** In this electronic age it's possible to list a number of different ways of contacting you (or your agent) quickly. Alternatives can be useful — they can also be confusing (especially multiple e-mail addresses). The important thing is to have a primary contact number/address clearly listed as such. If you have an agent, then that 'primary contact' should be them. Also, think about how many other 'contact points' you should list. It might look impressive to have a conventional phone, a mobile, a pager, an e-mail address and a website, but this plethora of electronic codes could make you look more like a techno-nerd than an actor.

This applies to letters, CVs, photographs and labels fixed to anything else that you send.

**Handwriting** Very few people have handwriting that is good, stylish and even enough. However, if you are blessed with good readable hand-writing, it can be worth exploiting. It can help convey more of yourself and can be a pleasure for the director to read in amongst all the typed ones. (I met one director who actively prefers hand-written letters.) I know an actor whose handwriting is not only beautiful to behold but also seems totally to contradict what he looks like (he's built like a heavy-weight boxer). This kind of apparent contradiction is a very simple and effective way to gain attention. Contrasts like this are always intriguing.

**Computers** If you haven't yet, get a computer — or, at least, access to one! And allow yourself several frustrating weeks to learn how to use it properly.

Computer technology is advancing rapidly all the time. This means that there is a booming second-hand market. You can pick up a perfectly reasonable one — with a printer — for a few hundred pounds. (You only need a very simple machine for working with words.) If computer and printer are beyond your means go for an all-in-one word-processor, which won't be as flexible but will be perfectly adequate.

A great advantage of computers is that there are an enormous number of different — and stylish — typefaces which can be fed into their systems, so you can easily create a very appealing letterhead. Don't be tempted, as you learn more of the clever manipulations that computers can carry out with type, to create a letterhead that is so 'whacky' it's semi-legible. ('Typefaces are the clothes words wear.' Beatrice Warde.)

The computer helped me as an author. I find it's much easier to 'scribble' thoughts down — as they come off the top of my head — onto my machine and then refine them later. If I do the equivalent on paper, the refinements are a great unreadable mess of crossings out, arrows and insertions which is very hard to read let alone refine further.

**Your personality** This has been growing ever since you leapt out of the womb (and possibly from conception) — it would take another lifetime to explain it. You can, however, evoke it — briefly — through things that you've done. These don't necessarily need to be 'acting things'. They can be 'happenings' that are now commonplace to you, but cause gasps when you mention them to someone new. Or, if you really don't think you've got anything that fits within this category, they could be the very ordinary jobs you've done before going to drama school, to fund your training, for instance.

For example:

Dear —,
My first job was as a waitress in a cocktail bar. This proved to be a little more tricky than I had anticipated, so I moved on from spilling things over tablecloths to manufacturing them. I spent four years working for a textile company during which I began saving money to go to drama school.

I have nearly completed my training at [*School, then details of current production and how to organise tickets.*]

I am enclosing a copy of my photo and CV and a s.a.e.

This letter got a 75% reply rate (from agents); contemporaries writing (less 'characterful' letters) received less than 10% response. Don't be tempted to copy it! Since this letter was first published in the previous edition of this book the clones of it have started arriving. It's the 'spirit' of it that you should seek to emulate, not the 'form'.

**Personalising each individual letter** If at all possible, personalise each letter by referring to someone the recipient knows well. Of course it is difficult and time-consuming to find connections with each and every individual but it is well worth it for at least some of your mailing-list. Remember that if you do mention someone you must make sure they are happy to act as an unofficial referee for you — and make sure they really are known to the recipient. Work out a basic format within which you can vary details for somebody you have that 'connection' with. Don't try to compose each letter separately. It'll take for ever and you'll go mad.

Invite directors to the production you are in at the moment — they probably won't come, but the fact that you are working will add energy to your letter. In fact, it's best to do your letter writing when you are working for this very reason. Even if you feel you've got no spare time at all because you are working, make some to organise those vital letters.

**Strong skills** Actors with strong skills in other areas are becoming more and more sought after. So if you play an instrument well, for example, it is well worth stating that in your letter as well as on your CV.

**Clarity** What is clear to you may not necessarily be clear to the recipient. Look at your letter again before sending it. Is it clear and does it make sense? For instance, if an incident is worth describing in your letter, can you be both brief and clear about it without having to explain too much about the context? I had to do this endlessly in the writing of this book. Friends were extremely helpful in pointing out the many things that were obviously clear in my head but not clear to the reader. As I rewrote I developed the discipline of asking myself at every stage: 'What am I really trying to say and to whom am I saying it?'

**Your signature** Of course you will put your signature at the bottom. (Some people stupidly forget this — I presume in the panic of mass-producing all those letters.) If your handwriting is really awful, it is well worth practising just your signature to get it into a good strong shape. It is curious how so many signatures look tight and resentful as though the writer was signing a cheque for the rent. Always use your full professional name, not an initial and surname. (See 'Abbreviations', page 71.) And use black or blue ink — red or green or other bright colours look childish.

**Be concise** Don't feel you have to cram too much information in. Let your CV take on the bulk of that load. Your letter should be the 'come on', your CV and photograph the details of the 'product'.

**Finally** Look at your letter and ask yourself if it's clear and expresses you and your personality.

## Some pitfalls to watch out for in your CV

All the comments above about spelling, layout, and so on, apply to CVs (or résumés). There are numerous other common faults.

**Padding** CVs padded out with amateur productions and exam results, for instance, don't communicate anything except a desire to make your CV look longer. If you are just leaving drama school, I know that they are probably a significant part of your life to date, but there is a general prejudice against amateur work and a recognition that the intellectual prowess implicit in a passing exams contributes very little toward good acting. Youth theatre work is probably viewed more sympathetically

but, even if you have played leads with the National Youth Theatre, put them in their place on your CV. Don't get paranoid because it seems too short. A good layout can solve that problem.
NB 'Non-professional' reads better than 'Amateur'.

**The obvious** Don't put 'Curriculum Vitae' (or 'CV') or put 'Description' before 'Eyes', 'Height', and so on. Similarly, don't put in sub-headings like 'Character', 'Play', 'Director' — or any other term that is inherently obvious.

**Damaging information** Some information can be positively damaging. For instance, giving your date of birth (or your age) can tie you down too much. Think carefully about whether you need to mention your drama school at all as prejudices exist about most of them. You are you, your performances and other skills and talents, not another walking, talking doll off a particular production line. If you have also directed, consider carefully its place on your CV. You are trying to sell yourself as an actor — to directors, and some don't relish the potential of being upstaged. Put any directing credits in their place — that may mean omitting them altogether.

**Irrelevant information** CVs cluttered with irrelevancies like 'Equity number', 'Weight', 'Hair Length', and so on, are boring. You are not attending a school medical. Your photograph will give sufficient information in these areas, and if you are extreme (in the useful sense) in any area you can put it in the letter: for example, 'I am a big actress'. (I once received a letter that started with this — and she was lovely.)
   The only important personal statistics that cannot be gleaned properly from your photograph are eye and hair colour, and height.

**'Playing range'** This is one of the most vexed questions in the actor-information area. I maintain that (perceived) age is in the 'eye of the beholder' and can be gleaned from your photograph. But The Spotlight insist that is the question they are most frequently asked. (They use the term, 'Age band normally cast'.) I suspect this query generally comes from 'blinkered' media people (see chapter 16). My suggestion is that you don't put it on your CV, but do fill it in (without compromising credibility — get a body of opinion) on your *Spotlight* form. (A friend, although 25, looked much younger and claimed that she was 14 in a commercial casting and got the part. When filming was completed glasses of wine were handed out. She was given an orange squash.)

**Abbreviations** Another common phenomenon is for people to use a sort of telephone-directory style by using initials for first names: 'M. Ellis in *Touched* by S. Lowe, dir. by S. Dunmore'. This so depersonalises the facts that it almost feels that the part, the play and director were all extremely boring (let alone the act of 'dir.'-*ing*). I know that it can be awkward trying to fit long names and titles all into one neat line, but you have to find a way. A computer or word processor with varying typesizes can really help with this. (See 'The layout of your credits', page 75.)

**'I've read this before'** Similar CV formats coming from a number of different people can get very wearing. Once again, find your own way of expressing yourself. This may seem impossible as your CV is a series of facts, but they are facts about you and nobody else — find your own way of expressing them. Don't resort to putting them in prose form; this makes it harder for the reader to pick out the salient facts.

It would seem that each drama schools preaches its own particular layout (or maybe it's those 'helpful secretaries', see page 22); these range from the very formal to the very jazzy. I know that not everybody is good at layouts, and it is important that the information is clearly laid out. But stylistic repetition when going through a whole pile of letters can become very tedious. A sudden piece of innovation like your name in a different typeface — can break the monotony and draw attention to yourself in a strong simple way. You have shown individuality and imagination — both very important qualities for the actor behind that CV. Especially early in your career, when you've done very little professional work, you'll seem very similar to several thousand others, but you are different, so find a way of expressing it.

**More scrap paper** CVs spread out over several pages make me wonder what the actor is trying to prove. You only need one side of one page — that's all the recipient has time to take in; and when you've done enough to fill that page you can start cutting out your less prestigious productions.

**Brochure-style CVs** These can look very good, and attract attention, but can also increase irritation. The fact is that we want to be able to turn over as few pages as possible — it all saves precious time. (If you only knew how much paper we have to deal with.) There is also a sense that such presentations are almost too glossy, almost 'over the top'.

**'Is this actor on drugs?'** Some CVs are so 'jazzy' that they are difficult to read. A CV decorated with artistically arranged extracts from favourable reviews or one utilising all a computer's type-manipulation potential might feel very clever, but is the important information it contains easily discernible? Remember that we only have time to give it a quick skim in the initial selection process.

There is a designer's rule that suggests that you should use no more than two different typefaces on a page. I am not saying don't put play titles in capitals or don't use the 'bold' or 'italic' forms of a typeface, but use these forms sparingly. On the other hand avoid using 'underline' — that was the only way typewriters used to be able to emphasise and now seems very crude; as does the computer's facility for putting boxes round things.

**Disguising the truth** Don't make vain attempts to try to pull the wool over people's eyes about your piano-playing abilities, for instance. Listing 'Piano' under 'Special skills' (or whatever) when the summit of your achievements is *Chopsticks*... need I say more? You might think that you'll gain attention points by this listing, but you'll have the reverse effect if put to the test in any way. Nobody takes kindly to being conned — it'll be remembered. It's better to omit 'Piano' altogether, if this is the case — or get lessons to bring it up to CV level.

**Exaggerated claims** Of course you want to present yourself in the best light possible, but bear in mind the actual level of your individual skills. For example, your Geordie accent may be reasonable, so mention it; but don't claim that it is 'excellent' unless it really is. You may get an interview on that basis, but you could easily be asked to demonstrate it there and then — to a Geordie.

I know an actor who claimed to 'play the flute very well'. She was somewhat taken aback when a director produced one from his bag and asked for a demonstration. She had reached Grade 8 in her youth but hadn't practised it for years.

**Referees** Unlike most professions, actors don't need referees and putting them on your CV can make you look as though you know nothing about how the profession works. Directors do talk to each other about individual actors, and reference is often sought between us. If necessary, we can always find someone to refer to from your credits.

## Creating a good CV

I've come to the conclusion that apart from good layout the most important things to include in your CV are the names; those of the parts you have played and the people who have directed you. (Teachers, if well-known, can also count.) The former are your achievements; the latter, the reader's reference points. A familiar name can be a point of contact with your reader and could be a good discussion-point in an interview. However, don't go into tedious and pedantic detail — you are being patronising if you list 'Macbeth in *Macbeth* by William Shakespeare'. A 'taste' of your work to date is all that's necessary — well laid out on one side of A4 paper. The other important element is what else you've done and can do.

It should also contain your name (numerous people omit this 'detail' from their CVs) and your 'primary contact' number (see 'Contact details', page 68) — paper-clips have been known to fall off and letter, CV and photograph become separated in the chaos of paper.

One of the most persistent criticisms I've had on this book has been, 'Why is there no CV template?' I shall persist with this omission, for fear of receiving too many clones (see 'I've read this before', page 72).

**Your approach to its contents** Curriculum Vitae means 'the course of one's life', which, to me, evokes a rather more personal image than the bald lists of facts that I usually receive. (Incidentally, 'résumé' means 'summary', which implies something less personal than Curriculum Vitae. It is also too often written without its accents, which turns it into an entirely different word.)

Your CV should be personalised; it should reflect your life, your personality your very soul even. It is not a shopping-list. Someone once included 'Created the part of Chantale in *A Bridge Too Far*' to upgrade her CV. I fell for it; I hadn't seen the film at that point. Strictly, she wasn't lying as there is no such character in that film. Chantale was indeed her 'creation'. I found this very witty. I'm not sure whether everybody would agree.

**Headings** There is no set list of headings (or sections). Of course you'll include (some of) the productions you've done, the other things you're good at or experienced in (apart from acting), any teachers/directors who are 'known' and anything else that might be relevant to playing any part you can imagine. For instance, horse-riding, keyboard skills, swimming and driving are often required in television.

**Your acting credits** It's convention to put these in reverse chronological order. What else should you list apart from character, production and director (also MD (musical director) and choreographer, where appropriate)? The playwright is only important if they and/or the play are obscure. How do you know what is 'obscure'? This is a nigh on impossible question to answer absolutely, as playwrights come in and out of fashion — apart from a few 'ever fixéd marks', like Shakespeare, Chekhov, Ibsen, and so on. The only thing to do is to ask those with more experience. And when it's an obscure play by a famous writer, you only need to use that writer's surname. (For instance, Noël Coward wrote numerous plays that have sunk into obscurity and John Galsworthy is now only really known as a novelist — he wrote some wonderful plays.) NB Translators are generally irrelevant in this context, but do remember who they are — for instance, some people are deeply interested in the relative merits of the Magarshack and Frayn translations of *The Seagull*. *Tip* If you're listing several productions with the same director, don't list them successively, list others in between — it looks better.

**Venues** These are only really relevant if they are prestigious. But if you only put venues against certain productions it will seem odd and make a mess of your layout. There are several solutions to this. You could have a separate list of venues and/or if you've done several plays in one worth mentioning then list them under that venue's name.

**Dates** In general, it's better to omit dates of productions on your CV as they can tend not only to clutter up the whole layout, but also might start the reader wondering why there's nothing recent there (if that's the case). However, see '*The Spotlight Directory (Your credits)*', page 36.

**Credits as a child** Think carefully before you include these. As I've said before it's very different acting as a child and most people recognise this. It might be worth including just the most prestigious of such credits.

**The layout of your credits** Lay your credits out in columns ('Part', 'Play', 'Director' — without those headings) with a reasonable amount of 'space' between them.

If you've got a title that's uncomfortably long (like *The Effect of Gamma Rays on Man-In-The-Moon Marigolds*), put it onto two closely spaced lines and make sure there's a bigger space between that title and the ones above and below. Or you can simply abbreviate it thus: *The Effect of Gamma Rays...*

In order to accommodate those writers' names that are necessary, put them in brackets after the play title — it'll save having an extra column.

**Character first** Put the character first, not the production! It's a curious fact that if you put the production first then the character is somehow dehumanised.

**Media and film credits** The problem with these is that there is so much attached information that could be promotionally useful that laying them out neatly is difficult. Obviously, 'Part', 'Production', 'Director' are important, but mentions of the producer(s), the star(s), the channel it was screened on, the production company (if different) and even the writer could be useful. You have to assess what will catch the eye — crudely, who and what are well known/famous? And then work out how to lay it out neatly so that it's easy to read — you'll probably have to go on to two lines.

Newcomers often encounter the problem of how to write down a one-line 'no-name' part to 'buck up' their CVs. If you were doing it properly you will have created a character history including a name for him or her. Use that name. That's not lying.

**Accents**  What to put under 'Accents' is another of those eternally vexed questions. It is definitely worth putting in a good, strong 'native' accent and any others that you are sure you can do well. It is better to avoid generalisations like 'American' or 'Scots' — be specific to an area like 'The Bronx' or 'Glasgow'. In theory all those voice lessons should have given you an infinitely flexible voice that could cope with any accent. In practice I've only ever met one actor who could do this — he had taken a degree in phonetics before going on to drama school. So, it is probably best to list (a) 'native' accent(s) and (b) those you've actually used in productions — provided the results were good. I'm afraid that expressions like 'Good ear for accents' just don't sound convincing; better to list specific ones.

**Skill levels**  You need to find the right level for a 'skill' to qualify it for CV status — that is, could you convince an audience (containing someone with that 'skill') that your character can really do it. There is rarely time to 'train someone up'.
NB Keep any 'skill' you do claim up to the mark — see 'Exaggerated claims', page 73.

**Hobbies, interests, experiences and other work**  These may not seem strictly relevant but do serve to give a more complete picture of you. Use this information judiciously to add 'life' to either or both your letter and CV and not as another piece of pedantic detail. 'Other occupational experience includes mortuary attendant, market research, gravedigging and helping to build the M25' attracted my attention at the end of an actor's CV. A friend has 'inventor' tucked in at the end; this is not invention on his part, it's absolutely true.

Many people say to me that they've got nothing 'interesting' in this area. If this is so, then look for something different to do that would enhance this section of your CV. You don't need to be an expert for it to qualify for CV status, but make sure you can discuss it in interview and carry it through in the 'field'.

**Adding recent credits**  This is easy with a computer or word-processor — watch that by adding it in you don't muck-up the overall visual impact. If you don't have the technology then add it in neatly by hand — it can give a good feel of recent activity.
(NB It can be a good idea to leave a bit of space to accommodate that hoped-for next job, when you have you CV typed.)

**Photographs on CVs**  Sticking on (or scanning in) a small copy of your photo to an upper corner of your CV might seem like a good way of saving paper. However, what happens is that — even if the combination is well designed — you defuse the individual impacts of both CV and photo. Also, many people like to look at photos (and CVs) separately.

## Some pitfalls to watch out for in your photograph

After talent good photographs are probably the most important part of an actor's professional armoury. Given their importance it is vital not to make mistakes.

**'My friend's got a camera'** Indifferent and amateur photographs are another excuse to put someone to the bottom of the pile. You'd be amazed at how many Bonus-print-style snaps I receive — often with the actor blinking into a strong sun or red-eyed from the 'in-your-face' flash — and prints with dust-marks or fixer-stains because they were printed in somebody's home darkroom. Make sure of your results before committing them to the post. An amateur photograph makes you look like an amateur actor.

**'Are you an actor or a model?'** The other extreme — the glamour shot — is equally off-putting. Is this a dummy or is it a living, breathing actor? Don't ask for bags under your eyes, moles, and so on, to be edited out. These phenomena are an essential part of you and cannot be removed for the hoped-for interview.

**'My head's falling off'** Before training, one of your major concerns may well have been with where to put your hands. You can laugh now, but why do so many of you pose for photographs with one or both at the side or back of your head or underneath your chin? I know that this kind of pose is often used for models, but they are often in full-length shots. Hands appearing in a head and neck shot can look peculiar because we cannot see the connecting links. More importantly, such photographs tend to look much more 'posed', unnatural and unconfident.

**Attitude** Too many people think that they should have an 'attitude' in their photograph — broadly, either strong or submissive. A shot, staring hard at the camera might be appropriate for a 'strong' part, but you are tending to restrict yourself. A shot looking too far down, or to the side (or both), can make you look like a frightened rabbit who would never be able to face an audience. As an actor, if you talk to an audience directly, you have to 'connect' with them — not try to stare them out or have your eye darting towards the nearest exit.

**Funny photos** Don't try to be funny in your photograph, either. John Cleese may once have had a *Spotlight* photograph of himself dressed as Elizabeth I, but he can get away with it — you can't!

**Mimicry** There is absolutely no point in mimicking the photo of a famous actor. It will simply demonstrate lack of imagination on your part. I once came across two photographs on the same page of *Spotlight* which not only had the same first name and similar surnames, but also were in exactly the same pose. The same unimaginative photographer had taken both.

**Pornography** I have never received an overtly pornographic photograph. I have, however, come across several examples of highly suggestive photos that have made me blink. My feeling is that, if you choose to advertise yourself in this way, you are going to such an extreme that I suspect you have very little else to offer.

**The last-minuter** Don't try to get your photograph done at the last minute. Like performing, you need to be in the proper state of mind to have a good photograph taken. It's not something that can be slotted into the odd spare moment — like going to the loo — either by you or by the photographer. Bear in mind that as the deadline for *Spotlight* gets nearer photographers become increasingly busy and it becomes more difficult to book a session. And make sure you've had enough sleep the night before or the results will add years to your face.

## Getting good photographs

Your photograph is a silent, static, two-dimensional representation of vocal, mobile, three-dimensional you. It will be in black and white and can be the most important part of your publicity package. ('A picture is worth a thousand words.') It needs a lot of thought.

Your photograph should be of your head down to your shoulders, reasonably stylish and well produced without necessarily being too glamorous. It should look natural and have life, energy and personality — especially in the eyes, the most important part of your face. Your photo should say, 'Here I am; I know who I am; I'm OK with who I am.' Also, it is very important that your photograph really looks like you when you arrive for interview.

**Choosing a photographer** Not every photographer suits every actor. The actor-photographer relationship — much like the actor-director one — must be good and positive to produce good results. Look through *Spotlight* and talk to other actors to pick out people whose work could suit you and then ask to see their portfolios. If one refuses move on to another one. Many photographers advertise with samples of their work in *Contacts* and more and more have websites.

Like acting, photography is a highly skilled art which cannot be measured by the complexity and virtuosity of the camera. Of course in going to an experienced professional you will probably be faced (currently) with a bill of around £200 — and that's before you've had all the copies done. (NB Many photographers will charge reduced rates for students.) Even if you feel you cannot afford such an investment, you have to find a way. Good photographs are essential for anyone who is at all serious about being a professional actor. It is probably the most important single investment you can make, especially at the outset of your career.

In my experience the best photographs come from photographer and actor getting to know each other, at least a little, before the first picture is even taken.

It is also important to check how many shots each photographer will take and how many 10x8in (25x20cm) prints are part of the overall fee.

**The photo session** Think carefully about what to wear, arrive on time and take a positive attitude.

*Clothes* The photographer may well tell you to 'wear what you like'. That's right, as it is important to feel comfortable, but be careful that your clothes — especially the top — help to emphasise your face and don't distract or blend in with it. Excessive patterns on a shirt or blouse, which look fine whilst you are mobile, can easily detract in the static photograph. Similarly, a floppy jumper with an unpredictable neckline or a collar that sticks out at strange angles can make you look most peculiar, and polo-necks tend to disconnect your head from your body. Take several alternative tops with you if you are not sure. I like V-necks as they provide classic 'perspective' lines that lead up to the face, but not everybody agrees with this.

*Make-up* Wear as much (or little) as you would for an interview. It's important that the natural 'you' shines through the photograph so it's probably better to wear 'little'.

*Hair* If yours is of a length that can easily move around, try to ensure that it doesn't mask too much of your face or cast too much shadow. NB It's a mistake to get a new hairstyle immediately before a session as it tends to take about a week to settle in.

*Colour* Your publicity photographs will probably be the only non-colour ones you will have taken if you were born after about 1970. A black and white photograph is mostly made up of shades of grey — it should really be called 'black to white'. What really counts is how well the tone and texture of the top you are wearing sets off your face and hair, so wear a top the tone of which contrasts well with your skin tones and hair colour, and won't blend too much into any background the photographer chooses to use. If you have light blonde hair, pale skin tones and wear a pale top, everything will tend to blend together. If you happen to

have such Aryan looks, then go for a darker, rougher top which will highlight them. Think 'black to white'; it's positive textures and colour tones that read well, not subtle shade variations on the same colour.
NB If you have red hair, remember it will come out looking either brunette or blonde on a black and white photograph depending on its tone. And don't wear deep red lipstick or your lips will come out nearly black.

*Glasses* If you wear these, it is a good idea to remove them about an hour beforehand, otherwise the pinch marks could show up in the final results.

*Attitude* You will need to bring energy and commitment, to feel happy and confident and totally relaxed for the photo session. You need to be able to treat the camera and the photographer as friends just as you would an audience — and aim to show the positive aspects of yourself. Aim to 'play' to the camera rather than lean away from it. This doesn't mean leaning towards the camera; your head could end up out of proportion to your neck in the two-dimensional photograph — something akin to the classic 'stick man'.

*Exterior or Studio* This is a much debated topic and is largely up to the photographer. I prefer natural light to create a more 'honest' look, but you may run the risk of a sudden breeze blowing your hair into a strange shape on an otherwise perfect shot. It's a good idea to discuss location with your photographer before the session.

If you are 'camera-conscious', like so many people, and find being natural difficult, take along your Walkman or wear your favourite perfume or just remember good times in order to make you feel good. (Don't let any comforting 'prop' appear in the photographs.) I believe the best photographs are often caught when the subject is doing something positive rather than stuck in a static pose. The word 'snap' is a very accurate one as it expresses that capturing of a 'real' moment which can be so expressive in the final photograph. However, you will have to avoid excessive movement or the final result could be blurred or out of focus.

The art of black and white photography has been downgraded in our 'colour' age. I think that the best of black and white photography is much more exciting than the 'literalness' of its colour counterpart. It leaves much more room for the viewer's imagination. See the work of the great French photographer Henri Cartier-Bresson for the most potent expressions of this.

**Choosing your photographs** Choosing from a 35mm 'contact sheet' can be difficult as the images are so small — there will be thirty-six of them in an area of 10x8in (25x20cm), so each will only be about 2% of its final enlarged size. (Some photographers will supply contact sheets enlarged to 20x16in (50x40cm), which makes this initial selection process much easier. Ask if this would be possible when making first enquiries.) I think that it's best to start by eliminating the obvious no-hopers and then examine the details of each of the remainder using a magnifying glass — ignoring any of the inevitable dust speckles; they shouldn't appear in the final print. Start with the eyes: make sure they look reasonably even, that is, one is not half-closed or focused in not quite the same direction as the other. This often happens; the sixtieth of a second (or less) in which the photograph was taken can often be just slightly the wrong sixtieth. (The human eye cannot capture a moment faster than about a tenth of a second.) Next look at the mouth. It should have strength and not be too open, revealing too many teeth — not everybody has sufficiently regular teeth to survive the close scrutiny of a photograph. Also, a really broad smile might be giving off a lot of warmth, but how many extra creases has it added to your face? Looking carefully at these vital areas can eliminate a number of frames and focus your concentration on a smaller selection.

The next stage is to ask the opinion of several other people and get a consensus from your 'smaller selection'. You are never the best person to select the photographs of yourself that will sell you best. You have become so used to your face and its tiny faults that you cannot see the wood for the trees. If possible, it is best to get a director, agent or someone used to looking at photos to help you choose. A (female) friend grudgingly suggested that it is probably better for a male of one of these species to help you as the majority of directors are male. I am not convinced of this, but I mention it for consideration. Never ask parents and/or lovers to choose, as they will select the 'pretty' photo that probably won't show your important strengths. (NB It can be a mistake to use the magnifying glass at this stage as they can tend to distort at the edges and don't necessarily give the best overview of each picture.)

**Final selection** Don't expect your final selection to be processed instantly. It may be possible to get your holiday snaps back within an hour, but getting the framing and contrast right on your important photograph is an art in its own right and takes time and concentration — like rehearsals.

The prints should be 10x8in (25x20cm) for the best impact and for subsequent copying (there is no point in bigger ones). Don't be tempted to use a slightly fuzzy one that otherwise looks good. An out-of-focus eye or nose can really throw the whole balance of the static picture out of joint. These final prints will feel very different from their contact-sheet counterparts, and you'll need a final selection process using the same approach as above — only it'll be much quicker.

**Subsequent copies** These can be cheaply mass-produced by one of the 'Repro' companies who advertise in *The Stage* and *Contacts*. It is worth checking other people's recent results to select the best as standards seem to vary from time to time. It really isn't worth attempting to save money by getting indifferent reproductions from a good original.

*How many?* Most people tend to underestimate their needs. They only allow for their initial mailing-list and not for follow-up letters and new contacts that suddenly emerge. Adding a postscript to your letter like 'I'll send a copy of my photograph when I've had some more done' sounds pathetic and disorganised.

A new photograph probably has a life of at least two years, so try to be realistic in your estimation of quantity and then add about 50%. The more you order the less the unit cost.

*What size?* In general you'll be fine with postcard size. One casting director told me he felt 'guilty' about the extra money spent on the 10x8in (25x20cm) prints he receives. But it is well worth also having a good stock of the bigger size for 'significant' submissions — if you are looking for a new agent, for example.

**Composite photographs** A sheet composed of photographs from productions and so on may illustrate your range but tend to look over the top. Your CV is a much better place to demonstrate your versatility.

**Copyright** Under the Copyright, Designs and Patents Act 1988 the photographer owns the copyright on any new photograph, even though you've already paid for the original. That means that you have to obtain his or her permission to have new photographs reproduced in *Spotlight* or anywhere else. Your photographer may be happy for such reproduction, but may not be so happy about any cropping or other alterations — you must get permission if you intend to do this. The other important new legal requirement is that your photographer must be credited on any reproduction of the original. Some of the repro companies are now doing this as a matter of course.

## Other things to think about before sealing the envelope

**Contacting you** Always make sure that your 'primary contact' details (see 'Contact details', page 68) are contained in your letter and CV, and on your photograph. It's very cheap to have personal sticky labels printed for this purpose. (Don't forget to enclose a suitably-sized s.a.e. if you'd like your photograph returned.)

**All those bits of paper** Paper-clip everything together — it saves the envelope-opener a little bit of time and trouble. It's possible that every-thing will be stapled together to ensure the continued companionship of your bits of paper when they are placed into the filing system. This will damage your photograph — yet another argument for not asking for it to be returned. Also, filing systems are generally designed to accommo-date standard A4 paper. If your entire sales package is significantly smaller it could get lost.

It is very annoying to open a letter and find each item separately folded and inserted. I don't know why some people do this, but they do. All this means is that precious time is wasted in putting them together in order to be impaled by the staple.

**Sticking your CV to the back of your photograph** I know that this ensures their continued companionship but it can be irritating to have to keep turning the sheet over and over. The ability to survey letter, CV and photograph all at the same time is very useful.

**Enclosing reviews** I often wonder about the value of these — unless they are very good and written by a very reputable national reviewer. An extra sheet of paper with your mention(s) highlighted may make you feel good, but can feel like yet another piece of paper to a recipient. I suggest that it can be much more effective to put a quote into your letter or in your CV.

**'My photograph is in Spotlight'** If it is, it could be unnecessary to enclose a photograph with your letter and CV. However, with so many letters to peruse it can be annoying to have to refer elsewhere. If you can afford to send a copy with your letter and CV, then you are saving the recipient time and trouble. If economies are necessary, referring to Spotlight is legitimate. Mention your current Spotlight number on your CV (remember this changes every year); it saves time to be able to turn straight to the page rather than having to go through the index as well. NB I know that some people now have the Spotlight CD-ROM and/or Internet access, making it simpler to access your photograph, but it still takes precious time on the computer.

**Other contents** Videos (short compilations of audition speeches) and showreels (short compilations of extracts from television appearances — not whole episodes) are another extra expense, and a lot of people won't look at them because it takes up too much valuable time, and they are hard to file efficiently. Before sending out one of these expensive items check whether it will be received with interest.

The same applies to singing tapes. They take time to listen to and don't really give an impression of you in the flesh.

If you do go for any of these, it is essential, like photographs and voice-over demonstration tapes, to label them clearly.

**Marking the envelope 'Personal'** Essentially this is another attention-seeking gambit to avoid. Even if your request is acceded to, you'll just get thrown into the pile of actor-letters anyway.

**Finally** When doing a big mail-out, make doubly sure that you put the right letters into their corresponding envelopes. You'd be amazed at how many people make this basic mistake.

## The following correspondence or lack of it

**'I wrote to you months ago'** If you want a reply, you should enclose a s.a.e. One second-class stamp doesn't cost much, but several hundred will add considerably to your budget, let alone the stationery and time costs. Even if you have enclosed a s.a.e., the recipient may well have been frantic ever since you wrote and only just found a little bit of time to go through the accumulating letters from actors. You can easily wait several months, and some people don't reply at all despite a s.a.e. Unfair, but it happens — even when an advertisement in *The Stage* has requested one.

**Replies to your letters** I sometimes wonder if the traditional s.a.e. is really worth it. All this really does is elicit confirmation that your letter actually arrived. If someone is really interested in you, he or she will write back anyway, s.a.e. or no s.a.e. Many organisations have standard responses for those who send one. These are almost always quite pleasant but finally noncommittal. Some actors take sentences like 'We will consider you when we are next casting' too much at face value. In general that means 'No, not for at least the next six months', but I have known people use it to blitz me with letters saying that I had promised to see them (see 'How often should I write?', page 65) when all I have said is that I would 'consider them'. The problem is that, at heart, most directors are too soft in this area and cannot write an outright 'no' to an actor.

If you want your photograph back, you must enclose an envelope that's big enough. A surprising number of people don't.

**Replying to replies** There is no point in replying immediately to a 'standard' response. All it means is that your details have been filed and that file might be looked at and even referred to at some time in the future. You have done all you can for now. Write again, with a fresh CV and photograph, in about six months. The exception to this rule is when your research turns up an opportunity for you to suggest yourself for specific casting.

**The reminder postcard** It can be a good idea to send out reminder cards — especially to people you know. A simple postcard with basic details (of your current production, for instance) is perfectly sufficient, and is quick and simple to read. You can get these made up with a scan of your photograph incorporated.

**Timing** The success or failure of your letter-writing can also depend on when you write. Of course you'll write when you discover there's a particular part you'd be right for, but it can also be worth writing in general terms. For instance, directors of theatres seem to be at their most receptive when they first take over, that is, in that honeymoon period when they are optimistic that the inherent financial problems can be solved. The same tends to be true after a well-earned holiday. There are also times when you can reduce your chances, like just before Christmas and at other especially busy times of year in that particular company's calendar. You should try to keep in touch with each organisation's pattern of work via *The Stage* to work out when the pressure will be off.

**Now forget about it** Once you've posted your letter forget about it. However confident you feel about its contents, the ball is out of your court now and there is nothing you can do. So why waste time and energy worrying about it?

**How important is it to write?** A friend of mine estimates that she wrote 500 letters when she was first starting out and ended up with three agents wanting to represent her and a small part in a production that eventually went into the West End. She kept up this letter-writing for two years and then decided that she couldn't be bothered any more, and her work-rate went down. Especially in your early years, you will probably have to keep this subtle pressure up — even if you have got a good agent. You might be lucky, but until your work is 'known' in at least some circles the only way to get work is to keep up the publicity campaign. Even then you should keep plugging away, but perhaps not so often and not in such volume.

## Targeting your submissions

The late Barbara Cartland managed to write about ten novels a year. That is equivalent to several thousand letters. She was rich enough to employ three secretaries to transcribe all those words. In theory there are as many agents, directors, casting directors and other potential employers for you to write to just as much, but it is an impossible task unless you spend all your waking hours doing it. You have to be selective.

**A hit-list** The only way to sort out a suitable 'hit-list' is by asking other people. Time spent sorting out potentially sympathetic ears, will save a considerable amount of time and money later on. It isn't always necessary to write to the top dog. An assistant or associate director, for instance, might well have more time. If there's a casting director in place, he or she should be your first port of call. However, check the relevant names as they tend to move around.

**Joint letters** It is always a mistake to write to two or more people in the same letter — unless you know that they work in close harmony. Sharing a building doesn't mean that they share philosophies.

**Writing to people you've worked for (or 'short-term memory syndrome')** There is a profession-wide complaint known as 'Short-term memory syndrome'. You've worked for someone and know that you've gone down well, but they haven't employed you since. It is almost certain that they would like to work with you again, but the other incredible pressures have squeezed you out of their memory banks. Don't be shy to write. Evoke the glow of your joint success and write with the energy of what you've been doing since.

**Keep records** It is important to have records of what you've said to whom and any responses (written or verbal) for at least two years so that you don't repeat yourself.

## Other promotional aids

It is now possible to have your CV, photograph, voice-clip and showreel all on one CD-ROM and/or on a website. However, any new technology — however exciting — takes a long time to be properly understood and widely accepted. At the present time, I suggest that it is unwise to invest too much money and effort into these new promotional aids. If you are thinking of 'diving in', try to work out how widely such innovations will be acceptable and carefully calculate whether you will actually save money compared to sending out conventional letters, CVs and photographs.

## A fundamental note

Always write with something positive to say and with a strong sense of purpose. Never write in desperation as in the following. This was a hand-written letter from someone I did not know. I haven't corrected any grammar, punctuation or spelling, and there was no CV or photograph.

[*Address and date semi-legible*]

Dear Simon,

I have written to you a few times in the past this time I hope I will be successful in my application for a job. I am 24 on 19 of this month 23 at the moment so it would be a very nice birthday surprise. I have been singing and touring with cabaret and show band, you have most of my details of file. I really want to be an actress but how can I when I get letters saying no vacancies at the moment try later without even chance of an audition if there are no vacancies as an actress then perhaps you could offer me some backstage work. Im a hard worker easy going and really like working in theatre so come on Simon spread a bit of Christmas Spirit.

yours sincerely

[*Name almost illegible*]

**Warning** Many people have found this, and the letter on pages 62–3, very funny. However, bear in mind they are the sort of thing you might write either when feeling lonely and desperate, or when feeling extremely cocky.

# Chapter Ten

# *The Internet*

You can't miss it — it's all around us, 'That ruddy great wall that any-body can scribble upon' as a friend described it. (It can also seem like a Tower of Babel.) I'm certainly a convert — now that I've got through the hair-tearing-out days of learning how it works. I have stumbled across old friends, opened up new friendships and indulged in some fascinating debates. How can the actor exploit this new marketing medium and can you find work out there? As widespread use of the Internet is so new to the UK I have been looking at the North American experience, where they are several years ahead of us. Over there tradit-ional methods of actor-marketing and work-seeking still largely rule the roost at the beginning of the 21st century. However, in anticipation of this changing in the future I offer the following:

## E-mail and websites
Now there is the potential to transmit your advertising-package cheaply and almost instantaneously.

**Sending submissions via e-mail** In theory an e-mail could replace your cover letter and you could add your CV and photograph as attach-ments, and send it for significantly less than the cost of its postal equiv-alent. The important thing to remember is that you should approach the text in your e-mail in much the same fashion as that in a conventional letter (see chapter 9). Don't use the foreshortenings and acronyms so beloved in this medium unless you are very well-known to the recipient. The other potential problem to consider is: will what looks good on your computer screen, (a) be viewable by the recipient and (b) if so, will it look the same as it did on your screen? In spite of advances, com-puters still cannot communicate seamlessly with each other via the Internet and many people don't know how to use them properly and/or are using outdated systems. (Also, there are a surprising number of people who still resist using the Internet at all.) The other problem is that the more actors who use this form of communication to blitz those with casting clout, the more the latter will switch off to anything but the conventional, less 'invasive', mailing system — it'll be their only defence. (That snowstorm of paper threatens to become a hailstorm of e-mails — I know which I'd rather be in.) To many a personal computer is private space and a submission arriving in it is nigh-on equivalent to the actor arriving on the doorstep in person, or phoning, without invitation. At present, it's probably inadvisable to e-mail a submission unless specifically requested. If you do, ensure that you send your attachments in a form that can be read by the recipient's system without loss of quality.

**Actors' Websites** There is a much better way of utilising the Internet for getting your CV and photograph (*as you would wish them to be seen*) onto someone else's computer screen: get a properly designed website. Then you can e-mail an invitation for someone to look at your details on your website. In fact, if you are in *Spotlight*, they can already check out your details on that site. However, it can be useful to evolve your own website to help you stick out from the crowd. Overall, it must be easily accessible and navigable to the first-time eye — just like a good letter, CV and photograph.

There are now plenty of people willing to design and maintain a website for you. However, as when looking for a photographer, check the quality of any potential designer's work and compare prices — because this is a new area of enterprise there are wide variations. (It's also important to check the cost of making changes. In fact, it's probably better to ask for a copy of the site on disk — with the appropriate access codes — because the website-design business seems to be very volatile.)

It's also not too difficult to build a basic one for yourself — it would take far too long to go into the ins and outs of doing this here and there are plenty of books about website design.

Here are some basics to consider:

- Look at other actors' sites to see what you like and what you don't. (There's a list of a lot of actors' sites at <britishtheatre.about.com> — some are fan sites, but many are individual actors' own sites.)
- As with letters and CVs don't go overboard with jazzy graphics and colours — let alone background music, quirky animations and advertising banners.
- Don't be tempted to fill your site with items that are irrelevant to your professional life — photographs of your dog, you at a wild party, or you surfing, may amuse your friends but don't promote your professionalism.
- Make sure that your site can easily be updated as you gain more credits and/or want to change your photographs.
- Make sure that your photographer is credited (see 'Copyright' on page 82).
- Make sure that you include an e-mail address and/or your 'primary contact' number (see 'Contact details', page 68). And make sure that that e-mail address is hyper-linked so that the viewer can just click on it to respond.
- Look at your site on lots of other people's computers. The content may survive but the layout could well acquire some odd quirks on

arrival on the recipient's screen, and photographs can lose some of their lustre.

**Printing out** If you've been asked to e-mail your CV and photographs as attachments or your invitation to view your website is accepted, and the recipient likes what they see, they will want to keep some kind of record. It's very easy to bookmark a website for future reference — however, at some point, the recipient will want to print it out. What will your e-mail attachments or website look like when printed out on the recipient's printer? The text may look fine, but will its formatting survive — especially on your CV? (There are several ways round this formatting problem: using Portable Document Files (PDFs), for instance.) More importantly, your photograph could easily lose a lot of it's original quality. (As most people are still sending conventional photographs by post, your Internet transmitted version could look tatty in comparison.) The reason for this 'quality problem' is that for a photograph to look good on screen it only needs to have a resolution of about 100 dots per inch; to look good on paper it needs a resolution of at least three times that. A photograph at the higher resolution will take about ten times longer to download (as an attachment or from a website) than its screen-quality equivalent. A further problem is that in order to retain the quality of the former, the recipient must be using a high-resolution printer. Modern ink-jet printers are very cheap and capable of near magazine quality reproduction if printed on the special 'ink-jet' paper. However, this is significantly more expensive than normal paper and high-quality print-outs take several minutes. All together the whole process of downloading and printing out a 'quality' 10x8in (25x20cm) photograph can easily take 15 minutes. Combine this with the expense of the special paper and the costs to the recipient begin to become significant. In short (unless specifically requested) it'll be a mistake to use the Internet to send out photographs – until speeds of transmission improve, unmetered (low subscription) Internet access is universal and high-quality printing is much quicker and cheaper.

**Extras** It is now comparatively easy to put a voice-clip on a website or send one as an attachment to an e-mail. There are also video-clips — however, these currently tend to be of indifferent quality and take too long to download. This will improve. The important thing is to make sure that — like your photographs — the recordings are made by someone who really knows what they are doing. Even the rapid advances of digital technology and editing do not remove the need for some expertise to ensure the necessary quality of your presentation.

**'Do I need the Internet?'** Access to e-mail is now widespread and extremely useful for transmitting basic messages quickly and cheaply. However, think carefully before going further into the expense (probably about £200–250 for a basic website design and 'connection' into the system) of the more sophisticated uses of the Internet, when an entry in *Spotlight* includes your appearance in their online directory. (NB Their 'screen-quality' photographs are subject to some degradation when printed out, but at least its the same for everybody.)

It's going to be a while before individual actor's websites will become common currency. However, a professional looking website might just tip the balance in your favour and once it's out there it's comparatively easy to update, and you should be paying nothing apart from the subscription to your ISP (Internet Service Provider).

**Summary** The principal point to remember is that e-mail and the Internet, require more time, equipment and expertise than that involved in opening a letter. Until the technology becomes as commonplace as the telephone it will remain prudent to use 'snail-mail' as the primary method of marketing yourself.

## A few actors' experiences and observations
An actor-friend has had a website since 1993 and has never got a job through it.

Another actor-friend did manage to get an interview with a casting director because of his newly installed website sound-clip. The casting director was new to the Internet and 'experimenting' — she had chanced upon the actor's site. He ended up 'being the latter candidate on a short-list of two', and hasn't had another interview since as a consequence of his very well designed site.

'A website is just like a telephone. Unless someone is motivated to dial your number then your telephone won't ring. The trick is to get people to know and use your website address. Reliance on random events does not have a good chance of success.'

'Can you imagine a casting director sitting down and typing "great actor play Hamlet" into a search engine?'

'Hopefully in the future things will change, and a website might be a good place to give an expanded showcase of yourself, but I think it would still only be used by someone you'd already made contact with.'

'I've used my site as an easy way for people to see me while my information is on the way. I have got the odd interview before my CV and photo have even reached them. I think of my site as an electronic business card.'

## Other uses of the Internet
Just as very little acting work is advertised in *The Stage*, there isn't much advertised on the Internet — and what there is, is on *The Stage's*

website <www.thestage.co.uk>. The traditional system of employers sending 'casting breakdowns' to agents (sometimes using a casting director) still largely pertains. However, some aspects of this 'system' (official and unofficial) are also using the Internet.

**Internet casting information services** There seem to be more and more of these advertising in *The Stage* every week. I'm told that the quality of the information is quite good in some of them. It's obviously cheaper for these services to use e-mail rather than ordinary post, but you still have to pay a subscription. The other advantage is that information can be sent more frequently and much more quickly. A friend recently received five e-mails in one day from one — all with urgent commercial castings. (The speed and cheapness of e-mail seems to be encouraging some employers to leave casting to even later in the day.) I think that the future will see these e-mail services become the norm. (Also see 'Casting information', pages 194–5.)

**Agents' websites** There are a growing number of UK agencies who are building their own websites. However, it is interesting to note that legitimate actors' agencies in North America typically don't have websites — they are seen as an unnecessary expense to set up and maintain. This seems to make total sense to me — for the moment. (However, as a friend in a co-operative pointed out: 'A website for a co-op is a sign of permanence and professionalism — if it's done well.')

I can foresee the possibility of it becoming the norm for agents to have websites. Instead of posting out small piles of paper in response to a casting breakdown, agents could simply send e-mails with a list of web addresses — and the recipients will be responsible for generating those 'piles of paper'. However, this 'paper generating responsibility' is at the heart of why agents' websites may not become the 'norm'. Whilst supply (of actors) far outstrips demand, those with casting clout can continue to insist on receiving submissions 'on a plate' (that is, on paper) — except where it's an unusual piece of casting. Anyway, agents can always refer people to *Spotlight* — and the rising number of competing Internet casting directories.

**Internet casting directories** I have yet to see one of these that comes anywhere near *Spotlight* for ease of use, quality of design and sheer number of entries. All but one were significantly cheaper than *Spotlight* and might be worth investing in — in addition to it. (There are several that are free and others that will list your website address for nothing.) However, can you envisage a casting director (for instance) surfing such sites with all the disadvantages listed above? This may change, and again I offer a few things to look out for on these sites — both free and charging:

- Read the small print of the application form ('terms and conditions', or whatever) carefully and look out for hidden charges — some that claim to be 'free' start charging after a trial period, for instance.
- Many are not just for actors, they also contain models, entertainers, presenters — sometimes all mixed in together, which can make it very confusing for the viewer.
- Does it work with all computer operating systems? A significant minority of sites only work with a certain world-famous operating system — which is very annoying to those of us who prefer one of the alternatives.
- Is there too much extraneous advertising which could frustrate a viewer?
- Are individual actor's credits well laid out and easy to read? Also, check the standard of spelling.
- Is the overall design pleasing to the eye and is the site easy to navigate?
- Does the site download reasonably quickly?
- Will it survive the test of time? At present 75% of 'dot.com' companies go out of business quite quickly.

NB It is not advisable to put your Equity number on a publicly accessible website because that number is the key to accessing the Union's Job Information Service — you could be letting non-members gain access.

**Newsgroups** I check my favourite ones first thing most mornings, and I've met some interesting people and engaged in some fascinating discussions — some of this chapter is based on these. Occasionally, work is advertised but it all seems to be non-Equity. This is hardly surprising as any employers offering Equity contracts would be swamped if they advertised in this way. They can be useful places for meeting like-minded people, and exchanging ideas.

**Whatever next?** There's no doubt that electronics will get even smaller, faster and capable of more complex operations — moving even closer toward the miracle that is the human brain. But as we move toward a 'virtual' world, reality will still be here — we won't be able to escape it. I think there will come a point when electronic communications will become so fast and so voluminous that there will be some kind of meltdown. We already can't take on board properly all the information that's thrown at us.

How is whatever happens in the future going to affect the actor in communication with the employment-brokers? A very perspicacious comment from Will Hutton (*Guardian*, 18/9/95): 'The best communicative use of the Internet is between those who already know each other, not between those who have never met face-to-face. It takes physical contact over a long time for human beings to bond; but once bonded, the Internet can be an extraordinary facilitator.' In short, I don't believe that new technologies will have any significant impact at the grass-roots level. However, watch this space!

Because the number of actors available will always far outstrip demand I don't believe that the Internet will supersede the traditional postal system for the work-seeking actor for quite a while yet. (It is a fact that reading from paper is less tiring than reading from a screen.) However, you cannot ignore it and future communication technologies. Things will change — in time, but not as soon as some people are claiming.

## Work in the Internet

This is an emerging area of work, particularly for voice-overs (see chapter 17). Also, there have been several attempts at interactive games (using actors rather than animation) and even a 'net-soap' with interactive elements via e-mail. Growth in this area of work is waiting for the development of widely-available, broadcast quality video-streaming on the Internet, which I'm told is not far off. I would expect that work of this nature will largely be available via the usual channels and be auditioned for much as for the other visual media (see chapter 16). I also suspect that there will be some 'dot.com' entrepreneurs starting such ventures who will know nothing about how to find actors (let alone about acting) — it could be worth keeping your ear to the ground for such emerging enterprises.

## Warning!

North America has long been the home of the 'scam' — essentially, a legal confidence trick. For instance, unscrupulous casting directors suggest that if you pay to attend their acting classes, they will consider you for casting — and then nothing happens. (I must stress that I have not come across this in the UK.) The Internet, combined with incredibly cheap Digital Video, has meant that the 'scammers' have been able (in various ways) to make enticing offers of parts for sale (or auction) in 'movies' to be shown on the Internet. There are numerous variations on this ('movies' cast only from specific Internet casting directories, for instance), but these 'movies' are all but useless in terms of career advancement. I know there are legitimate examples of utilising Digital Video on the Internet, but you should not risk significant funds in an attempt to be part of one. The Newsgroups are very useful for checking the legitimacy of anything like this.

Chapter Eleven

# *The Mechanics of Casting*

For a director, casting a production is as traumatic as a first night. It is full of agonising decisions, disappointments as well as triumphs. Before even thinking about casting, the director gets to know the script, talks with the writer (if available) and begins discussions with the designer and anyone else who is part of the whole evolutionary process of a production (producer if it's a commercial production, musical director and choreographer for a musical, for instance). In television and film there are many more people with whom to start discussions and logistics to consider. Meanwhile at the back of the director's mind ideas for potential casting will be fermenting — actors already known, others seen before. He or she will flip through *Spotlight* for half-remembered names and faces. Perhaps a 'casting breakdown' has been sent to selected agents or that job has been delegated to 'Script Breakdown Services' (SBS), which lists much of what is being cast and is only available to agents. Perhaps there's a casting director with whom to hold discussions. Apart from the director's own ideas there will be many more suggestions to go through, from which lists for serious consideration are drawn up.

## Casting directors
It used to be only the biggest theatre companies, who along with most television and film companies used the services of casting directors. (Also see 'Casting agents', page 51.) The last few years have seen a considerable growth in their numbers — both full-time and freelance. The freelancers have their own section in *Contacts* and those with companies are usually included in that company's entry. You can also find the CVs of some on the website of the Casting Directors' Guild <www.castingdirectorsguild.co.uk>.

In fact the title 'Casting Director' is somewhat misleading as they 'facilitate' casting; it is the director, and sometimes the producer, who actually 'direct' the casting decisions. Their precise functions vary, but broadly they are the link from the director to the actor (usually via an agent) and take on a lot of the nitty-gritty work involved in casting. This is not meant to give the impression that they just do the dirty work; they are expected to come up with bright ideas for casting that can take ages to formulate. An empathetic, intuitive and imaginative casting director has immeasurable value to both actors and director.

It is important to remember that in an interview a casting director especially wants you to succeed, may even give you hints about what the director wants or give you some advice about how to approach the interview, because your 'performance' in the director's eyes will reflect on the casting director's ability to make good suggestions. And the director is the casting director's employer.

In general, I think that casting directors are better than directors at spotting potential, but just like directors their judgement is subjective. David Leland, who wrote and directed *Wish You Were Here* told a story of working with two casting directors on the film: the one he started with had to cry off after a while because of pressure of other commitments (most casting directors will work on several productions at once). It was the second one who finally introduced him to Emily Lloyd, the film's eventual star. Months later, during a break in filming, it transpired that the first casting director had met and rejected her.

With their growth in numbers there has been a rise in actors' cynicism about casting directors: of the 'They never go and see productions; they cast from the television' variety. All the ones I know go to see at least three or four productions a week, keep careful notes about anyone who interests them and have a passion for finding new talent. I have heard stories of power-crazy rotten apples, but like their director and agent counterparts they are in a distinct minority.

## The casting process

Once a list of 'possibles' has been drawn up, somebody has to check whether people are available for the dates — a time-consuming and tedious process. This may not start until several weeks after the suggestions came in and some actors may have become unavailable and new names come into the frame.

Once again, I will use the term 'director' throughout to cover them and casting directors.

**Availability checks** A lot of actors seem to take these too much to heart. Directors, when thinking about casting, like to check a string of people for a part to help gain a perspective on how they might cast it. That's all. It's a 'private' process. There is no point in dashing off letters when you hear you've been 'checked' to say how wonderful you'd be in the part. You are in the running and are at least of some interest to the director concerned.

**The actor without an agent** Doing an availability check on an actor without an agent can be embarrassing, even for a secretary, if the actor treats it as 'all but an offer'. Too many actors jump in and start asking what the money is, the domestic arrangements they'll have to make, and so on. Don't jump the gun; there's a way to go yet. (This can be even more embarrassing with an actor already known to the director. It's so much easier when there's an agent in between.)

**An interview?** At the same time as an 'availability' is done there may be a request to come for interview, or perhaps that will come in a later phone call — the director may want to rethink who he or she wants to see now that the list of who is actually available is clear.

If you're known to the director you might get an offer without interview. Whether you know him/her or not there could simply be a deafening silence — you didn't make the interview-list for reasons you will probably never know.

Then the interviews are held and the agonising decision-making starts. (However, you, the actor, mustn't wait around agonising — best to forget about it.) Crystallising decisions can take several days' thought and research. This can sometimes involve recalls — making the process even more long-winded.

Some directors like to phone actors directly about doing a part — sometimes even before the formal offer is made. This usually happens between friends and is really to establish interest, or not, before spending time on the money side.

**Slowly, slowly...** Any responsible director will cast gradually: offer the lead first and when that actor accepts go on to offer the other parts in whatever way is appropriate. The director wants to build a company of actors who individually feel 'right' and will work well together. This is comparatively simple if it's a small cast of two or three, but is complicated when it's above about six and requires an enormous amount of work for above a dozen. For example, X may seem perfect to play the husband of A, but if she turns down the offer and B accepts the director may feel that Y would be the better choice. If the process of A and/or B thinking about whether or not to accept has taken too much time, Y may no longer be available; the same may be the case for X. The director may well have other options; if not, more interviews will have to be held and there still may be other smaller parts to cast. Each stage of this process can take days, which grow into weeks, and it can all become very complicated. (Working to create a good 'company balance', especially with a large cast, can take months.) In practice there is rarely time to cast in this slow methodical way, so several offers will usually go out at once — but rarely all of them at the same time.

**The offer** When you do get offered a job don't just blindly say 'yes' — without any thought. If it's your first one, of course you'll probably take it. But just take a moment to think twice, because once you've said 'yes' you have made a verbal contract which is morally (and possibly legally) binding. If you turn round a few days later, when, say, you suddenly realise the holiday you've booked coincides with the middle of rehearsals, you will throw the organisation into turmoil. Directors don't just make offers willy-nilly. They give a lot of thought to each one they make. If you've got a legitimate problem, which it might be possible to work around, discuss it with the director at this stage rather than at the beginning of rehearsals when there's so much else going on.

**Changing your mind** A director generally expects anywhere between 10%, and 50% of offers to be turned down — for all kinds of good reasons. That is respected, but if someone says 'no' after at first saying 'yes' it upsets carefully thought out plans, throws the whole process out of joint and wastes several people's time. All the organisation's departments — wardrobe, wages, publicity, and so on — have then to be told of your change of heart, which takes up more of administrative time. If a significantly better offer does come up, or some kind of personal difficulty arises, and there is decent time to recast, most directors will release you from your contract, but the reasons have got to be good. Be sure before you say 'yes'. Actually signing the contract is almost a formality.

**Thinking about an offer** It is usually perfectly acceptable to ask for a few days to think about an offer, and you are well within your rights to ask the organisation to send you a copy of the script to read. Don't feel pressured. The ball is very firmly in your court, and you can take reasonable time to read the script and weigh up the pros and cons. I've only once heard of a part being 'gazumped', so think about whether you like the part, can sort out any domestic arrangements, and so on — usually a day or two from the receipt of the script is reasonable. There are numerous circumstances in which you may need longer — another offer 'in the wind', for instance. You should negotiate that extra time with the management — via your agent if you have one. Just because the work doesn't start for a while it doesn't mean that the director can wait for your decision for too long. If you do take too long — without good reason — you are asking to be put down in his or her 'black book'.

**The late offer** The effort put into 'building a company', can mean that some offers go through a long time after meeting the actors. At other times a whole string of successive offers for the same part get turned down, or the director just needs time to think. It may be that you are the second choice, but there is absolutely no point in feeling miffed. Directors do try to keep this kind of fact confidential, but sometimes that's impossible. You have to get on with the job as usual and forget there was any other choice but yourself.

**Turning down an offer**  You don't have to give reasons for doing this, but it is a good idea. After all the thought that's gone into choosing to make that offer to you, it is the least you can do. Make sure your 'reasons' are good and don't appear petty or arrogant or in any way insulting. Follow up your decision with a brief letter.

The decision-making involved in making offers can be an emotional one for a director — like watching a football match with your heart very much on one team. Everything should be fine but sometimes the full cast won't be known until the last moment before rehearsals start. It is as nerve-racking as it can be for you the actor waiting to hear whether you've got the job. Casting is probably half of the creative work involved in a production.

## Other issues

**The money**  Thank God this is usually not the director's job. Most organisations have their well established scales of payment, and in many cases there is no room for manoeuvre. Most organisations are keenly aware that actors talk with each other and any apparent unfairness must be avoided at the outset. Generally, the actor who can negotiate more than an extra 10% has either a lot of publicity clout or is in some way indispensable to the production.

Agents will know the going rates and should do their best to get you more than the offer, depending on what arguments can be presented (you'll have to help with this). If you haven't got an agent, check with The Spotlight; it has been known for unscrupulous managements to try to offer under their normal rates to actors without agents.

It is almost always counterproductive to say 'no' because you want more money. You will be marked down as someone not worth bothering to ask in future.

**Nudity and simulated sex**  Think very carefully before accepting a part that demands anything like this. Under Equity agreements a management is supposed to warn you even if it's only a possibility, at the contractual stage, but I have known several actors, when faced with actually revealing themselves, trying to 'bottle out' after initially going along with the idea. Some directors will be sympathetic, but it is yet another example of potential time-wasting. Consider it properly before you say 'yes'.

**Silence**  It is quite normal not to be formally told that you haven't got a job for which you've been seen. If you are told, that means that you came very, very close.

# Chapter Twelve

# *Interviews*

What is an interview? *The Shorter Oxford English Dictionary* gives, amongst others, the following obsolete definitions:
'Inspection — 1586'
'Mutual view (of each other) (rare) — 1667'
'A view, glance, glimpse (of a thing) — 1719'

I try to conduct my interviews according to the 1667 definition. However, I constantly hear stories from actors suffering the 1586 version, sometimes with the brevity and attitude implied by the 1719 modification. *The Penguin Dictionary* contains the following: '... formal meeting and conversation; meeting to test the suitability of a candidate for a post...' Ideally an interview should be an informal mutual testing in the best possible sense. It should really be an equal assessment session of whether you'd both like to work together. After all, rehearsing a production is probably one of the most intimate of shared human activities. Unfortunately for you, the actor, there are almost always too many people after the same job, and the privilege of deciding whether you'd like to work with a particular director or not is afforded to very few actors. You are in the position of having to sell yourself subtly but effectively to him or her, and not vice versa. Perhaps if all actors decided to make interviews a 'mutual testing' the more obdurate directors would have to respond and the whole system might become more satisfactory. However, whilst things remain as they are, here are some preparatory observations.

**Interviewers** Who is this person to whom you are going to talk and demonstrate your skills? Directors (and casting directors) are as varied as any random sample of people. They make many of the mistakes that I castigate actors for elsewhere in this book. (I was once interviewing with a colleague and we were playing Backgammon in the many gaps that appeared that day — we didn't know that a bomb had ground central London to a halt. The level of absenteeism was so great that the game became more important than the remaining interviewees. It must have been very hard for them.)

Some can be just as nervous as the actors they are interviewing. I've also heard stories of others almost cruelly exploiting their positions of power, including one horrendous story of a friend asked to strip for a part that required nudity. The director wouldn't consider her unless she did so. She had the courage to refuse. There are those who seem to have a 'take it or leave it' attitude — almost as though they didn't care about what they're doing; others who hide behind assistants, the table or their glasses, or at the back of darkened auditoriums; and I know one whom I would classify as quixotic, if not downright eccentric, in his rapidly changing attitudes.

Many are not very good at interviewing, that is, giving you the 'room' to show yourself off at your best. There are those who are so nice that you cannot believe you haven't got the job; those who go as far as to say 'I know I could use you in my season' to everybody — perhaps because they cannot bear to be resented. If it is a good atmosphere, then it will be easy to give all you've got; if it is a difficult one, you cannot let it get you down. You have to be stoical and give the best you can. Treat interviewers well without being obsequious or grovelling, or you'll come out feeling badly compromised. Would you want to spend time working for such an appalling individual anyway? Save your feelings about the session and your interviewer until afterwards.

Most do recognise the potential dangers of casting purely on the basis of an audition speech/reading. Talking with the actor, discussing and/or working on the audition piece or reading are useful. In fact the chat can be over 50% of the session and in some cases more influential on the final decision than anything else. It can be useful to think of the interview as a chance to promote yourself. Even if you find yourself in a situation where the chatting-time is minimal, you must focus just as much on that 'promotion' as you do on the product: your speech/reading.

**Interviewers are only human beings** They could well be as shy as you are (for instance) and will almost certainly be embarrassed for you if something goes wrong during the session. They often won't have an assistant to sort out the pile of CVs and letters, have probably had to get up extremely early to catch a train which was probably late, denying them that vital cup of coffee. Personally, I find interview days even more exhausting than technical rehearsals. Lunch-hours usually end up being twenty minutes, and there is absolutely no time to relax when you have to bring fresh concentration to bear on each new person every ten or fifteen minutes.

**'You could be just what I'm after'** Most interviewers start with the hope that you could be just what they are looking for. This is partly because they have very little reason to have anything against you as yet (but see 'First impressions', page 112) and they rarely know exactly what they are looking for. It is true that some do have a preconception of the type of actor they want — especially in television and films; but I don't believe that anybody has it completely worked out. You can show such people that you could come somewhere close to their preconception and bring your own special talents as well.

A few directors are downright cynics and start out with the idea of specifically looking out for what's wrong with you, but they seem to be in the minority and you simply have to work harder at proving yourself and not be put down.

## Notes

1 The words 'interview' and 'audition' are commonly intermingled. Strictly speaking, an audition (from the Latin *audire*, 'to hear') is the speech/reading and the interview is the chat between you, but, excluding musicals and commercials, generally the word 'interview' is used to cover everything.

2 Much of what applies to directors also applies to agents, casting directors, and so on, unless otherwise stated.

## Preparations for an interview

You will never finally know what you will walk into — even when you are a seasoned interviewee. However, there are certain ways in which you can prepare and certain mistakes that you can plan to avoid making.

**A call is a call is a call** You must never be late. This is the cardinal rule of the whole profession, and it doesn't just apply to a working call; it also applies to an interview. Interviews may start on time but almost always run later and later as the day progresses. You, on the other hand, must still be on time. There will be a carefully calculated schedule with each actor slotted in at ten- or fifteen-minute intervals (longer is a luxury). There may be contingency-times, that is, deliberate gaps to allow for the almost inevitable overrunning. However, you cannot rely on this. Some actors on the schedule might find they cannot attend at the last minute, thus creating spare time. So, you could go in early. Your job is to make sure you're ready and willing in good time for your appointment.

You should plan your journey to the interview location. In general, don't try to travel into any city centre by car to meet a deadline unless you have a real instinct for finding parking-spaces and your car is utterly reliable. Use public transport and work out how long it will take — then double your estimate to allow for delays. If you don't know central London (or wherever) get to know the bus and Underground systems and how to use an *A to Z* and Tube map. Also, check travel reports in order to anticipate transport problems. Of course, an interviewer will be sympathetic if a bomb scare has suddenly ground traffic to a halt, but try to help by setting out extra early and beating the chaos. It doesn't matter if the schedule goes out of order; at least they will have fewer people left at the end of the day to interview in the cafe down the road because the hired room has been booked by someone else.

Always have a note of a suitable contact number, so that if something unforeseen occurs to delay you, you can get a message to your interviewer. Also carry a collection of change suitable for ticket machines, parking meters, and so forth, and/or plastic cards fulfilling the same functions.

**'What have you been doing recently?'** The interviewer will probably start off with this question (or variants). It is the most popular way of getting the conversation going. Don't think less of your interviewer for being so unimaginative and don't have your response so well rehearsed that it trots out without any 'passion'. It's your life you are talking about. Don't respond with 'It's on my CV.' That will kill the conversation stone dead, and it's difficult to get it going again. Get together a mental check list of doings with which you could respond. Don't write a script, however! The specific question could be marginally different.

Don't presume everybody will start with this question, either. 'What's been your favourite part so far?' is another popular starter, and 'How do you see yourself as an actor?' and 'What do you want to be doing?' are all opening gambits I have come across. You have to be prepared for anything.

**Time passes more quickly when you're trying to sell yourself** Sight-readings and/or audition speeches can easily take half, if not more, of your time. That doesn't leave very long — and can feel even less — for the interview part. So aim to be concise, but not so precise that you appear calculating and cold. Principally, you need to find a way of 'opening up' as early as possible, and the rest should flow from there.

**Talking too much** The majority of interviewees talk too much — a few talk far too much — and it is either a very rude or a desperate interviewer who will cut you off in mid-flow. Where is the dividing-line between too much and too little? That varies enormously and depends on (a) your interviewer's willingness to listen, (b) how relevant to the question each element of your response is and (c) how much time is available overall. For many it is terribly easy to amplify too much on a basic answer. For instance, an actor was introduced to a director by a close friend who also happened to be the director's assistant. A natural opening question from the director was, 'So how do you two know each other?' My friend launched into the complex series of events that first acquainted them. The assistant, realising what was happening, cut in tactfully by saying: 'It's personal as opposed to professional.' Then they got down to the interview proper. If you are a talker, then work hard at sticking to the subject and resist any little deviations that 'won't take a moment'. Develop an 'end-of-subject awareness' — the ability to recognise when a particular subject is covered sufficiently for now, and it is time to move on.

The truth — or one's perception of it — is infinitely complex. Theoretically, we could talk for ever on a single subject, and it is easily done if it is of great importance to you. You have to resist the temptation when those subjects come up. Think beforehand what your personal 'talking' danger zones are, and think how you might paraphrase without losing the essence and 'passion' for that subject.

Some directors talk too much. If this happens to you, then look for ways in which you can tactfully, but firmly, bring the subject round to yourself.

**Talking too little** A few actors talk too little. Monosyllabic answers do not help to give a good impression. Your response to even the most banal question should aim to convey something of the positive aspects of yourself.

Nerves can make some people tongue-tied. An unsympathetic interviewer or even a shy one can make it difficult for you to find words to express yourself. But 'find words' is what you have to do. Anticipate this possibility and work out a scenario of what you could talk about beforehand.

**'What are they writing?'** Your interviewer(s) will probably spend a lot of the time writing notes. Give him or her just enough time to do so; don't get paranoid about it and don't, under any circumstances, try to read what is being written. (Often it's simply your basic physical details — hair colour/style/length, clothes, and other distinctive marks — all very useful as memory joggers, when going through the notes later.)

Some write very little, if anything. 'Does that imply a total lack of interest in me?' It might, but you have to ignore this and plough on regardless. Some people like to write their notes immediately afterwards. There is absolutely no point in worrying about what they write or think. If you do, it could inhibit your efforts.

I am also very aware of this phenomenon in rehearsals. However, what most actors fail to realise is that the note does not necessarily relate to the moment that pen hits paper. Many notes take time to formulate at the back of the mind before going down on paper, and the moment they do get written down may well have nothing to do with the immediate circumstances.

**Mutual friends** Try to find some kind of personal contact with the person(s) you are meeting and make sure your information is correct. On several occasions I have been told by an interviewee that A, B or C 'sends their love', when I may have met the 'friend' once but cannot remember them from X, Y or Z. Also be careful about how you phrase a greeting. 'Love' is a commonly used word in this profession, but you should be sure of yourself before using it. Perhaps, something like 'wishes to be remembered' might be a better salutation.

If it's the case, be wary of admitting that the third party concerned also happens to be your lover. This somehow opens up other connotations that are unnecessary and can cloud the central issue and/or take the focus away from you. Marriage is different, but it still should only be a passing reference. The interview should be about you and not about some third party whom you both happen to know. In general it's better to keep intimate relationships out of the discussion altogether — you never know who might have known who.

**'I want work!'** Never be overtly desperate for a job; it can colour the whole session in totally the wrong way. A classic example of this was the actor I was seeing for the part of Mozart in *Amadeus*. He expressed his enthusiasm for the subject-matter by saying: 'I've got all his records.' He was deadly serious. Acting requires objectivity as well as subjectivity, and dispassion as well as passion. A director must see that 'objectivity' in you.

Several people have suggested that it is better to approach the session with the idea of not wanting the job: for some that can be the best way of coping. For others, that attitude can make you seem so casual it might well turn the interviewer right off. Somebody else suggested to me that it's probably best to go in thinking that the job is yours for the taking and, when you've left the room, get it into your head that you haven't got it and forget about it. Or 'Care when you're in there; forget it when you're out of the door.'

**'Acting' confident** Some people find it very easy just to go in and be totally relaxed and confident they can enjoy the session and be totally open, and show easily that they care about their work. If you are the sort of person who needs to act 'confidence', be very careful because an acted confidence can come over as arrogance, which is very alienating. It is essential not to overdo confidence and/or be too assertive. I'm afraid this is especially true for a woman being interviewed by a man. Some of my sex are too easily put off by the apparently assertive woman. Essentially, assert yourself but don't make it look as if you are doing so.

If you find your mouth dries up with nerves, scrape you tongue hard along the back of your teeth surreptitiously; that soon gets the saliva circulating again.

**Role-playing** In spite of what you might feel about interviews, enjoy being there. Role-playing because you get nervous isn't necessarily wrong or insincere. It's not 'not being yourself'; it's your way of dealing with the interview situation. In taking on a role you will be showing at least part of yourself, which is all that can be expected in that short space of time.

A friend takes the role-playing even further. She will adapt an aspect of herself — where she lives, for example — to come closer in reality to the character she's up for. This may be a good idea — she works a lot — but you must be sure you can carry it through and don't get found out. There is also the danger that if you go too far that particular interviewer will only think of you in that kind of part when considering future casting. (To some extent the clothes you wear will dictate the role you play: see 'What shall I wear?', below.)

**General presentation** I used to do a lot of hitch-hiking. I learned that I stood a better chance of a lift if I didn't look too scruffy and didn't overplay my hand — in both the physical and the presentational sense. Just make your point — 'I would like a lift, please' — and that's it. On the other hand, don't just sit there looking bored and fed up, limply 'waving your thumb'. There has to be energy behind each request. The same ideas apply to your general presentation in an interview.

**What is your face saying?** Too many people seem to think that the best way to sell themselves is by sitting there with a forced, fixed and blasé theatrical smile on their faces: the 'eyes and teeth' approach. I've known others sit there looking totally vacant. Concentration does strange things to some people's faces (I'm told I can look angry), but nobody maintains a fixed expression if they are listening and receiving properly (see 'Listening and receiving', page 114).

Don't start 'putting on' faces. If your brain is connecting properly with what's going on, then simply use your actor's training and instinct to inform your face and your whole body.

**'What shall I wear?'** Dress comfortably and not over the top or very scruffily, unless you can carry it off with style. Extremes of dress can totally dominate your interviewer's perception of you. Don't wear large eye-catching earrings — hypnotists are supposed to use similar objects to put us into trances. The fashion for padded shoulders was also distracting, especially when the wearer was doing an audition speech. (I'm sure other people have other dress prejudices.) Make sure that your shoes are clean and in good condition. I have been riveted by numerous pairs that looked as though they were auditioning for a remake of *The Gold Rush*. Also, avoid noisy heels: they can upstage any audition speech on a wood or concrete floor.

*For television, commercials and film* You need to dress as close to the part as is possible, whilst still being yourself. (See chapter 16 for more detailed considerations.) Several experienced actors have said to me that you need to go in 'looking successful'; you need to look as though you'd be at one with the stars who will be playing the leads. That doesn't mean dressed as though you are going to a society wedding. If it's a dowdy part, then go 'designer dowdy'; scruffy, then 'designer scruffy', and so on. Don't wear clothes that will upstage that most important part of you — your face.

Be aware of the details. It is no good looking right to play a business person but walking through the door with a carrier-bag full of the trainers, jeans and T-shirt you've just changed out of.

*For the theatre* You will get more of the benefit of the doubt in what you wear — provided you don't go to extremes. In general, avoid excessive make-up and formal suits. Go feeling comfortable in what you wear and looking as though you'd be prepared to work there and then.

I once turned somebody down for a part and subsequently realised I should not have done. I met her and then recalled her to read again after she'd read the entire script (along with five others). She was very keen to play the part, but on both occasions she appeared very sloppily dressed — the same jumper each time — with no 'energy' in her appearance. From her television work I felt she'd be right, but in taking the final knife-edge decision against her I subsequently realised that I was deeply influenced by that sloppy jumper. Your visual impact can easily upstage what you say because human beings take in far more information through their eyes than through their ears. You are your own shop-window; you should dress it well. If you are a tall woman or a short man, seek to minimise your out-of-the-ordinary inches with your choice of footwear; it could make the difference. And remember: lipstick on teeth is one of most people's 'least favourite things'.

**Women and trousers** A subtitle for this paragraph could have been, 'Trousers can hide a multitude of sins'. If you are going for a part that specifically requires skirt-length above the ankle, then it's probably better to wear a skirt. Sexist but true. If your legs are excessively thin or fat, then you'll be used to finding a length that disguises as much as possible; this is probably your best option as trousers worn for an obvious 'legs' part could make the interviewer suspicious. For instance, good legs are important for the traditional pantomime principal boy, for Louise Page's *Golden Girls* (a play about female runners) and I'm sure there are other examples. I've also met a director who wouldn't employ women who wear trousers in interview.

**Hair, perfume and personal hygiene** You may have long and beautiful hair, but can we see your face properly?

Strong perfume (like strong colour) provokes strong reactions — positive and negative — so be wary of using it. And body odour will put anybody off.

**Sex** Don't be sexually provocative in your dress. One woman semi-exposed her bosom to me by the surreptitious undoing of an upper blouse-button — I have no memory of the rest of her. The same is true of the man in tight, revealing trousers pointing his crotch at whoever might be interested. Don't, as someone once did to me, take all your clothes off as part of an audition speech. The striptease may have been justifiable for the speech, but I — a broad-minded, red-blooded, hetero-sexual male — did not know where to put myself and could hardly continue. I don't remember anything else about that session beyond mumbling, 'Perhaps you'd better get dressed' and my hurried exit. A strip can be effectively mimed or not be nearly so extensive.

**Injury and illness** It is awful to have to miss the chance of an interview if you are injured or ill. Sometimes it is possible to get another appointment, but most interview-times have to be limited because of the costs involved. Of course, whether you cancel depends on how incapacitated you are and in what way. If it is something obvious like the spectacular broken leg I once saw then struggle in there and use it as a talking-point. However, don't 'milk it' or go to the opposite extreme of trying to ignore it as she did. (Somebody had dropped a stage weight on her foot, which would have been a good talking-point.)

My wife got an interview only a few days after she was involved in a car accident. She shuffled painfully along the corridors of Television Centre assisted only by a walking-frame — and her own determination. Her face was still showing obvious damage but it didn't affect her spirit and she got the job. That is the central point to consider about whether to go or not. Your body may be affected but is your 'spirit' capable of rising to the occasion?

If you feel that adrenaline will not be able temporarily to restore you sufficiently, it is better not to go. Interviewers are sympathetic but they won't be able to judge much and you will be wasting their time, which could even count against you for future reference. It is much better to turn down the invitation to interview and write a brief, and positive, letter explaining why.

**Forewarned is forearmed** You should get as much information about the job, about the interviewer(s) and what will be expected of you as you reasonably can. Your agent should be able to supply most of this for you, but any extra research you can do could be useful. However, never entirely trust the information you receive, and use it judiciously. It could be that you discover that an interviewer likes cats, for instance. You may also discover, after you've spent several precious minutes extolling the virtues of your ginger tom, that your interviewer is only interested in pedigree Siamese and despises common or garden 'moggies'. This is a true example.

**State of mind** It is crucial that you focus on the fact that you are a skilled and accomplished professional, not a hapless beggar desperate for work. And, if it is necessary for you, find that positive interview 'state of mind' and be prepared to sell — but not oversell — yourself. A friend does workouts to get himself up to that 'positivity' level before he goes to an interview, and another sings along with her favourite grand opera arias. Prepare well and then be prepared for anything and everything.

**Modern technology** Mobile phones, digital watches, and so on have nasty habits — they emit unpleasant sounds when least expected. Make sure your electronic bits are firmly switched off before you enter the interview room.

**Portfolios** These are collections of production photographs, reviews and press-cuttings neatly displayed in a portfolio. They can be useful to show a range of your work, but too many people try to hide behind them and use them as a substitute for talking about themselves. An actor once handed me his in answer to my 'Tell me a bit about yourself' without saying a word. It contained some riveting photographs of him and a rather elegant naked woman. I asked what the play was — he couldn't remember. Others have had modelling shots, badly photocopied reviews, even holiday snaps. If you go for this extra encumbrance, make sure that all the material is 'quality', that is emphasises your acting work (neatly labelled) and that it's not too long. In an interview the stress should be on you, in the flesh. It is probably better to reveal your portfolio later on in an interview — if it feels appropriate — and it can be briefly skimmed through. Be warned: some people do not like them at all.

**CV and photograph** Always take spare copies of these to any interview. You never know.

## Some things to consider on the day

Every interview is different — as is every audience. There can be all kinds of unknown factors that determine the course of events. Treat each interview afresh and anticipate nothing specific. Essentially, you should aim to be as relaxed and real as possible within the confines of what is essentially an unreal situation. You can exploit the fact that you've only got a short time just to put over your good points. That is not lying, it is being 'economical with the truth', which may not be legitimate in a court-room but certainly is in a brief interview.

You should present yourself as a confident human being who has the sensitivities and skills of an actor. Stay centred and honest, and sustain yourself through all the doubts and fears that are an actor's lot with that life force of humour. Don't find yourself forced into a corner where your soul starts lying. 'It's your job to enjoy talking to people' sums up the general attitude necessary.

**Signage** So you've found the building. Next you have to find the interview-room. It might be easy and there is an obvious gaggle of actors crowded into a small, scruffy waiting-room. Wait a moment. Are they waiting to see the same person as you are? Hopefully there's a notice on the door indicating the organisation concerned. There might be a friendly caretaker to tell you — or, even better, a receptionist who knows the difference between the Belgrade Theatre, Coventry, and the Library Theatre, Manchester. But be warned: there are several popular (and cheap) places to rent that can house several companies at one time in their rabbit-warren of rooms.

Essentially, look for the signs and arrive early enough to find them. They will be badly scribbled and Sellotaped on to walls, pinned up next to the Alcoholics Anonymous notice. The crucial thing is that they will rarely be larger than A4, and in a vast Victorian building they may not be obvious and will probably be easy to miss in a panic. You may suddenly come across a door marked with the obscure name — probably one of the founding fathers of the institution — that you were given in your instructions. Think before you knock, let alone barge in. You may be late, and silence seems to reign; but if there is no sign beyond that faded nameplate — wait, relax and think. Look around the vicinity more carefully. There could be two doors to the interview-room. Look for a waiting-room or area (it might be a corridor). Only in the last resort should you knock. It is always better to be in a situation where you can wait to be called.

**Aim to arrive early** Apart from the possibilities of finding useful information there's a more fundamental reason to aim for this. Most people need a 'period of adjustment' to settle into new circumstances. Even if you've been there before, there could easily be something different — not the usual room, for instance.

**Waiting and listening in** Once you've arrived at the appointed place you will usually have to wait. Some actors need to be quiet, some need to talk, but natural curiosity insists that everybody will be after clues as to what's going on in the interview-room. Of course hints might be useful, but they might also be misleading as no two human interactions are exactly alike. A glimpse through a door, loud laughter permeating the walls, a snatch of conversation as somebody is ushered out might generate presumptions on your part. You may be right — the interviewer is 'nice'; but it could be that he or she was very jolly with the last person because they already knew each other well and just wanted to chat about a part or simply that two strangers suddenly 'clicked'. You will never be able to get anything like a complete picture of a previously unknown interviewer, and a strong presumption on your part could easily lead you up the garden path.

I was once having a very good and jolly chat with someone after having done the 'business' side and ran late because I was enjoying myself. That session over, I admitted the next person, with apologies for the delay, and suddenly she came out with a barrage of chat and jokes in the manner of the previous interviewee. I had, quite firmly, to call a halt because it was getting me nowhere and by then I was running significantly late. She protested: 'But I thought you were such a nice man from what I could hear.' I am — usually — but not when I'm informed that I have been monitored for the previous ten minutes through a private conversation. It was very difficult to establish any kind of relationship after that.

On the other hand, a friend was waiting peacefully when he suddenly heard the sounds of a terrible row emanating from the interview-room. After a few minutes, somebody came flying out and passed rapidly through to the outside world. Then my friend was aware of a red-faced and shaking presence standing at the door of the interview-room. 'You're next, I presume,' it said and stalked back inside. My friend decided that he would subtly have to work at calming his interviewer down. He succeeded, the session ended very happily and he was offered the job. You may be able to capitalise on your perceived assessment of the atmosphere inside the interview-room or you may be catastrophically wrong.

**The waiting-room full of beautiful people** Sometimes you'll walk into the waiting-room to find it full of people who look 'perfect' for the part. It is true that the 'look' of someone (which *can* include their looks) can count — especially for commercials and often in television and film — but, generally, not as much as you might think. Anyway, the first thing is not to let it get you down. If your spirit flies out of the window at this early stage, you are doomed. If their presence really starts to bug you, look for things that might be wrong with individuals. How someone gets up from a chair is a good test of their 'cool'. There are others — watch out for them. As a friend pointed out: 'You have to work on convincing people that you're glamorous.' She also observed that 'Great British actresses aren't known for their looks'. Another said, 'You're as glamorous as you feel'.

**A friend in the waiting room** It's often a relief to find people you know in the waiting room — you can help each other ease the pain of waiting. However, don't make the fun of the renewed contact take from your focus for being there. I'm not suggesting that you ignore them and

sit in stoical silence — that's an even worse preparation for what's to
follow. Look to helping each other to prepare and arrange to meet up
and compare notes afterwards.

Similarly, don't let casual waiting room conversations get out of
hand. I've had, on several occasions, to quell persistent, loud conversation that was disrupting my interviewing.

**The earliest impressions** Whilst waiting outside the interview-room
don't try to draw attention to yourself by attempting to make eye
contact with the director/assistant each time he or she comes to collect
the next person. This kind of attention-seeking is terribly alienating and
typifies the bad, but generally unfair, public image that actors have. An
actor is a real person with special skills, not an attention-seeking child.

**First impressions** As you walk in to the interview-room, try to assess
the atmosphere inside the room in which it's all taking place and the
people it contains. Try to measure the energy of the space and aim not
to go above or below it (see 'Energies', page 203). That walk from the
door to the table, however long or short, can be an invaluable time to
assess the atmosphere and to absorb it for your own purposes.

Your interviewers will also be assessing you — unconsciously perhaps
— in those first vital seconds. I know one director who claims to do
most of his casting on that first impact — 'After all, that's how the
audience will react.'

**Baggage** Be wary of any baggage you are carrying in these first few
moments (see 'The natural rhythm of an interview', page 117). Don't
let depositing your belongings take away from the vital beginnings of
getting to know your interviewer(s). It can often be a good idea to leave
anything inessential by the door of the interview room as you enter or
with someone remaining in the waiting room.

**The long walk** The interview 'area' is often on the opposite side of the
room from the door; this is to cut down the chances of being overheard.
If you are nervous, it can seem miles to your chair. Not only should you
use this time to 'assess the atmosphere', but you should also use it to
begin to establish yourself — just as you would when making your first
entrance on to a stage.

**Introductions** Listen carefully to introductions especially if there's an
army of people there. Make sure you take in those names, even if it's
only first names, and try to take in what each one does. It doesn't
matter if you have to ask for one to be repeated — it's easy to miss one
through nerves or individuals slurring them. (It is curious how many
people seem to do this.) Anyway, you should aim to get all the names

when contacted about the interview — you can help yourself if you learn them beforehand.

If hand-shaking is in order, do it positively. There is nothing more off-putting at the very start than a limp handshake. (You, on the other hand, mustn't be perturbed if you receive one.) The act of shaking hands is an act that suggests mutual trust. It is also your opportunity silently to say 'I am me!' But don't be too strong or hearty either — your interviewer has probably got to write with that hand. Know your own physical strength, or lack of it.

If there are several interviewers, don't try to shake hands with everybody unless offered: it can take for ever. Don't just shake hands with the men, either; I've seen that happen far too often.

Sometimes the odd person may be left out of introductions. This can be oversight or it might be deliberate. If this happens, don't exclude them from what follows. Everybody is there for a purpose.

When you have finally settled after the introductions, your interviewers' opening smiles will probably turn to what look like frowns: it is strange what concentration does to many people's faces. Don't let that throw you.

**Your chair is not glued to the floor** A surprising number of people will sit in a chair that is found slap bang up against the interviewer's table, threatening an eyeball-to-eyeball confrontation rather than a pleasant chat. A few cowardly souls will sit in one that's on the other side of the room. (How does the chair manage to get into such strange places? It was moved by the previous interviewee.)

You should move your chair to a place that suits you, from which you can talk easily with all of your interviewers. That is, so that you are not so close that you invade your interviewers' space, and not so distant that proper personal contact is difficult. You should do this without asking (see 'Politeness', page 118). It shows you have a personality of your own and are not a complete wimp who will do nothing beyond what you are actually told.

The position of your chair is especially important when you are facing a gang of interviewers. You have to position it so that you can take in as many of them as possible without finding yourself constantly 'watching tennis'. Place it centrally so that everybody is within good 'contact' range. However, don't spend hours fiddling with your chair's position. This should become an instinct as natural as breathing.

**Sitting down** Sitting in a familiar chair needs no thought; in an unfamiliar one — in 'professional' circumstances — it does.
• It can be good manners to sit after whoever ushered you into the room — unless this would cause you to hover for too long and you begin to appear 'creepy'.

- Although many chairs are of a standard height, a significant minority are that little bit lower. It can be quite throwing to make contact with the seat that fraction later than you expected.
- You'll appear more positive if you sit up reasonably (but not ram-rod) straight.
- Try not to cross you legs — you'll seem more 'open'. If like me you find it difficult not to do so, then aim to cross them 'lightly'. I know it can feel comforting to wrap one leg round the other, but what happens is that you start compressing the blood vessels in the upper leg and in a short time it will begin to go numb. Then the attached foot will take on a mind of its own and when you try to stand up the numbing effect will make you unable to walk properly until circulation is restored.

**'Who's in charge?'** Never act on the presumption that one person there is more important than all the others. You may well be right, but don't let that presumption make you direct all your answers to that person to the exclusion of the others. I have known people direct all their answers to me, as senior person present, even when some questions were coming from the trainee at my side. The trainee was most put out and so was I.

Everybody in the room will have at least some influence over the casting — even a secretary or assistant stage manager. Don't alienate one apparently lowly person for the sake of giving your all to whoever's in charge — even the person ticking off names outside. He or she may be an employee of the organisation that runs the building and nothing to do with the interviews, but even so comments will be made, especially on intolerable behaviour.

Assistant stage managers and trainees might become powerful directors in days to come, and memories are long for those that hurt us unnecessarily.

**Your native accent** If you happen to have a strong accent and the part is not in that accent, should you do the interview in standard English? Opinions vary. Some say it is a 'denial of your roots' to do so. Some directors will switch off immediately if they hear an accent, believing that standard English is an impossibility for such a person. You have to learn to judge each circumstance, but it can be very exciting to hear someone change from one to the other at the flick of an internal switch.

**Listening and receiving** Listen carefully to questions asked and be positive and concise in your responses. You may be nervous, and nerves tend to stop people listening properly. If this is the case, then try concentrating hard on this 'listening' and it could help calm you.

And don't just listen — receive! That is, receive the message that is being sent to you. Too many actors seem to concentrate so much on giving little nods and smiles that I know full well they are not taking on board fully what I am saying or asking.

**The same old question** Don't respond to 'What have you been doing recently?' with a basic telephone directory of facts which can be gleaned from your CV and letter anyway. Use it to show your wit, charm and personality. You will be asked this basic question frequently — never let your response get stale. (See 'What have you been doing recently?', page 103.)

**The sin of being out of work** Obviously you try to disguise those great grey patches of unemployment when talking about your recent career, but some interviewers are very sharp at reading between the lines and, if it's the case, will detect that you have in fact been out of work for too long. If they comment (which I'm told is unusual) to this effect, don't worry or be embarrassed; just be positive about the painting and decorating, the temping, and so on, you've been doing to keep the wolf from the door. Talk about the amazing characters you've met and what useful studies they've been. In fact, you should go into non-acting jobs (and about life as a whole) with your actor's antennae alert for such useful observations — after all it's those real people that you have to bring to your craft.

**Excuses and apologies** Don't make excuses unless some kind of genuine apology is necessary: for example, if you are late. If something does require an apology, do it simply and straightforwardly. Over-apologising can easily waste precious time and can embarrass.

There is no excuse for being under par because of a hangover, for instance. That is your fault and, if it prevents you from interviewing properly, it is unprofessional.

**Mumbling** 'When in doubt, mumble' seems to be some actors' way of covering a hangover or other embarrassing fact. You are only undermining yourself further.

**'Only connect'** Do your damnedest to 'connect' with your interviewer(s). They should be trying to do the same with you, but in practice the onus tends to be on the actor.

Every interview is different. Even someone you have met before will — to at least some degree — seem different in a different context. You have to find a rapport with each individual in each circumstance. You should try to 'interact' with each interviewer — just as with all your fellow actors in rehearsal.

**Non-acting matters** Interviewers sometimes like to talk about these. There doesn't seem to be any consistency in this, but it may have something to do with boredom from the same old questions or with challenging further someone who seems to be very right for a part. For instance a friend was told, 'That's an interesting T-shirt' at the start of an interview.

**Status** Apparently some directors are actually afraid of actors. This makes 'connecting' difficult. Certainly I often feel in the first interview of the day that I don't know what the hell I'm talking about and can start thinking that the actor must think I'm stupid. I don't care a damn about being thought stupid but I know that some interviewers do like to 'maintain their status'. Whatever communicates, never let them know that you know — unless it's obvious they don't sit on their status. They are your only route to the job. You can help your interviewers. They may get into a muddle about information they're trying to get over about the play — when one is repeating the same thing over and over again that's very easy to do. Listen carefully, and if something doesn't make sense to you, then ask.

**'Power tends to corrupt'** It is also true that for some the power inherent in being an employment-broker can tend to corrupt. If you do meet this phenomenon, there's only one thing you can do. Be strong!

**When there's someone in the room you know** The strangest thing can be the interview between two people who already know each other reasonably well which takes place with nobody else in the room. There can be all kinds of reasons for this to occur: a director who feels he or she doesn't know somebody quite well enough, a 'dangerous' piece of potential casting, a casting that is outside the actor's perceived range. As a friend said, 'It felt extremely odd' when I asked to see him for the first of those reasons. Don't feel offended. Your director-friend may also feel embarrassed, but you can help by aiming to treat the session as 'professionally' as possible and put the relationship to date in perspective. Some (but not all) directors think even harder about employing friends than strangers. I know at least one director who won't employ his own wife as a matter of principle.

If there is more than one interviewer, and there is someone there you know very well, then you have to push that personal relationship to the back of your mind. That is not to say that you should ignore them, but you should treat them as another interviewer and then not miss things out that they know well but the other interviewers do not.

**Instant friendships** Yes, one aims to make friends with one's interviewer, but don't be over-friendly. This can often happen when interviewer and interviewee have a close acquaintance in common. It can lead to the presumption on both director's and actor's part that they are therefore already close acquaintances and don't need to go through those essential early 'connecting' stages. They do. Don't, as I have known people do, dive in, in the first moments, treating your interviewers as long-lost friends when you don't know them from Adam (or Eve). It will crowd them, and they won't be able to start off as they want. At the beginning the field is your interviewers', so let them make the running and set the pace.

**Diplomacy** With some more open friendly interviewers it's easy to feel very relaxed and open yourself, and you may well find yourself coming out with a minor piece of bitchery. This may be fine, but there's a chance that he or she might be friendly with the person you've just bitched about. I know of someone who was distinctly unkind about his drama school to a director. What the actor didn't know was that the director's wife had been one of his teachers. Be careful. Diplomacy rather than candour.

**It's easy to be negative** Don't give negative reasons for anything unless you can be positively negative. That is not a contradiction in terms. For example, if you didn't enjoy a particular job because of the laziness of some of the company, be positive in your criticism of such unprofessionalism. Beware: spreading doubt about others can create doubt about you.

Especially, don't complain about one director to another even if pushed. In fact don't run anybody down — ever. Even if your interviewer seems to be enjoying it hugely, it's not worth the risk.

**Generosity** If you know somebody who is perfect for the part you're up for — and you're patently not — then say so. This kind of generosity, in this fiercely competitive world, could reap rewards in time to come.

**The natural rhythm of an interview** Two people who are genuinely getting on find a natural rhythm to their dialogue — just like that natural rhythm that actors look for in a scene. This will partly come through trying to 'connect' with your interviewer and partly through being aware of natural hazards. For instance, you could be offered a cup of tea. That's probably a good sign that things are going well. But, however parched you may feel, you should usually politely decline. Why? Because this encumbrance can suddenly make the whole session take on another course. Consider the analogy of a scene from a play. You've rehearsed and rehearsed, and it's going well, then comes the moment when you stop miming and use real tea in a real cup. The whole scene suddenly falls apart because you find there is a great pause whilst you drink the hot liquid. You may have marked this moment in rehearsal, but virtually no one leaves long enough. Of course, a short amount of rehearsal-time will sort this out, but in an interview there is no rehearsal-time. The pause whilst drinking can strain, or even sever, the gossamer thread that is the connection you are building with your interviewer(s). You have interrupted the natural rhythm of the all too brief session. (Once, a nervous actor missed his mouth completely — through concentration on the conversation — and poured orange squash all over himself.)

**Eye contact** Don't overdo eye contact. Be natural about it. A lot is made of 'eye contact' in acting; that doesn't mean you try to do it throughout an interview. Of course you make eye contact in the first instance, but don't hold on to it like a limpet; that seems to be the prerogative of the newly in love. If you push it with the idea of making even better contact, the interviewer will probably feel that you are invading his or her space and may even feel threatened. Remember playing 'stare-you-out' games as a child?

Also bear in mind that the director will often be looking down at papers and writing notes. (See 'What are they writing?', page 104.)

**Make 'em laugh** Yes, a few laughs are a good way of 'connecting', but don't overdo humour and don't force it. Humour is not always the art of making jokes; it is that zest for life that made you become an actor in the first place and without which you'd have slit your wrists long ago. It is the way we get through the months whilst we're waiting for Godot to offer us a job.

**The balance of humour** Like the 'balance of power' you must be careful that it doesn't tip too far one way or the other. Early on you need to assess whether your interviewer has a sense of humour or not. If he or she has, then be careful that your combined 'humours' don't take over the interview too much and detract from your other efforts.

**Politeness** Be pleasant, but don't go to the extreme of being over-polite, even formal: for example, by addressing your interviewer as 'Mr X' or 'Ms B', asking if you may take your coat off, and so on. You may have been 'well brought up', and there is nothing wrong with the basic rules of politeness, but you should use them to suit each circumstance. Regard the situation as if you've been invited into a vague acquaintance's house for a social drink. Don't be too casual, however; it is also very important that you come over as someone who cares about your work.

**Flattery is base** Don't plead or flatter. Both are more alienating than anything else I know. Essentially avoid extremes of behaviour (which can happen through nerves). Never get to the extremes of either subservience or plain bloody-minded cockiness. Never flirt with your interviewer. Even if you do suddenly find yourself fancying them, and you think you feel it reciprocated, concentrate on the job in hand, which is to get a job. The casting-couch is an extremely rare phenomenon.

**'You remember, we met...'** Tolerate with good grace a director who cannot remember meeting you before, even if the meeting was recent. Directors meet an amazing number of different people, in all kinds of different contexts, day in and day out. There is no way, even possessed of very good memories, we can immediately remember each and every person we have ever met. It can also be very confusing if you've changed your hairstyle, grown a beard or acquired glasses since our previous meeting, or are simply dressed completely differently.

The reverse can also happen, with directors saying they know you 'from somewhere' but you cannot for the life of you remember them. Don't worry about it; this profession is an ocean of ships passing in the night.

**'You turned me down for...'** If it's the case, don't bear a grudge against your interviewer for previously rejecting you. Most directors do feel at least a little bit guilty about those they liked but rejected in favour of people they liked even more. You probably wouldn't be in the interview at all if you hadn't come over well at the previous meeting.

**Superstitions** A lot of people would deny being at all superstitious, but in this profession that is generally not true. If you are asked about current job prospects and you don't want to discuss anything about possibilities in the pipeline, that will be respected.

**Interruptions** Anything might happen during an interview: the phone might ring, someone might interrupt with an urgent message. Don't let this throw you. Concentrate on where the session was interrupted to help your harassed interviewer pick up from where you left off. The interruption will have wasted precious time and has probably made the interviews run even later than they were. Don't feel rushed by this — that is the interviewer's problem, not yours. (I was once severely embarrassed by a director-friend barging into an interview in order to arrange lunch. The actor in the middle coped extremely well — even ending up with a job with my [rude] friend.)

**Politics and religion** Never discuss politics unless absolutely sure of your ground with your interviewer. A significant number of directors are at least moderately radical, but a significant silent few are not. You may think you will be on safe ground if you take a swipe at whichever politician or party is today's joke; in all probability you will be, but bear in mind that an awful lot of people voted for him/her/it and some of them do work in this profession.

Treat religion (or lack of it) in exactly the same way. The silent majority of directors are probably apathetic agnostics, but there are a few devout believers and some angry atheists amongst us.

I do know actors (and directors) who maintain that they could not work with somebody who held diametrically opposed political or religious beliefs. This may well be true, but unless you are prepared to sacrifice the chance to work for your beliefs there is no point in waving a flag of extreme colour. Even if the director does agree with you, your viewpoint usually has nothing to do with your acting ability.

**Taking the initiative** Don't try to go on the offensive too much by asking the interviewer about his or her theatre, the productions, artistic policy, and so on, too early on. You may want to glean some information, but it's not helping the interviewer to get to know you and you might inadvertently tread on some sore spot — for example, the production that went disastrously wrong.

Always let interviewers take the initiative to start with, even if it does not seem very imaginative. Ask your questions if invited, or if appropriate, when the main business is done with. (See 'Any questions?', page 121.)

**'I don't agree with you!'** You may find an incautious interviewer commenting adversely on something or someone you hold dear. Some directors are prejudiced against some drama schools, for example. If you feel you need to disagree, do so! But do it well. I once had a very 'spirited' discussion with an interviewee on the subject of her drama school and its methods. She was strong in its defence and I was strong in my attack. There was no resolving our disagreement, but it had nothing to do with whether I wanted to work with her or not. In fact, her 'spirit' warmed me to her, and it has been pure circumstance that has prevented me, so far, from working with her.

**Smoking** If you are a committed smoker, try not to. Even if the room is thick with smoke and the ashtrays are overflowing, don't join in unless you really can limit yourself to only having one. In these nervous circumstances one can lead to another, and another... I know! The interviewer, even if a committed chain-smoker, could think 'I have got a real neurotic here', and you will go right down in the employment stakes. If there are no cigarette-ends at all, then don't even think of smoking.

If you're a committed anti-smoker, it's better to hide your feelings — much as with politics and religion.

**Don't bump into the furniture** Accidentally walking into doors and chairs (for instance) might be ignored, but the director might wonder how you will cope with similar items on a set. Somebody once walked into an interview with me and bumped into a large and obvious piano near the door. 'Sorry,' she said, 'but I've only got one contact lens in, and that's not my own.' I don't remember her name, what she looked like, her interview or her speech — just the incident and that remark. If she had laughed at her stupidity, she would have put the incident in perspective and taken the first step in 'connecting' with me. Inconvenient shafts of sunlight suddenly hitting you between the eyes, and so forth, are understandable natural hazards to be dealt with simply and acknowledged briefly before getting back to the main point.

**Don't let the cat out of the bag** There will often be certain things it is tactful not to mention — for example, your acquaintance with an actor you know the director does not get on with. Or it might be something more prosaic as the following example illustrates.

A friend once went up for the part of Miranda in *The Collector*.

'Do you know the book?' she was asked.

'Oh, yes! I know I haven't got blonde hair, but I could always wear a wig.'

'Is she blonde? I missed that.'

It was a pleasant interview and a good reading, but the director then concentrated on the blondes.

I'm not saying that you shouldn't talk about the background knowledge you've acquired, but try to avoid something that might affect your suitability for the part. That's tact, not lying.

NB Wigs are a very expensive answer to hair problems. One that moves well, and looks real, costs an awful lot of money.

**Singing** No, this paragraph is not in the wrong chapter. It's here because you might be asked to sing unaccompanied if you claim singing as a strength. You need a song prepared whose first note you can hit accurately — and remember that when you are nervous your voice automatically rises.

**'Any questions?'** Many interviewers like to round off with this invitation. Usually, it's fine to respond positively with the negative, but it has been suggested to me that it can be good idea to take a suitable question in with you. The important thing to remember is to keep your question simple and straightforward — there is not time for complicated discussion. And whatever you do, don't ask what the money is or when decisions will be made unless it is important — for example, you are considering another potential job. (Also see 'Taking the Initiative', page 120.)

**Don't overstay your welcome** Some people are very bad at ending interviews. Things are going well, you are prattling away and your interviewer seems to be having a good time. If all the usual processes have been gone through, then it's time for you to go. Develop an end-of-interview awareness. Remember that ancient theatrical cliché: 'Leave 'em wanting more!' And when you do go — go! Don't try to cram in more irrelevant information as you are leaving. It will be a waste of time; the interviewer is already thinking about the next person.

This is true even if your time has been very brief. Don't feel short-changed; it can be a good sign.

**Leaving things behind** Leaving things behind can be very irritating for your interviewer(s) as well as embarrassing for you. I have known people do this deliberately to draw attention to themselves. It does not work and it could well mark you down as potential chaos and not worth employing.

## A few final notes

**Recalls** Sometimes a director will go in for what seem like endless recalls. You may think that he or she must know you, and your capabilities, sufficiently by now. What else can you do to prove yourself? But you go on being asked back. There can be any number of reasons for this. You have to go on exactly as you did in the first interview doing whatever is asked of you. Don't let it frustrate you.

**Producers** These are the top dogs when there's real money involved — generally films, television and commercial theatre. They will usually cast the stars and often be involved in interviews and auditions for other parts. React to them as you would to anybody else.

**Casting and assistant directors (or the 'in-betweenies')** You may meet one of these before going on to meet the director in a position actually to give you a job. Obviously you treat the first round with the casting/assistant version as per usual, but meeting the top person can have some peculiarities. The director must have a fair degree of trust in the lesser mortals to employ them, but I have heard numerous stories of enthusiasm from the junior and virtually nothing from the senior partner. There are two fundamental problems.

1 The presumption on the actor's part is that the interview is going to be similar in mood to the one with the junior and there is very little more to prove.
2 The over-enthusiasm of the junior alienating the senior, who consequently sets out to be sceptical.

The answer is to focus on the senior without excluding the junior. Don't keep giving the latter little familiar smiles, or looks for confirmation, or constant prefacing of remarks with 'As I told [*the junior's name*]...'

This phenomenon is much more common when assistants are involved, but I have heard of it happening when a casting director is the link.

**Children** I'm told that mothers with small children are advised not to admit this fact to potential employers on the grounds that if something serious happened to a child at a vital point in production, then her priority has to be with that child. However, doesn't the same apply to a father and also to the serious illness of a parent or spouse? Unfortunately there are directors who don't realise that a working parent will ensure that there is someone in loco parentis whilst she or he is away. Anybody who feels they have to run home at the slightest childish sneeze is acting unprofessionally whether they be male or female and shouldn't be in this profession. I agree that children shouldn't be an issue, but discretion probably has to be the watchword.

**Gate-crashing** Most will see gate-crashers if there's time. But always have a copy of your CV and photo for them to keep and, as you wait patiently for a gap to appear, don't try to blackmail your way in with whomsoever when they appear to collect the next person.

**Children's theatre and Theatre-In-Education (TIE)** The principal difference for these is that you will know far more about what is required from you beforehand — especially for TIE companies, who tend to go in for all-day workshops to assess how well you would work with their team.

**I hate interviews** I'm told that the very words 'interview' and 'audition' are to the actor synonymous with the word 'exam'. You have to go in with the idea of giving all that you can offer. Be vulnerable but don't display your insecurities. In a sense you need to drop a little emotional 'blood', but be able to recover easily. Don't get so wound up that the whole thing becomes a great blur and you cannot respond properly to anything that's asked of you. Be relaxed, assured and open to anything and everything. Treat the interview like a joyous improvisation, but make your interviewer feel as though he or she is just one step ahead of you.

Through everything don't let your actor's instinct desert you, and remember your interviewer may well be ill-prepared, suffering from a hangover, worried about an unfinished report, and — crucially — he or she has probably just done another interview concentrating on somebody completely different.

**Consequences** If you are not what they want, then that's fine. Don't feel cheated because you felt you'd done very well. You haven't failed if you are not right in their eyes, and a good session could lead to work at another time — you never know. By going to interviews you are initially looking to get that particular job, but you are also sowing seeds for the future. (My wife got a very good job nearly twenty years after first meeting a particular director.)

Unfortunately, too many directors wind actors up at the end of interviews by all but promising them the job. I think I've done it myself. If a director meets someone who feels 'dead right', there is a terrible temptation to say so — there and then — almost to ensure that they'll take the job. But then someone even more 'right' comes along, and the first disappears from view. You have to be sceptical after you leave the room, even if they've promised to 'get in touch' or 'let you know'. (Note to directors who do make such promises: Stop it! It is one of the worst cruelties you can inflict on an actor whom you don't subsequently employ.)

An unlikely, but true, story: At the end of an interview a director went as far as to say he 'really wanted' a friend of mine to play the part. Already quite experienced, she knew that she had to remain sceptical. But it hurt her deeply to read a few weeks later in *The Stage* someone else's name against that part. Several years and some success later she was having her new house decorated. One afternoon she returned from filming and went round to view the improvements. Upstairs she found that director at the top of a ladder painting her ceiling.

**60%** You will often come out of an interview thinking of ways you could have done it better and cursing thoughts that didn't come out right, moments blown, and so on. There is nothing you can do now except learn for future reference. Anyway, if you've done 60% of what you feel you are capable of, you've probably done as well as anybody else. This rule applies to audition speeches, sight-readings, musicals auditions, and so on.

**Everybody's different** Elaine White, an actress, received sponsorship from The Geoffrey Ost Award and The Mary Henniker Heaton Memorial Trust for a research project on *Auditions, Interviews and Casting*. She circulated numerous directors with a questionnaire asking what each felt about interviews and auditions, what they expected from actors and what general advice they could offer. She incorporated all those essential questions that every actor would like to, but most never dare, ask (and that I have tried to cover in this book). For example, question one was 'Please describe the usual procedure at your auditions/interviews.' Individual answers ranged right across the spectrum from 'informal interview' only, through the full works of not just an interview but also 'pieces and/or reading and work with the actor', to an emphasis on the 'use of recalls'. Question seventeen was 'What should an actor bring to an audition (photos, CV, and so on) and will you usually ask to see these?' The answers included 'Bring reviews or portfolios/videos' and 'No reviews or portfolios'. Question eighteen was

'Does it help if an actor follows up an audition?' Again answers ranged widely, from 'Yes, it shows interest' to 'No, it's irritating/embarrassing and time-consuming'.

Elaine received over two hundred responses from directors, including a few very well known ones. Not only was there a wide range but even contradictory responses from four pairs of directors working in the same theatres. Her statistical analysis came to no definite conclusion and as she commented, 'At the end of the day it seems that auditionees must suit their presentation to that particular director, working with that particular company on that day,' *but* 'It does seem that an actor's personality could be as important a factor as his technical ability.' She has circulated copies of her report to interested parties including Equity and the Drama Schools and I am extremely grateful to Elaine for allowing me to quote her.

**The final touch** Do thank your interviewer at the end and if you've enjoyed the session say so. Or you can write a brief but not creepy letter afterwards.

**Postscript** A piece of basic advice from someone I met at drama school and then invited to interview (her very first, but I didn't know that until later) and subsequently offered her a job. She wrote to me later:

> 'I am currently dipping into your book (ugh! what a creep I am), but it appears you missed out a vital piece of advice — "The A, B, C — X, Y, Z formula for auditioning: Always Be Clear and (more importantly) Examine Your Zip!"'

She'd done the complete interview, a song and a sight-reading with the zip in her jeans undone. Fortunately she didn't realise until after she'd left the room.

## Chapter Thirteen

# *Audition Speeches*

Audition speeches may be very well established as a method for actors to demonstrate their talent, but I am constantly surprised at how few people make a real impact with them. This is generally through poor choice of material and/or bad staging. It is true that you will probably only be asked to do them for drama school and in your first few years in the profession and virtually never for the media. (Although I have come across several examples of audition speeches being asked for in television interviews — one actor was told 'I just want to see some more.') But a surprising number of theatre directors still ask for them from experienced actors as well as, or even instead of, a reading (hopefully you will be warned of this beforehand). I also know a number of experienced actors who would prefer to do a speech instead of a reading.

Many actors argue that doing them is a desperately artificial way of having their worth assessed. I would tend to agree but, however much you may hate them, you will periodically have to do them. Of course it's an artificial situation, but isn't acting about making artifice seem real? There are ways of making them work. (Think of Bob Hoskins in *Who Framed Roger Rabbit* and Steve Martin in *Dead Men Don't Wear Plaid* — both acting with beings who weren't really there.)

Essentially audition speeches should be self-contained, well chosen, well researched, well staged and well gauged for the room you are in and for whoever is watching you — just like a good production of a play. In fact an audition speech should be a 'mini-production' (of a 'mini-play') in its own right.

NB The transatlantic term, 'monologue', means a one person play — which is slightly different.

## Selecting your speeches

**Length** An audition piece should be no more than 2–2½ minutes long (that's roughly 300 words), which feels very short whilst you are doing it. (It is considerably shorter than the 3½-minute average in a mini-survey I once carried out.) You may argue that there is no way you can show enough of your skills as an actor in such a short time. True, you can't show everything, but you can give a very good indication of your potential — like a good television commercial. And you don't want to use up too much of the overall time allotted to you on one thing.

It doesn't matter if it's less than two minutes, provided it's self-contained. In fact it is probably better to aim for less, but don't compromise your speech for the sake of brevity. Doing it fast, simply to crack the two-minute barrier, will get you nowhere. The impact of a short speech that contains all the parameters listed elsewhere in this chapter can be tremendous. Also, directors can generally tell if you are of interest to them within the first thirty seconds or so.

If you time your speech yourself you are probably about 10–20% under the actual playing-time. The sheer act of self-timing makes most people speed up.

**How many?** If you are just starting out, you should have at least six completely different pieces (if not more) of which you are very sure, on instant recall. This might seem rather a lot, but you need at least that number to ensure a good range to choose from. (When Janet McTeer first auditioned for The Royal Exchange, she eventually did six speeches because they 'liked her so much'.) Even if there are protestations from the interviewer that 'It doesn't matter', if your speech is too much at variance with the play on the schedule it takes that much more time and effort to change gear. An audition piece does give some idea of your ability as an actor but doesn't necessarily indicate whether you'd be right for the part in question.

**Categories** There are an enormous number of potential audition speeches to choose from, and a great range of plays to choose them from. Here is a rough suggested list of categories from which you could start selecting your repertoire:
1 a 'modern' comedy piece;
2 a 'modern' serious piece;
3 a 'classical' (Shakespeare and contemporaries) comedy piece;
4 a 'classical' serious piece;
5 at least one 'period' piece;
6 something that can demonstrate any special skill like an accent, singing or juggling.

Don't see this list as all you need to prepare — it is a starting point to build from and is subject to all the caveats and qualifications listed in the succeeding paragraphs.

**'Modern' and 'Classical' (and 'Period')** I think I'd been using these terms for nearly twenty years before I started to think about what they actually meant. To me, 'modern' means a speech in which the language is easily comprehensible to the modern ear; 'classical' where it's not immediately so. By these definitions the dividing line lies somewhere around the middle of the nineteenth century. I suggest that we need another, in-between category: 'Period' — that is plays written in 'comprehensible' language, but from a time when the general social mores were very different from now. It is wise to check specifically what will be required — usually this is only important for drama schools.

Incidentally, does a modern translation of a foreign 'period' or 'classical' play count as a 'modern'?

**'I hate doing speeches'** If you are one of the numerous people who find doing speeches extremely nerve-racking and prefer to read, then ask. The majority of people will go along with this request, but a few will not and insist that you do a speech. So, if you are in this category, aim to have just two contrasting ones that have been so well worked on that you can do them in spite of those cursed nerves.

**Keep an archive** It is a good idea to keep a copy of every audition speech that you have ever done, for whatever comes up — especially if you are one of the significant few who are not very good at readings.

You might suddenly be asked to prepare a speech from a specific play, period or playwright, and one could be quietly yellowing away to itself in that dusty folder you've kept since drama school. Of course, some will no longer be within your 'playing range', but there are speeches that can be remarkably elastic in this respect. However long ago you originally did them, it is amazing how little work is usually required to bring them quickly back to life.

**Stick within your 'playing range'** Your speeches should be varied and within your 'playing range'. At drama school you will have played all kinds of parts, in many different age-ranges. You will rarely play far outside your age-range in the profession, so there is no point in doing a piece that is significantly younger or older than you are, however well you do it. This is sad but true. (Also see 'Playing range', page 71.)

**Content** Too many people fail because they choose to do an indifferent speech. Even if they do it well, it somehow doesn't have much impact because of indifferent writing, lack of content, and so on. Essentially you should go for pieces that tell good stories and/or have exciting and interesting emotional developments. Look for pieces with surprising juxtapositions of idea or emotion — opportunities for what I call 'sixpence' (as in 'turning on a...') acting. Each speech needs to show off as many of your skills as possible, but don't try to cram so much in that the sense is lost in a firework display of technical virtuosity. At the other extreme avoid something that requires performance at one pace or on one note.

**Soliloquies** Some people do find it hard to play to somebody who isn't actually there, so it can be a good idea to find soliloquies; there are plenty of them in modern plays as well as in Shakespeare.

**Poems** In general, don't choose poems, not even Shakespeare sonnets. They might show that you can speak well, but they rarely have the emotional range to tell your interviewer much about your skills as an actor. There may be a few exceptions to this, but I've only ever come across one, and that was from a play.

**The 'novelty' speech** I have seen speeches from sex comedies, films and even one from an Agatha Christie. I have enjoyed their 'novelty' value, but with some notable exceptions from films they tend not to have very much emotional range — and not everybody appreciates 'populist' drama.

**Speeches from novels** I've seen several interesting speeches from novels, but more that were simply very ordinary descriptions. Like plays they contain characters with potential for you to bring to life, but novels were written to be read and plays were written to be performed. (The novelist includes the 'stage directions'; think of those being read out in the course of the performance of a play.) If you are selecting from a novel, you need to do some very careful editing to make a piece of theatre.

**Speeches from life** I developed this idea from something that Shakespeare did. He adapted other people's words. For example, in the court scene of *Henry VIII* (Act 2, Scene 4), Queen Katherine's wonderful speech beginning 'Sir, I desire you do me right and justice...' is an almost direct copy of what she actually said, according to the historical record. I have taken this idea further and found for my students a dramatic description of a mass killing, a 'musing' on the pleasures of working with wood by the playwright Arthur Miller, a description of the hellish fighting at the siege of Stalingrad by a Nazi commander, and many more. I found most of these by listening to Radio 4. It's an almost limitless field that is well-worth exploiting.

**Stringing together** It is possible to make a complete speech by 'stringing together' short speeches from a piece of dialogue, but make sure that the end result no longer relies upon responses from other people. It is absolutely useless to leave pauses whilst you say the other lines in your head, yet people do it. I've known the odd 'eccentric' think it all right to ask the interviewer to read in the other person's lines, and one who threw them in, like asides, himself.

It is legitimate to change the order of dialogue so used, provided it makes a complete and comprehensible speech. However, the art of such editing is quite difficult and can take some time and experiment to get right.

I've also seen a wonderful rendition of a speech that was constructed from three characters talking with each other via intercoms. The actor very excitingly switched instantly back and forth between characters.

**Know the whole play** You must know the whole play (but see 'Journey', page 135), not just to inform the particular speech you are doing but also to be able to discuss it afterwards. When an original and intriguing speech surfaces any director will want to know more about the whole play. (It can also happen that the director knows the play and wants to discuss it.)

**Books of audition speeches** These are the main resource for those who don't yet know enough plays. An editor has done the hard graft of seeking out good speeches for you, but once you've fixed on a speech from one of them get a copy of the whole play! This is where the problems start, as they often come from plays that are out of print or, although performed, were never published. The other problem with these books is that too many people use the speeches from them — which can become tedious. You will probably be safe with a selection from a new book but, after a few years, auditioners will have seen the bulk of its contents.

NB See the 'Bibliography' for details of my *Alternative Shakespeare Auditions* books.

**Finding speeches** If you don't know many plays and don't know where to start when faced with all those shelves full of them, try focusing on the writers of speeches you've liked — they almost certainly wrote other plays.

It is possible to find out-of-print plays via libraries, book finding services and combing second-hand book shops. Some publishers (even a few playwright's agencies) will organise a photocopy — for a fee. Also, The British Library (in theory) has a copy of every play ever performed in this country but there can be complications in actually getting hold of a copy. Start with your local library if you're determined to find a specific play, but be prepared for it to take a long time.

**Shape** Make sure that each of your pieces has a decent shape. In a sense it should be like a good play, with a beginning, middle and ending. Generally, avoid choosing something which is a section taken from a longer speech; such pieces tend to do nothing for you because they usually don't have a good shape. This is not always the case, but it is often better to take snippets out of a long speech so that the essence, or overall journey, is still there. Don't be beguiled by beautiful language; be ruthless in order to achieve that shape within your target-time. Your speech should be a 'mini-play' in its own right.

**'I identify with this character so closely'** Some people are tempted to go for a character which is very close to themselves. In my experience this rarely succeeds because the most difficult part to play is oneself.

The first significant thing I learnt about acting was that, although it may draw from real life, it is not the same as real life. The 'onion layers of subtext' that are your personal emotional make-up have been growing throughout your lifetime. It is almost impossible to be properly selective in order to project (or communicate) this character, which is so close to yourself, beyond yourself. Anyway, acting is about becoming other people, and there is nothing more exciting to watch in the audition-room than an actor suddenly appearing to become somebody completely different. (See 'Contrasts', below.)

I know that there are a number of well-known actors who seem simply to play themselves. However, in almost every case, that's not how they started out. They worked at projecting a personality that now appears to be themselves; in reality they are subtly, if not significantly, different.

**'This has happened to me'** Be very wary of doing a speech whose content is very immediate to you. It could be that one corresponds exactly with your political or religious convictions or closely with some traumatic experience you've had. (Be especially wary if it's recent.) If something is too important, or too close, it can easily confuse and hence defuse the impact of what you are presenting. All drama is a paraphrase of real life, and real-life experiences need the objective skills of an actor to bring them alive for performance. This doesn't mean that all those lovely 'onion layers of subtext' gleaned from your personal experience aren't valuable; but the playwright's subtext, even if the events are precisely the same, will always be different.

I've known people write their own speeches based on deep personal experience. This also rarely works because very few actors are good playwrights. There are notable exceptions, but are you really one of them? It is a general rule that most writers need years to separate themselves from personal experiences before they can write about them with the objectivity necessary for presentation.

**'But you seem just like...'** Some directors ask for pieces 'close to yourself'. This saddens me, but it's a fact, so you should find pieces which appear to fill that criterion as part of your armoury. This is especially true if you look like an obvious type — for instance, a dumb blonde or a macho male. I know you're probably fed up with being cast to that type, but give in gracefully with the selection of at least one of your pieces.

**Contrasts** One of the most memorable speeches I have ever seen came from someone who came in dressed in a pretty flower-print frock looking like 'Daddy's little girl off to a party'. (She was in fact going to an interview for a commercial immediately afterwards and had dressed for that more lucrative part, not for me.) After a lively chat she proceeded to do the miscarriage speech from *Ashes* — a very bleak speech from a woman in her hospital bed, who describes in graphic detail the loss of the twin babies she so desperately wanted. I've seen that speech many times, but she succeeded in reducing me to tears at ten o'clock in the morning.

This is just one example of my being knocked sideways by speeches whose character seemed totally to contradict the impression of the actor I'd gained in the interview. To me that is what acting is fundamentally about: the ability, with apparently very little effort, to become someone completely different.

**The shocker**   Never set out to shock deliberately. That is not to say don't do them; rather, don't set out with the specific idea of shocking your interviewer(s) as many people seem to intend — we've heard most of it before.

**F'ing and blinding**   These traditional 'Anglo-Saxon' words may be very true to life, but become extremely tedious when over-used. Listen carefully next time you hear someone in full flow. Part of a writer's craft is not to bore the audience with over-repetition. The problems arise in audition speeches when actors add more expletives than were written — that is, they get too close to life. Examine the text carefully and don't go overboard when you are in full flood.

Some people don't like them at all, regarding them as 'vulgar and unnecessary'. A friend has a speech that he's been using for over ten years — he finds it easy to adapt the tone of it for each circumstance. This speech contains the 'c'-word, which he drops when he judges it inappropriate.

**Sex and gynaecological matters**   Be very careful about speeches that describe explicit sex or related matters. Some people find the former offensive and the latter (like that *Ashes* speech) too upsetting. I agree that a director should be able to discuss or 'take' anything, but a remarkable number find these specific areas difficult. (You never know what might have happened in their private lives recently.) I know one director who is sick to death of being made to feel that she's 'just been to the gynaecologist again'. I am not saying don't do such a speech; rather, find a way of assessing whether or not it would be suitable. Attitudes in these areas have changed radically in the past few decades. After the swinging 1960s and sexy 1970s, Victorian values tried to invade the 1980s. Now, at the disillusioned start to the new millennium, who knows which way the pendulum of political (and social) opinion is going to swing. Acting is generally a 'liberal' profession, but it doesn't mean that everyone in it is that way disposed. I am constantly surprised at how conservative (with a small 'c') some of my colleagues can be.

**Political correctness**   It is inevitable that there will be 'non-PC' elements in plays — social attitudes change gradually all the time and contemporary drama is often about current 'tensions'. For instance, I recently saw a 'brilliantly' homophobic character in a play — the audience was almost hissing him like a pantomime villain; only they were very serious. He was necessary to the play — essentially a plea for acceptance. However, when you isolate such a character from the play, you run the risk of some taking you too seriously. Be wary and have plenty of other speeches in reserve if you sense that your 'non-PC' one will not go down well in this particular circumstance.

**Laugh or cry** On the whole it is more relaxing for the interviewer to laugh than to cry, and some would be highly embarrassed at the thought of doing the latter, so in general go for comedy. In fact some of the best speeches are those which start as comedy but end up as tragedy — or vice versa. This doesn't rule out the totally humourless speech, but you are less likely to make a good impact with it unless you do it extremely well.

**Shakespeare and the classics** Traditionally you have to have at least one of these in your armoury. The fact is that most people perform them indifferently. Too many renditions seem as dead as their writers. The problem is that they are remote — in language and in content — from our direct experience and therefore usually require much more research, thought and preparation than a modern speech.

On the plus side there is no doubt that Shakespeare not only had a great understanding of mankind, but also managed to communicate it in the most wonderful language. Many of his contemporaries (and those that followed) are also worth exploring for something 'different' — especially for women. (There are some excellent female speeches in Jacobean and Restoration plays.)

**Speeches from the ends of plays** There are some seemingly good audition speeches to be found at, or near, the ends of plays. But be careful. These often rely on too much knowledge of what has gone before, and can be confusing. (Also, see 'Explanations', page 139.)

**Accents** If you choose to do a speech written in a regional accent, make sure you can do that accent well. (It is important to have at least one in your repertoire that features your own accent if it is a strong and 'characterful' one.) Some people choose to 'translate' a speech into an accent with which they are more comfortable, and this can work. I've seen an excellent Jerry from the great American writer Edward Albee's *Zoo Story* done in a North London accent with barely a word changed. However, watch that in doing this you are not sacrificing too much of the quality of the original language. Some directors can be quite purist about this, and will only countenance speeches done in their original accents — particularly, well-known ones.

A writer who doesn't seem to 'translate' is Tennessee Williams — something to do with all that heat and humidity. And there may well be others.

NB It's very tedious to see comedy Shakespeare speech done in a 'cod' West Country accents. If you can genuinely do one of the many variants of this accent, then that's fine, but his language works in every other regional accent in which I've heard it done.

**Physical skills** If you are physically very adept, then go for a piece that allows you to show this skill off; it can be very exciting. But don't clutter up your piece with too much action; it's the words that are finally important, and we must hear all of them.

**The 'personality' speech** There are some wonderful monologues written by well-known writer-performers like Victoria Wood and Alan Bennett. It is generally better to avoid these as they were specifically written to be performed by the writer or another well-known performer. It is very, very hard for the viewer not to compare your rendition with the original. You'd be better off looking at monologues by a writer like the relatively unknown, but brilliant, Peter Barnes.

**The popular speech** Don't worry overmuch about the piece that is done by a lot of other people. It's done frequently because it is a good speech. If you are committed to it and feel you do it very well, then go for it. If unsure, you can test the water by giving your interviewer several alternatives including the popular one to choose from. (But see 'You choose', page 140.) If they have already seen eight speeches from Jim Cartwright's *Road* that day, you'll probably be asked for one of your other options.

**The 'original' speech** It is always useful to have 'original' pieces — provided they're good and fulfil all the parameters listed elsewhere. There is no doubt that a good performance of an unknown piece can advance your cause significantly. This is simply because if we've never seen it performed before then we have no 'benchmark' against which to assess you — and assessing good acting is a highly inexact science.

## Rehearsing your speeches

**'What are you bringing on stage?'** You must bring your character's life history, up to the moment before the speech starts, into the beginning of your speech. It is the 'ignition' that kicks your 'engine' into life. In particular, focus on the moments immediately beforehand that 'provoke' your character into talking. Try running a brief 'film' in your imagination culminating in the event that is your cue.

**Your invisible partner(s)** If you choose a speech involving another character, think carefully where you place them. If you place them directly across stage you could end up too much in profile, if you place them in the direction of your interviewer(s) you could become intimidating or embarrassing. In general, find somewhere in between.

There is no point in placing a chair specifically to mark this other person — or even the hat-stand which I once saw used as the object of some singular passions. If you do use such objects you'll usually find yourself concentrating on that object rather than your 'partner(s)' — they should be clearly lodged in your imagination so that the interviewer can 'see' them through you.

Remember, you don't have to stare at that place continually just to make it clear that he or she is there. (See 'Eye contact', page 118.)

**Your invisible circumstances** You should also bring the set, costumes and props with you — in your imagination. I believe that actors neglecting these is the cause of a high proportion of failed and indifferent speeches. It's not just the visual images, it is also what the other senses give you. Actors tell me that this is hard — I don't see why this should be. Plays are not performed in 'real' rooms (there will be at least one wall missing) and every play has at least one non-appearing character mentioned — these absences are filled by the actors' imaginations. Do the same with these 'absences' in the audition circumstances — especially with 'your invisible partner(s)'.

**Lots of other characters** I have seen electric presentations where the placing of several other characters was so precise that it was very exciting, but in general if a speech has a lot of other people onstage only 'see' those who are specifically named in the speech (unless it's a generalised crowd). An actor 'placing' too many invisible individuals round the stage can be very confusing. And that confusion can detract considerably from your efforts.

**Journey** There will inevitably be some variations between characters as they appear in the play and how they appear in your speech when it has been separated from the play. The journey travelled in that speech within the context of the play will be different from the journey you have to travel when doing the speech on its own.

**That voyage of discovery** Be aware of the 'voyage of discovery' that shapes your speech. Don't anticipate the end at the beginning. This is a common fault in rehearsal, which is easily corrected — but a remarkable number of people fall into this trap when performing their audition speeches.

It can be very useful to write a speech out with each sentence on a separate line — then it appears less of a 'block' of words on the page; more a series of separate, but connected thoughts and ideas.

**Beginnings** If you start your speech nebulously, your interviewer probably won't take in what you are doing for the first few seconds and may miss vital information that could make the rest of it a complete puzzle to them. You need to find a way of starting your speech that will grab their attention from the very beginning. This doesn't mean that the beginning has to be loud, simply that it should be positive and effective — almost as if the house lights were faded down and the curtain rises on... You! (See 'Starting', page 141.)

**Staging** Think carefully about how you stage each piece. Too many people seem inclined to put in extraneous moves either to compensate for the lack of the other character or because they think the speech is boring if it doesn't contain enough movement. In general, the fewer moves it has the better, unless it's one in which you make activity a feature (see 'Physical skills', page 134).

It can also be very useful to incorporate a simple movement to start a speech — a turn of the head, for instance.

**Acting past cuts in speeches** I have very often found that a 'hiccup' in the performance of a speech can be caused by the last echo of a cut still lingering there. You get it sorted out on paper and then work on it only to discover that it's too long, doesn't quite make sense or whatever, so you cut it further. However, the thought behind that which was cut can linger on and can be caught by the discerning ear. (It's that moment when your brain says: 'Cut here!') It is important to rethink and rework a speech after such cuts. This usually takes longer to do properly than most people realise.

**'I do it my way'** If your interpretation of a speech is unusual, be prepared to justify it. There's usually no harm in honest disagreement.

Sometimes you will find that a director has done a production of the play that your speech is from. That's fine, providing you have researched well enough to discuss your approach. Be prepared to discuss the interpretation and details of all of your speeches.

**Chairs** A warning about chairs. There is a common variety of chair, as familiar as the bollard is to the motorway, that inhabits many popular audition venues. It can serve all kinds of functions as well as the simple one of being sat upon. However, don't rely on the well-known weight and balance of these plastic and steel functionaries for crucial elements of your well-prepared speech. You may suddenly find only chairs with arms or a room filled with wobbly ones. That is not to say don't have speeches that rely on such a chair, but also have alternatives that don't.

**Props** Avoid using props. These usually get in the way of the acting and can be mimed. As you haven't got a proper set or lighting, too much of the visual emphasis goes on to the prop and consequently away from you. It is amazing how riveting even a small piece of paper produced for one of the numerous 'letter' speeches can become. I was once mesmerised by the meticulous (and time-consuming) laying out of a complete tea service (without the tea) before a speech, but have no memory of the acting.

If you feel that a prop is crucial, think again! A good piece of mime can add considerably to your presentation — that mime doesn't need to be brilliant. And think how much easier it is to put down an imaginary glass down on an imaginary table, without making a sound at the wrong moment.

The only exception to this can be a prop introduced briefly and then quickly discarded. Even then, make sure its impact doesn't take the focus from the rest of the speech. I have seen a brilliant rendition of Major Giles Flack's funeral oration from Peter Nichols's *Privates On Parade* where the actor held a small bible between his hands. He found the speech much easier to 'get inside' with this prop and it was hardly noticeable in his large hands.

**Mimicry** Don't do a speech in the manner and voice of a famous actor. Mimicry is not the same as acting. I have seen too many 'Ritas' that were simply clones of Julie Walters. Her performance was wonderful but not definitive. It is probably better to avoid any character who is generally remembered through a specific performance.

**New speeches** It is essential to try a new piece in front of someone else first. If you don't have a friendly director to help you (and, even if you have, be wary: directing a play is different from directing an audition speech), almost anybody else in the profession will do as a first-time audience. A speech always feels different when done in front of an audience — just like a play.

**A six-month service and an MOT** Be careful your speeches don't go stale. (The better the writing, the more chance of them staying fresh; there will always be more layers of that 'subtextual onion' to peel off.) Audition speeches, like cars, need regular servicing or reassessment. If a favourite old banger has done you good service in the past, make sure it's still road-worthy before you bring it out again. If not, trade it in for something new.

Essentially, each time you do a speech it should still have that freshness, that need to communicate and that willingness to give blood that personifies a first night. A second-night performance will not do. It is no excuse to blame the cold ambience of the room you are doing it in.

**The last-minuter** Don't try to get a new speech together at the last minute. An audition speech, like a performance, needs a good gestation period to come to full fruition. The rehearsal-time needed varies from person to person, and from speech to speech, but the 'last-minuter' rarely succeeds. A half-known, half-prepared speech — however suitable — will waste everybody's time and put you right out of the running. I would suggest that a new speech needs at least a month — conscious and unconscious — preparation before its first airing in the 'field'.

**'Should I take a copy of my speech with me?'** Some like to carry a copy of their speech with them as a security blanket. Most directors won't want to know about it. In fact offering one can label you an 'amateur' with all the dreadful prejudices that professionals have against that group. However, I have heard of occasions when one has been asked for — usually when the speech is obscure. So it can be handy to have a copy of such a speech with you; even better, take the complete play with you.

**Finally** Ask yourself: 'Is my speech and my presentation of it a good piece of "Theatre"?'

## Performing your speeches

Each presentation of a speech has to have the raw energy of a first performance. Unlike a first night where the only new factor — at least, in theory — is the audience, you have to face numerous new and possibly unexpected factors when doing your audition speech. You need to be not only well rehearsed but also well prepared for how to cope with all the peripherals that are other people's responsibilities when you are actually doing a production. You are your own stage-management, wardrobe department, front-of-house manager, and so forth.

**'Act in here?'** I don't think any audition-room is entirely satisfactory. They can be dirty and unkempt, too hot or too cold, too big or too small, have inconvenient echoes, have barely adequate waiting facilities and/or be hard to find down a maze of corridors. You'll be very fortunate if the whole session has only road traffic as a background noise. You have to be prepared to adjust the presentation of your speech(es) to each context — by fractionally slowing down and enhancing your diction slightly if there's an unavoidable echo or scaling down your movement in a small room, for instance.

**It's your space** You should regard the space in which you are doing your speech as your stage with which to do whatsoever you wish — as long as you have due reverence for the fabric of the building, for your interviewers and their goods and chattels. Move the chairs if you need to, take your shoes off if that's necessary, and so on — but don't ask if it's 'all right' to do so. It can get very tedious for an interviewer if you keep on asking permission every time you want to change something. Providing it doesn't affect your audience directly, just get on with what is necessary for your performance. (See 'Politeness', page 118.)

Don't ask where to stand; your actor's instinct should tell you the optimum place for what you are about to do. Especially, don't ask permission to start, even if it's only with one of those pathetic little enquiring looks — another way of undermining yourself in your interviewer's eyes. Once you've been given your cue, it's all yours and in your own time. (See 'A pause for thought', page 140.)

**Natural hazards** Be aware of natural hazards in the room: for example, a low afternoon sun pouring through the windows that blinds you as soon as you happen to turn into it. Don't, on the other hand, stand in the deepest shadow; nobody wants an actor who cannot find his or her light.

Your interviewer will probably be sympathetic if the unexpected suddenly interrupts you, but it really is your responsibility to spot this kind of thing beforehand and adjust accordingly.

If it is something impossible to anticipate, then aim to recover as quickly as possible and get back into your speech. After all, if something goes wrong during a performance, you don't just stop until it's put right — you continue as best you can, and 99.9% of the time nobody in the audience will notice that anything went wrong.

**Explanations** Minimise explanations about your speech. Ask yourself if you need them at all. In fact the best speeches are self-contained and don't need explanation beyond the character's name and possibly the title and the writer of the play. Whatever their individual faults, most directors do know a lot of plays, the characters within them and who wrote them. Be careful not to insult directors by telling them what they already probably know. (For example, 'Hamlet from *Hamlet* by William Shakespeare'.) On the other hand, make sure you know the title and writer of more obscure plays and be prepared to discuss them.

Sometimes, in the process of getting inside the character, actors forget to give these basic details. I don't think this matters (I enjoy trying to work them out for myself), but some directors have a nasty habit of interrupting actors' preparations with demands like 'What are you doing then?' If you do forget and are so interrupted, don't be so thrown that you rush into your speech.

**Your interviewer as the other character** Many people try to use their interviewer as the other character for the purposes of their speech. This is not necessarily a good idea. It can work but is fraught with pitfalls.

First of all, do you need to ask permission beforehand? Politeness dictates that you should. After all, you are asking the director to do the job of being in your play. He or she may say, 'Yes, of course', but has probably been asked the same question in every other session of the day; it can get very tedious. Even if it is all right, the director is probably not an actor, will become self-conscious in the process, may well want to drop out of character to write notes and consequently won't be a consistent partner.

Even if everything seems fine, your interviewer certainly won't react the way you'd always imagined, which could throw you. A sympathetic director once volunteered to be Brutus to a friend of mine's Portia, even going as far as to stand up and move it with her (*Julius Caesar*, Act 2, Scene 1). She'd rehearsed Portia starting by approaching from behind. The director dutifully turned his back, and she started. After one line he turned round, totally throwing my friend who had envisaged Brutus turning at a later point. They started again. My friend, then only just starting in the profession, was getting quite nervous by this time, and when the director turned after the third line — again too early! — she was a heap on the floor and could not for the life of her go on. The director was still sympathetic. 'But', he said, 'I've got to watch what you're doing!'

So, in general, don't use your interviewer — unless you feel it happening during your speech. (I've enjoyed being part of a number of speeches in which this has spontaneously happened.)

Finally, if your speech has sexual intent, be extra specially careful about using your interviewer as the object of your character's passion. This can lead to irritation and embarrassment. (Also, see 'Sex and gynaecological matters', page 132.) Some men seem to take great delight in pointing speeches of male sexual superiority straight at a woman in the room. That is very stupid.

**'You choose'** Actors often come up with several alternatives on being asked: 'Well, what speeches have you got?' That's good — they are well prepared — but they often trip up when they cannot make up their minds which one to do. This may not matter — the director may enjoy choosing one for you to do — but don't then suddenly say: 'I don't feel like doing that.' If a speech is not going to feel right for that particular ambience, don't suggest it. Be crisp and positive about the decision-making.

**A pause for thought** Do give yourself that moment of thought before starting a speech — a moment to 'get inside' your character and circumstances. Almost everybody understands that it can be hard to change gear from chatting to acting. Don't think that you are wasting time; it'll only be a few seconds, and your interviewer will almost certainly have something else to write down before concentrating on you again. (For most actors a 'few seconds' feels much, much longer in these stressed circumstances.)

However, don't take too long to wind up into your speech with lots of heavy breathing or pacing about or even just standing quietly in a corner. That may be what you have to do before you go on stage, but most directors, however understanding, will begin to wonder what kind of lunatic you are and are you going to take up precious rehearsal-time with these warm-ups? Your 'pause for thought' should be as brief as you can make it without showing your inner turmoil. Properly done, this can be riveting to watch.

**Starting** One of the hardest aspects of doing a speech is starting it from cold. If you are onstage at the beginning of a stage-production (especially on a first night), you'll experience an immense (and, for some, terrifying) feeling of excitement and power as the audience goes quiet. (As a student I silenced two thousand people — simply by appearing — at the beginning of a production. It was a wonderful — and terrifying — experience.) You should aim to recreate this feeling just before you start your speech. It'll give you tingles up your spine and a real 'kick' into your speech. This will 'communicate' to your auditioners and make them really look at you — even if they've had their heads down scribbling in the preceding seconds.

*Tip* To help stimulate this process, get the smell of dust into your imagination — it's the pervading smell of any theatre.

**Communication** You may well 'feel' your speech, but are you communicating it? Just because you are in a small room with only one person watching don't mutter your speech at below conversation-level. How do I know you can fill a stage — however small — if you are not filling the room we're in? You have to make that room your stage, the interviewer(s) your audience. Think of them as being in the best seats in the stalls (the ones reserved for the critics on a first night) and aim just beyond the limits of the space. Only a lazy actor will give a smaller performance on stage just because there is a small audience.

Don't blast your interviewer out of his seat, either. Measure the acoustics: a lot of audition-rooms are part of church-hall complexes and tend to have high ceilings with the inevitable echo.

**'Memory' pieces** The tendency to 'underact' is especially common with 'memory' speeches: a character recounting an incident or series of incidents that is particularly personal. A lot of good audition speeches are of this form, but be very careful in the intimacy of the audition-room that one of these doesn't become so low key that it disappears.

Keep the energy and the 'need' going; bring the memory alive for your tiny audience. I know that the privacy of such a piece demands an intimacy, the truth of which can be destroyed if you force it out too much. But it isn't a matter of 'forcing out'; you should 'think' it out to your audience — even when you are in close proximity to them.

**The 'need'** All of this is not so much a question of volume but much more of what I call the 'need' that informs any speech. A long speech is a series of connected thoughts and ideas; underneath there has to be the 'need' to talk at such length. We all know people who 'go on' too much in everyday life — the odd person is able to sustain attention because of the energy and 'need' to communicate. The same is true on stage and in the audition.

Also, remember that your character hasn't usually planned to say so much. Essentially, the circumstances provoke the 'need' for them to add more, and more, and... (Also see 'That voyage of discovery, page 135.)

**Your whole body** Another trait of auditionees is to forget about their bodies. Maybe it's because of the 'artificiality' of the situation and they wouldn't do it on stage — but how is the director to know that? Just because you haven't got the proper costume, props and furniture it doesn't mean your body isn't part of your speech. What were all those movement lessons for?

**Stopping** If you do need to stop during a piece — you've dried or it's started badly — do it positively and calmly, and do it without a grovelling apology. You may feel terrible but you have to get yourself out of the mess without becoming embarrassing. You can even capitalise on having handled it well. A brief 'I'll start again' or whatever won't be held against you.

Bear in mind that most interviewers do not know how acting works — so if, say, your breathing starts going haywire that's not a reason to stop unless it really is affecting the speech badly. You have left your teachers behind at drama school.

**'Where from?'** If you do have to go back a bit, don't ask 'Where from?' The interviewer almost certainly won't know the exact words of the speech, with the odd famous exceptions. Make your own decision.

Again, be in control of your stage area and solve your own problems without recourse to your interviewer. You wouldn't ask an audience what to do if something goes wrong during a performance.

**Clever tricks** If you've got a novel way of introducing your speech, make sure you really can carry off this trick and don't leave your interviewers so bemused that they aren't taking in the first thirty seconds or so of the speech. For instance, one woman started her speech outside the room. She simply said, 'Would you excuse me a minute?' and walked out of the door. She suddenly started yelling — at her imaginary husband as it transpired. It was all so real that none of the four of us quite realised that this was her speech, in spite of the fact that she'd been given her cue. She'd have been better advised to start inside the room — probably with her back to us — and then all would have been clear. Or she could have simply said, 'I'm starting from outside the door.'

It is probably better to have a novel way of finishing. For instance, I once interviewed someone who did one of that day's 'Ritas'. Her first attempt was very inhibited, so we discussed it for a few moments before I asked her to try it again. Very quickly she started to 'fly', and I found myself roaring with laughter. Her pièce de résistance was to jump up and sit on my table to punctuate the end of the speech. It was very exciting. She claimed it wasn't premeditated, that it simply came out of the new impetus she'd found in the speech. Whatever — it worked! Not every director would have been happy about that. You should assess very carefully whether you can do such a thing to your interviewers. And be careful of their precious — and confidential — pieces of paper.

**Finishing** When you finish you should keep the final thought in your mind and gently freeze for a moment. Then fade the imaginary stage-lighting and close the curtains — and then relax back to your normal self, ready to move on to whatever your interviewer wants to do next. That may well be to write notes on what you've done. Just settle down and let them get on with it. There may well be an aching pause, but you should quietly wait — the 'ball' is now very definitely in the interviewer's 'court' to restart the conversation.

**'Thank you' (a)** There may be a vague 'Thank you' or 'Right', even 'Mmmm' from the interviewer at the end of your speech. Don't read anything in to these vague expostulations. If you do you'll start to undermine yourself. We directors are usually thinking about what we're going to write down about your efforts. That thinking process is dominant and what comes out of our mouths is merely our acknowledgement that you've finished — an attempt at politeness that doesn't come out quite right. (I hear myself doing this constantly, but have never found a way round it.)

**That apologetic little smile** Too many actors tend to give an 'apologetic little smile' to indicate that they've finished their speech. That smile tends to seem like an expression of how badly you did the speech. You may feel you have done it badly, but that's your subjective view. Let the director be the judge of that and find a positive way of becoming yourself again.

A friend offered the following analysis of this: 'The English are not supposed to "show off". Performing at an audition is different from performing on stage, in that the audience at a theatre is listening to the contents of a play rather than making too many value judgements about the acting. The audition speech should be a "mini-play", and involve the director as audience, but the actor feels the difference and artificiality, hence the "apologetic little smile".'

I understand this, but it doesn't alter the fact that 'the apologetic little smile' is a particularly undermining phenomenon to any actor's credibility. After you've been through the 'finishing' process don't make eye contact until the interviewer speaks.

**'Thank you' (b)** Some actors opt for a 'Thank you', or 'That's it', at the end. Sometimes this is combined with 'that' smile, on others it comes across as sheer arrogance (watch the way some actors do curtain calls). If you've got a good enough 'ending', you've given the cue. The director may not respond to it immediately, but you should have clearly established that the 'ball' is now firmly in his or her 'court'. It's much better to say nothing.

**Switching off** It is respected that it can take a few seconds to come back to reality, particularly if it's a very emotional speech. But it's fundamental to acting that just as you can 'switch on', you can 'switch off' with apparent ease. I will never forget a woman who did a wonderfully passionate speech from Arnold Wesker's *Four Seasons* and ended up in buckets of tears. She had done it extremely well but when it was over she simply could not stop crying and had to be taken from the room and given time to recover. What would have happened if she'd had to get similarly emotional on stage and then immediately had to go on to do a comic scene, as can occur? This is an extreme example which exemplifies the need to look very carefully at how you change back to reality.

**'Why did you choose that speech?'** This is probably one of the most common of questions afterwards. Often, it's simply the interviewer's way of continuing the conversation and sometimes it's because the speech seems radically different from your perceived personality. Whatever the motivation, it's much better to have some positive explanation beyond the often limp, 'I like it' or 'My teacher suggested it.'

**'Why don't you try that again? This time standing on your head'** Don't get so stuck into a way of doing a speech that you cannot do it in any other way put to you. Some directors like to work on speeches. You should understand the insides of each speech so well that you could do it 'standing on your head'.

**'That was dreadful'** It is rare for interviewers to tell you exactly what they thought of your efforts — even rarer for somebody to say: 'That was dreadful.' If you know, without paranoia, that you've done your speech (or reading) badly — and know you are capable of doing it very well — and the director is on the verge of saying 'Next, please', try to find a way of discussing your failure positively. This is very hard to judge properly, but it is worth looking for the opportunity without seeming pushy or paranoid. (There may even be time to do it again.) You could climb some way back into their esteem.

**Another speech?** If there's time, and the interviewer is inclined, you might be asked to do another speech. Some actors come in with the idea that this will automatically be the case. Not necessarily! A director may well feel that he or she has learnt enough from just the one — this is not necessarily a bad sign and can in fact bode well. Anyway, it will take up more precious time.

If you are asked to do another speech, make sure it's sufficiently contrasting. If the idea isn't mentioned, don't suggest it!

And don't, as I have seen several people do, go straight from one to another with hardly a pause between — let alone asking whether the second was wanted or not.

**Advice** Some directors give constructive advice. In general, take that as a compliment, even if they are critical. Nobody will waste time and energy giving notes if they didn't at least like some aspect of you and your work. However, one director's constructive notes can become another's criticisms. In rehearsal an actor will take a note and try it out. Sometimes it doesn't work, and the moment has to be looked at again. Maybe it was only half-right. In an audition there is usually no time to rehearse that note to see if it works for you. So, when you do try it, and it perhaps doesn't quite work, you have no recourse to its originator for further amplification. Take such notes as suggestions to be utilised or discarded as suits you and your speech. That's how rehearsals should be anyway.

An audition piece is usually just the route to the next stage. Some directors — if there's time — will ask you to read something or maybe work on your piece with you. If they employ you, they want to be sure that they can communicate with you. The final decision could easily turn out to be a toss-up between you and somebody else. The person who seems the best to work with (and will be a good company member) stands a much better chance.

**Final note** Working on audition speeches can be a wonderful way of keeping your 'acting juices' flowing through periods of unemployment.

# Chapter Fourteen

# *Sight-readings*

Sight-readings (usually known as 'readings' and sometimes 'cold-readings') are at the heart of the casting process and different people expect different things from them. Most will say they 'don't expect a performance'. This doesn't mean doing it without any 'life'. 'Performance', in this context, means one that appears fixed and final with no room for change. You should try to show as many as possible of the aspects you could bring to an eventual performance without that sense of a 'final coat of varnish' that can stultify it. A director worthy of that title will look for potential rather than for perfection.

Don't use the lack of rehearsal as an excuse to show virtually nothing and just read the words out loud with no inflection as some people do. Approach the text with all your instincts humming and respond to notes given and clues discovered. Then make what sense you can and give a life to the piece.

Some people are not good at sight-reading. This is not necessarily through dyslexia or some other technical problem. It is simply a fact of their working lives. (I know an actor who feels he has to learn the entire play before the first read-through — something I would normally discourage as pre-learning tends to make most actors somewhat inflexible — he isn't.) A sympathetic director may let you do an audition speech instead or even be happy just to chat — but you are making it that much more difficult for him or her to assess you in comparison to those who have read. (However, see 'No reading at all', page 155.) Others will insist that you read anyway, so you have to try. Work at reading out loud from unseen texts and find your consistent stumbling-blocks (fading out at the ends of sentences, for instance). Use a cassette and find tricks to overcome them. It is also well worth reading to a child; you'll soon find out if you are communicating well. Nobody, except the chronically dyslexic, is incapable of reading out loud. Your big problem with doing it is almost certainly a combination of several minor ones that with perseverance can be ironed out. If necessary, seek advice. Don't use it as an excuse. (See 'Dyslexia', page 152.)

## Before entering the room

**The published play** If you are invited to read for a part in a published play, you must get a copy and read it thoroughly, but without forming fixed ideas that you cannot change. The former may seem obvious, but it is surprising how often actors don't even try. This is sheer laziness and no director wants to work with a lazy actor. (On the other hand, some people do seem to find it easier just to dive into a reading with no fore-knowledge: see 'Or jumping straight in', page 148.) If you are not sure whether it's published or not, find out! If it isn't, don't ask for a copy from the management; they probably won't have enough to go round.

**Glasses** If you need these to read, then don't forget them! I've a strong suspicion that a few actors deliberately forget these in order to avoid reading or excuse a poor one. I'm afraid that even legitimate excuses will get you nowhere.

**The script in the waiting-room** Sometimes scripts will be left out in the waiting-room. There may be even more information than you were given beforehand: a description of the play and a character-breakdown, even a list of sections from which readings will be done. It can be worth arriving especially early to take advantage of these possibilities.

If there is just a script then look for your character's first entrance for some kind of description and then for the first big scene or long speech; you will probably be reading either or both of these. It is less likely you'll be asked to read from near the end as it is harder to assimilate the rest of the play's build-up. When you do light upon what seems to be an appropriate section, don't start forming fixed ideas; you don't know what extra brief you're going to get.

**Listening in** It may happen that you can hear the previous person doing his or her reading and it's from the same character as yours. You can now feel fairly sure of what you are going to be asked to do and can learn from his or her mistakes and/or decide what you might do differently. Be careful, though; that person could be 'spot on' in the director's eyes, and/or there may be another section to read from. Listen for clues, but don't rely on them. (See 'Waiting and listening in', page 110.)

**'Who played the part originally?'** This could give you another hefty clue. However, once again the director's interpretation could be different — and beware of mimicry. (See 'Mimicry', page 137.)

## Whilst in the room

**'What do you make of it?'** Some directors like to ask this question as part of the 'getting to know you' process. You may be one of those who can't answer in an intellectual way. Why should you? Acting is primarily about communicating, not discussing, a text. You are not sitting a literary exam. Give your 'head' reaction if you have one and give your 'gut' reaction without feeling pathetic about it. Then the interviewer may well start to 'open up' and give you clues that you haven't so far been able to uncover. I'm not suggesting that such clues are necessarily being hidden from you. He or she has been living with this script for weeks/months/even years and ought to know it much better than you do. Things which are now as obvious as breathing to them are not so to you with only a short study-period.

**'I'm not right for this'** You may feel this, but now is not the time to say it. Even if you are right, you haven't yet shown off your skills and you don't know what they are casting next. If you do say it now, you'll be introducing a negative element that could easily cross you off that director's lists for a long time to come. If you feel you do need to say it, wait until afterwards and do it simply and positively with coherent reasons.

One of the problems when reading for a specific part for which you are obviously wrong — in that particular person's eyes — is the tendency for you to be dismissed entirely from future considerations. It's unfair but it happens; I've done it myself. I'm not sure what the solution is — it can be very hard to see beyond the part one is casting — but perhaps you should try to convey as much of yourself and your various qualities as possible so that I and my colleagues are not as blinkered as we can tend to be.

**Take your time!** If your first sight of the dialogue is inside the interview-room, then take reasonable time to study it calmly. It is natural to feel pressured and rushed in these circumstances, but stand your ground and take what time you can reasonably expect.

Don't just take in what your character is saying; also take in what the other characters are saying and doing. Don't feel pushed by that aching silence whilst you are studying; ignore scratching pens, heavy breathing, and other distracting forms of human behaviour, and ask if there's something you don't understand. A friend suggested imagining that 'you've paid for the director's time — so exploit it'.

Look through the text carefully and ask yourself questions as you would when rehearsing a part. Try to find keys to latch on to so that you can make something of what's there. Look for the central energy of the scene. Use aspects of your own life that fit the part — just as in a rehearsal. Make sure you've got some idea of the emotional as well as factual history that leads up to the section you are reading. Create in your mind a location (possibly one you know) and images of the other person/people involved, but don't rely on the person you are reading with having the same pictures in mind.

**Or jumping straight in** Some people find it easier to jump in blindly without considering it first and then, after discussion, read again. I see no harm in this; it is amazing what can happen by just diving in, antennae alert and instincts buzzing. Essentially, you need to know which method suits you best. (Also see 'Respond!', page 152.)

In either case don't let the circumstances make you rush the reading itself.

**Guiding thoughts** You will probably be given some guiding thoughts, but in the short space of time available these are likely to be brief and superficial, and your interviewer is probably fed up with repeating — yet again — the same information. On the other hand, it can happen that you're given so much information that it's difficult to take it all in. If you find this beginning to happen, politely stop the flow and write notes of what you find most important.

If you feel you're getting very little from the text through nerves or because it hasn't been explained well, open up a dialogue about it.

**The trauma part** If discussing a 'trauma' part, don't indicate that you've recently been through a similar experience yourself. Even if you have, keep it to yourself, as many directors believe that recent direct experiences may kill a performance. (See 'This has happened to me', page 131.)

**Cliché performance** Don't just latch on to a superficial idea of the character, which is probably all there's time to give you. Don't just produce stock performance number 7 or silly voice 18 in the hope you'll come over well. It'll probably be quite showy but it will almost certainly be to the detriment of the thinking that is necessary. Sometimes you will get what appears to be an obvious cliché character to read. There has to be more than just the superficial there (nobody is completely good or completely evil, for instance); look for the subtext — underneath, these stock characters have blood, hearts and feelings like everybody else. Even if the text is apparently superficial (as most musicals are), you should aim to make it three-dimensional. It can be a good idea to look for the opposite to the obvious: for example, the character is overtly strong, look for that inevitable Achilles' heel. A good director will probably choose sections with a good variety of mood and emotion; look for those changes. Don't generalise because you haven't got enough time for study. Every script is a new journey.

On the other hand, don't make your thinking so complex that the reading you are about to do lacks clarity. I find that this can happen when the actor has obtained a copy beforehand and given it too much thought. The result is often the kind of performance one sees about halfway through rehearsals — when everyone is beginning to get a real grasp of the text but it's not really coming off the page yet.

**Punctuation** Commas, semi-colons and full stops all provide possible clues to shifts in thinking (often only slight). There is no definitive set of rules as to how spoken language should be punctuated on paper. (Virtually nobody speaks closely observing the rules of written grammar.) So think of punctuation (apart from the obvious question and exclamation marks) as possible pointers; not as specific orders to pause for a set amount of time. Shakespeare, amongst others, used very little of it.

Be wary of dots and dashes. I have not yet come across a playwright who uses '...' or '—' consistently. It seems that both can mean either the speaker ending up in mid air or being interrupted (by someone else, or if in the middle of a line by oneself). Be decisive about what you think each means and go for it.

**Stage directions** Largely ignore stage directions unless they are crucial to the action ('She shoots him'). Some others might be useful, but be selective: concentrating your energies on 'moving upstage' because Samuel French tells you to will demonstrate a singular lack of imagination on your part.

Stage directions are not 'gospel', but possible pointers. Some of those (from a performed play) come from how it was done originally. (Those from a new play are how the playwright sees the action in his or her mind's eye.) Your 'reading' (or production) will be different — maybe only subtly — but because you're different from the originating actor, it inevitably will not turn out in the same way. There is no one definitive way to play any part.

*'Pause' and 'silence'* 'Find' these moments; don't feel you have to 'impose' them — use them if they feel right there and then.

*Italicised,* **bold,** <u>underlined</u> *and* CAPITALISED *text* Do your damnedest to ignore these unsubtle instructions. You may end up stressing the particular word(s), but if you simply do so because that stress is there, you will find it harder to come to terms with the whole line.

*Emotive stage directions* These are very disruptive — especially for a first time reader. It is impossible to react instantly with genuine 'happiness', 'despair', or whatever. The actual words you're fed and the words you say are much more important indicators toward how you say your lines. Again, 'find' these feelings; don't feel you have to 'impose' them.

**Pause-sounds, like 'Er' and 'Um'** Try to find these sounds naturally, and don't add more than there actually are in the text. A good playwright will have found the right 'pause-sound' for each character and circumstance. The more usual 'Um' and 'Er' are comparatively easy, but take care with exactly what is written.

**Other vocalisations** Scripted sounds like 'Arrrrgh' and 'Tch' are more difficult to vocalise at short notice. The most important thing is to focus on a motivation for such a sound — don't get bogged down in trying to vocalise it exactly as written.

**Apparently unsayable words and names** Again, an 'approximation' will suffice. Don't find yourself tortuously trying to get them right to the detriment of the sense and your flow.

**Abbreviated words** It is the playwright's job to abbreviate words appropriately for each character; it is the actor's job to respect the degree of abbreviation inherent in the script. Too many actors think that a sloppy speaking character can abbreviate even further — which can be to the detriment of communication. For instance, 'It is like...', 'It's like...', 'S'like...' and 'Like...' represent different degrees of sloppiness — it is important to adhere as accurately as you can to the playwright's intentions.

**This is not a rehearsal** Don't ask endless questions about how to play this or that line or what the character is thinking at a particular point in the text. There isn't time for that kind of rehearsal discussion, and by concentrating on such detail you can lose your essential perspective on the whole piece.

**An accent** If you are asked to read in an accent, don't make getting that right the dominating factor. (You should be told about it beforehand.) Get as close as you can, but don't worry about it. Good dialogue, written in an accent, will have the rhythm of that accent embedded in the lines — find that rhythm and you are halfway there with very little effort. If the director likes your reading, but the accent wasn't quite right, he or she should concentrate on that separately and may ask you to come back another time when you've had a chance to work on it. If you know an accent is required beforehand, then you must do some preparation. If you know that you really can't do that accent, consider carefully whether you should go at all.

In fact you really should know clearly what you can and can't do in terms of accents. Too many people are too optimistic about their range. Of course new accents can be learnt, but each one takes time — and once you know it can you act in it? I have worked with several actors who could demonstrate facility with an accent not their own but couldn't give flesh and blood to it in performance. (Learning an accent is like learning to drive — it's one thing to learn the techniques, it takes a lot of practical application to do it convincingly.)

A friend went for a part in a long-running television series. The brief from his agent was vague. 'Could you read it Geordie?' asked the director. 'I don't do Geordie,' replied my friend. Far from being put off, the director enquired about my friend's accent-range, and they read in several different ones. He got the job in the accent of his choice. Straightforward honesty can reap dividends.

**Dyslexia** If you're a sufferer try asking for more time to study the piece — suggest that the director sees the next person and you'll come back later. Whatever happens, don't let the extra effort you have to put into reading the words take away from your ability to perform.

I sometimes get the impression that some people use a 'degree of dyslexia' as an excuse to justify an indifferent reading. They seem to think that this 'fact' will excite a degree of compensation in the director's final assessment. Well, it won't. Medical science has made great advances in this area — with specially tinted glasses, for instance. It can be well worth getting your eyesight properly checked. You can check with The British Dyslexia Association, 98 London Road, Reading, Berks. RG1 5AU; (0118) 9668271; <www.bda-dyslexia.org.uk>.

**Your voice** Make sure that you are not slumped over your script and that all your vocal apparatus is as free as possible.

**Scan ahead** Scan ahead as you are reading it. Try to be on the phrase or sentence following the one you are actually saying.

**You don't have to be word perfect** If you stumble over words, don't over-apologise and worry. Don't go back unless you really have made a mess of the sense. Just don't lose the essence of it.

Do go back over part of a reading if you realise that you have made a real mess of it. Don't ask permission: just do it — but not too often.

**Respond!** You'll get a lot more out of a reading if you look to 'respond' to what you're given. Too many actors seem to charge in with the next line immediately their cue comes — just because it's there. (The same happens — too much — in early rehearsals.) Don't do it! Imagine each line given to you and your character's perception of its subtext as a ball thrown (by the other reader) in your direction. Look to how you might 'catch' it and 'respond' to it with your gut reaction to the next line. This will take a moment, but that 'moment' — if you are properly connecting — can be very powerful. ('Good actors are good because of the things they can tell us without talking.' Cedric Hardwicke.) The overall reading will be slower than a performance, but you will be able to give much more 'substance' to your part of it.

A character is gradually created through absorption, which is a slow process — a bit like eating a sumptuous meal. If you take your time and savour the food you'll feel much better than if you bolt it down quickly.

Similarly, lines chewed over carefully will contribute far more to your evocation of the character. I believe that a playwright's words and phrases should be treated like good food and 'savoured' accordingly.

**Crisp and clear** Aim to be neat and crisp, not all mumbly and method. Good acting is very precise and clear as well as containing a deep inner truth.

**Eye contact** Don't try to make eye contact with your reading partner at every possible moment. (See 'Eye contact', page 118.) A lot of people try to do this — perhaps in an attempt to 'connect' better. It really isn't necessary and can appear intimidating. It is just as important that you use what space you have to look ahead. (See 'Scan ahead', page 152.)

On the other hand, don't avoid eye contact altogether as other people do. I know you are concentrating on unfamiliar words on the page, but there will be spare moments when you will be free to take in your reading partner as you would in rehearsal.

**'Is there someone hiding behind that script?'** Don't hold the script right up in front of your face; it's very off-putting not to be able to see your eyes at all. If you can't be seen properly, it is much more difficult to listen to you. As a general rule: script down, eyes up.

**Your reading partner** The people you read with may well not be very good at it. They will probably mistime things, almost certainly won't interrupt on cue, and certainly won't slap or kiss and may even read some of your lines by mistake. Also they will probably read some lines with what seems like crass disregard for the sense. Occasionally I've known directors to read deliberately badly to test people. I don't see the point of that. More often than not, your interviewer's apparent lack of ability is because he or she is (a) not an actor and (b) concentrating on watching and listening closely to assess you. You have to aim to do everything for yourself — all the interruptions, slaps, kisses, and so forth. I don't mean literally. Do them in your imagination, which is secure in your imaginary space with your imaginary partner. However, don't let this imaginary world cut you off from your reading partner; use it as a springboard from which you can fly and balance your acting with the 'acting' you are given.

On the other hand, some reading-partners seem to fancy themselves as actors. I've even heard of some choosing pieces of dialogue which had far more for them to read than for the actor. You can exploit this absurdity by concentrating harder on working with them — however badly you may think they are performing. Acting with someone whose work you did not respect must have happened to you before; use the devices you employed then.

**Reading with another actor** Some directors like to do this in an attempt to find the best 'chemistry'. It can also occur when you're up for a take-over in an established production — in this context you could well be reading with an understudy. Aim to work 'with' your fellow actor — don't think of it as a competition.

**Moves as well!** Occasionally you'll be asked to 'move' a reading. Some actors like to move during readings; this is fine, but unnecessary. Moves come from a deeper understanding of the text that only comes with rehearsal-time. To include them in a reading may take away from what you are able to do with it at this early stage. This is not true for everybody; some find moving around enhances their immersion in the text. Know what's best for you and use your own instincts. It is not laziness just to sit whilst you read.

**Under-reading** Young actors are often better at readings than the more experienced. I suspect that some of the more experienced among you can see far more of the possibilities to be gleaned from the text and try too hard to cram in as much as possible, ending up with a kind of blur. Others, I know, instinctively feel that they don't want to commit themselves yet, just like at the start of rehearsals. I am very sympathetic to this in principle, but in practice it doesn't help anyone decide whether you'd be right for that part in that production. Of course the chat should help, but there has to be at least a little bit more than that. You may have a 'track record', but if directors have never seen you in something akin how are they to glean whether you'd be right for them and their way of working?

I sometimes get the feeling that some experienced actors are thinking: 'Well, you should realise what I'm doing.' Not true! Once again, most directors don't finally understand how acting works, and all actors have different ways of doing it. It is highly personal to each individual. You should regard directors as members of the general public who don't properly understand the need for sufficient rehearsal — so give them something. If it feels clumsy, that doesn't matter. That is where the director is not a member of the general public and knows that you will refine it. A child's first attempt at walking is inevitably clumsy but, you know that with practice — and a few accidents — it'll come to fruition in time. If in doubt, do more rather than less; they can always pull you back.

**Take risks** A reading is another artificial situation. Try treating it like an improvisation. Take risks! Experiment as you would in a rehearsal. Feel free! Of course you will have to rely on past experiences, but aim to find that magic synthesis between what you know and what is suddenly a new experience.

Doing a reading the 'right' way is impossible. You have to use what you know and not worry about what you can't be expected to know yet. There is no definitive way of playing any part, no definitive interpretation. You have to listen, think and bring you, your skills, imagination, instinct and energy into what you are doing.

**A second try** You may well be asked to read a second time. This doesn't necessarily mean the first reading was bad; rather, that the director wants to assess your flexibility as an actor or try out a different way of doing the play. If given direction, don't throw out everything you've done in the first reading by exclusively concentrating on the notes you've been given. Those notes may well have come from what you did in the first place.

**No reading at all** Assessing readings is another highly inexact science. Some may not ask you to read at all, fearing the 'good reading — bad performance' phenomenon. (And vice versa.) That is about as true as 'a bad dress rehearsal means a good first night'. (And vice versa.) Providing all other factors are taken into account, I do believe it can help to assess an actor's suitability by including a reading. Everything helps. Each piece of the assessment has to be put in perspective with the others to form the whole opinion.

**Finally** If you write later to a director for whom you felt you did a bad reading (or speech), don't mention that poor performance. Too many people use such self-deprecating comments in order to 'highlight' the memory of the previous meeting. This tack will only lessen your chances of being seen again. In all probability he or she won't remember the specific reading, so you just need to mention that you've met — and perhaps add something good that happened on that occasion.

## Chapter Fifteen

# *Musical Auditions*

Musical auditions can range from the 'cattle-market', run by disembodied voices at the back of a darkened auditorium stopping most people after a few bars (most West End musicals), to those where all are allowed to complete their songs, read from the script and perform a dance routine (most regional theatre musicals). Of course there are degrees of indifference/professionalism in between these two extremes, and each is not restricted to the respective types of managements. Usually, if you turn up to an 'open audition' advertised in *The Stage* it will be a 'cattle-market' and if you attend 'by appointment' you will usually receive much more humane consideration.

## The cattle-market
These are usually for large-scale productions costing millions of pounds to put on, let alone run. There will almost always be a large cast involved, which means that a lot of people need to be auditioned — and auditions cost money, especially in time taken by director, MD (Musical Director) and choreographer.

Most musical auditions will start with singing. An experienced MD can tell whether a voice is suitable within two or three bars, so it is possible, and makes financial sense, to eliminate people long before they get to the end of their songs. There is no point in complaining about this approach. You just have to face up to it and make sure you are on top form when you start your song.

Here is just one of the horror stories I have come across: A friend went up for a very prestigious new musical. She is very experienced and was fully prepared. Within a few seconds of starting her song she was keenly aware of people talking in the audience, which included a prominent subject of tabloid interest — who was laughing and talking very loudly. She completed her song, in spite of the obvious lack of attention, and was summarily dismissed. 'If I'd had my wits about me, I'd have gone down there and told him what I thought and perhaps made the front page of the *Sun*, let alone *The Stage*.' If she had, she would have struck a blow for all actors treated in this way. I regret to say there is nothing you can do in this kind of situation except do your damnedest and dine out on your horrendous experiences.

If you do get past this first hurdle, then you will be put through a dance routine and, possibly, a reading. If you are fortunate, you will get recalled in one or more areas. It could all take a long time. I once met someone who did six months of recalls for the lead in a West End musical, during which she had to learn the whole score — she came second.

For some parts — especially those in the chorus — the dancing will come first. Often this audition will resemble the London Tube in the rush-hour. If you are rejected in the first round, you can try the 'hoofer's ploy'. This is common practice amongst specialist dancers. After rejection they rush to the loo and change completely and come back into the next available session. I've known people, initially rejected, get jobs this way.

## Considerate musical auditions

For the more conscientious director, MD and choreographer, auditioning for a musical is time-consuming bloody murder. Each specialist has to wait whilst the others have their turns with the auditionee. (Not that each has no interest in the other departments.) A director will have selected a MD and a choreographer who can work well together as a team, and each individual will have a view on each auditionee's skills in his or her non-specialist areas. This can all get very complicated and has to be very tightly scheduled; it is vital that you do not waste any time.

A musical is not a series of songs, each with a dance-break in the middle, all interlinked with dialogue. All three skills are interwoven. So focus on each specialist in turn, but not to the exclusion of the others. Don't, as some people do, give your replies to questions from the MD and choreographer to the director. Yes, he or she is the final arbiter, but you will alienate the other two in that way. (See 'Who's in charge?', page 114.)

There is no standard order in which each skill will be tested, but the reading probably won't be first. Most of the other notes on auditions and interviews also apply, but here are a few extra thoughts.

## Songs: preparing

A singing audition doesn't mean just standing there and hitting the right notes in the right rhythm at the right moments. You have to think and prepare carefully in order to be able to sell yourself well.

**Your repertoire** You should have at least six (if not a lot more) suitable and varied songs well prepared. In general your selection should be from musicals. Pop songs past and present (even the beautiful Palestrina piece I once heard) are almost always unhelpful in the assessment process.

Here is a list of categories on which you could base your repertoire:
1  a slow ballad (the ultimate singing test) such as 'If You Walked into My Life' (from *Mame*);

**2** an up-tempo song from a show like *Cabaret* or *Hello Dolly*;

**3** an up-tempo, more modern rock song from a show like *The Rocky Horror Show*;

**4** a slow modern rock ballad from a show like *Fame*;

**5** a patter or comedy song, for example, Noël Coward, Tom Lehrer, Victoria Wood — a definite option for those with limited ability;

**6** a song that will show off your range — if it's a good one (but be careful; if you can hit a top C on a good day, then remember that an audition is rarely a 'good day'. Play safe and go for an A);

**7** a song within which you can show off any special abilities that you have — like speaking Russian, playing the trombone, or tap-dancing.

NB The above-mentioned songs are well-known examples. I suggest that you don't actually use them — they're done a lot. As with audition speeches, don't try to write a song yourself or do one written by a friend unless you're supremely confident of it. An indifferent song can make you seem indifferent. Also, make sure each of your choices will make a good piece of 'theatre'; if they come from good musicals, then they should do.

**The accompanist** It won't always be the MD who accompanies you — and not all accompanists are good sight-readers — so make some of your songs ones that are not too complicated if they're not generally known. For example, obscure Sondheim, Bernstein or Weill songs are intriguing but are probably out for all except the most accomplished accompanists. That is not to say avoid these composers completely, but select the less complex of their songs — 'Send In the Clowns' or 'Being Alive' would be fine in this respect. (Again, these specific songs are done too much.) Some of these more complex songs have had their arrangements simplified when reprinted in song-books — but beware: 'simplified arrangements' can be banal. Essentially, if a specific song makes the accompanist 'glaze over', have a simpler one in reserve.

You will probably have a good accompanist if it's an expensive production, but you cannot rely on it.

**Length** Make sure your songs are not too long. There are some wonderful songs from *A Chorus Line* but they go on for five minutes or more. Like speeches, songs can be cut. They should be no longer than 2–2½ minutes — and preferably less.

**Interpretation** Don't just copy the famous performance of a standard or the interpretation of a current hit. You may prove that your voice is right for the show, but, again, it will show singular lack of imagination on your part. For instance, as a devotee of early Elvis Presley I get very bored with people who do pale imitations of his songs. There is absolutely no point in trying to imitate the inimitable. On the other hand, I once heard a marvellous — totally original — rendition of 'Heartbreak Hotel' that led to a job for that actor. Aim to make it your own without just being quirky.

**Presentation** Give the presentation of your songs as much acting-thought as you would a speech — if not more. There is no point in just singing it — in an acting-vacuum. You must think about the lyrics and what they are saying. You must link your moves to the music; a surprising number of people fail to do this. Don't overdo the presentation with so much movement that your auditioners cannot hear the words. Make sure each song is well presented, but not over-presented. You can help yourself by choosing songs you feel are 'actable' in the first place.

If your singing voice is limited, good presentation can still keep you in the running. There are plenty of brilliant singers who can't act and/or move.

**The 'dots'** You should think of the sheet music (or 'dots') as the player's 'map' — he/she will have to 'drive' the piano at the same time as reading it. So, you must take the sheet music in the right key. (Transposing may be a simple mathematical process, but it is hard to do whilst playing.) It must be in a convenient form for the accompanist to read and easily turn the pages — with one hand. If your music is in loose sheets it can be a good idea to stick them together. It is essential that you do this neatly so that the page-turning can be accomplished with ease. And make sure that the resulting 'fan' is not too long.

If you are not singing the whole song, mark very clearly where you are starting, finishing and what you are missing out. A friend not only sticks her music on pieces of card so they don't flop about; she also photocopies any repeat and inserts it at the repeat mark so that the accompanist doesn't have to turn back. The way in which you present your 'dots' also reflects on your professionalism.

Don't fold your music (to fit in a pocket or bag) either. It can tend to want to return to it's former compressed form at the wrong moment. It's wise to keep it flat in a folder to avoid any possibility of structural collapse.

**Final preparation** Of course you will rehearse each song with a teacher before exposing it to the rigours of audition. Even if you can read music, a song always feels different when performed with accompaniment. It is advisable to refresh every song you might use before each subsequent audition. This can get expensive, but could make the difference between success and failure.

Don't try to get a song together at the last minute. Amazingly, a lot of people try this. Perhaps they believe that all that it is necessary for them to do is to demonstrate their vocal capabilities in isolation. This is not true. The actor who doesn't know the words to a song won't get far.

As with audition speeches, you should periodically 'service' your songs (see 'A six-month service and an MOT', page 137.) As well as 'servicing' the vocal side with your singing teacher, periodically take another look at the presentation — that could also go stale. Look for new songs and get rid of old ones that you no longer feel happy with. You should periodically revise and add to your repertoire to cope with any circumstance.

**Choices for a particular audition** When you are going for an audition you should have been told what kind of songs to bring. If you don't know, then you must find out. It's probably better not to do a song from the show you're auditioning for at the first audition. It may seem logical to do so, but the creative team's interpretation may be different from yours; that shouldn't matter, but it can. You will almost certainly be asked to sing something from the show if you are recalled, so keep your offering from it up your sleeve for the moment.

Don't forget to take the 'dots' of all the suitable songs to each audition.

## Songs: performing

**Warm-ups** If you know that you'll need to do this, make sure that you arrive in sufficient time to do what you need to do.

**The popular as opposed to the 'pop' song** As with audition speeches, there are a number of very popular audition songs. The same parameters apply. If you can sing 'Summertime' extremely well, then go for it, but have a viable alternative if you see dark clouds of 'Oh, no, not again!' passing over the corporate faces of your interviewers.

It is highly likely that you will be able to hear the previous auditionee's effort. If you have prepared the same song, forget it instantly — unless you feel you can do it significantly better — and dig another suitable one out from your repertoire.

**Alternative accompanists** Don't bring a taped accompaniment, your guitar or electronic keyboard, or sing unaccompanied. The MD will want to know whether you are capable of following tempi that are given to you; a surprising number of people may be able to hit the notes and sound good, but are wildly inconsistent with tempi given by someone else. Singing, like acting, is not just about what you can do but also about a creative partnership with everybody else.

Sometimes people bring their own accompanist. This can make you feel more comfortable and give the incumbent a chance to relax for a bit; but the MD will also want to do some work with you if he or she is interested.

**The eternal cold and other excuses** Don't start apologising for the cold (or whatever) that's affecting your voice. They'll know! They can still glean enough information even with your blocked sinuses. The cold is too often used as an excuse and is a very quick way to alienate your interviewers. Remember that, however skilled you are, they want somebody they can work well with, not somebody who is always making excuses. We've all got problems, but we have to leave them at home. If your cold is so bad that you really cannot sing, you are wasting their time if you go along 'just to meet'.

If you can't sing at ten o'clock in the morning, get a different appointment; that shouldn't be too difficult if you ask early enough.

**The tempo** Give the accompanist a good indication of the tempo you want beforehand. It doesn't matter if you haven't been quite clear to start with — just stop and quickly and calmly rework it with him or her.

**'Where shall I stand?'** This question gets asked too often at musical auditions. Don't be a wimp! You need to stand where everybody can see and hear you properly.

As with audition speeches you should be aware of natural hazards that might interfere and don't be so close that you blast your interviewers out of their seats.

There may be an interesting echo at some point in the space. Look to avoid it. It'll probably be somewhere in the middle.

**'Don't shoot the pianist!'** Don't criticise the accompanist. He or she may well also be the MD of the show and, even if not, will have some influence on the casting.

In my experience the problems that arise come from (a) unreadable sheet-music Sellotaped together into a too-long and unmanageable fan and (b) the appalling condition of some audition-room pianos.

Do thank your accompanists — especially if they have had to cope with both those problems.

**You might be recalled** Recalls are an almost inevitable part of musical auditions, so plan ahead and don't necessarily use your best song at the first stage. The recall stage is where you'll get more individual attention and where you need to produce your blockbuster.

## Sight-readings

All the same parameters hold that apply to reading for a straight play, but in reading for a musical bear in mind that the writing will probably be very thin and you almost always have to generate your own subtext.

Don't just launch into some stock characterisation. Think about it. (See chapter 14.)

Very often, the climax of a scene will be a song, so you will have to end in mid-air. Don't cop out that fraction of a second before. Make your interviewers believe you are going to launch into the song there and then. Again, remember that in musicals the three skills of acting, singing and dancing are not separate; they interweave, and you should show that you can make the transition into a song with consummate ease.

## Dancing

Whether you are asked to do a few steps or even a routine by the choreographer will depend entirely on the nature of the show and how the creative team intend to stage it. You should have been told if you are going to be required to dance or not. If you are not sure, ask beforehand.

### If it's just a chat, then:

**Your dance training** Be honest about your training and experience. I have known too many people make exaggerated claims in order to get a job, and then take up time in rehearsals because they weren't up to those claims. Yes, you might get away with it on one occasion, but your name will be marked down and bad news travels very fast in this profession. Also, remember that most choreographers and dance teachers know each other quite well; it's a very small world. Don't claim to have been trained by somebody famous when in fact you went to only one class.

**'Pick up steps quickly'** Don't claim this unless you really can. Choreographers know that it takes most actors time to grasp a routine and respect that fact. There are a few notable exceptions, and you may be one, but be sure before claiming this.

**'Just a few steps'** Sometimes the choreographer may want to try a few gentle steps with you when you have not been warned. You don't need to come in full dance gear, but it is a good idea to avoid articles of clothing, such as tight skirts or heavy boots, that will inhibit free movement too much. You won't be asked to dance, just to move a little.

**'Oh God, I'm hopeless!'** On the other hand, don't just freeze up when it's the choreographer's turn to chat with you. I have too often heard 'Oh God, I'm hopeless!' from someone the MD and I have just spent time on. If you really are hopeless on your feet, then why have you been wasting our precious time?

### If you are required to dance, then:

This session might be run by the choreographer or by a dance captain or an assistant — I have used choreographer throughout this section to cover all options.

**Research** Individual choreographers have their own styles: 'classical', 'busy, and looks like directing traffic', 'improvisational' are just a few. It can be extremely useful to find out what kind of routine you could be faced with in audition for each individual choreographer.

The other thing to do is try and find someone who has already auditioned for the show and cajole them into teaching you the routine used. This is easier with the long-running shows where they tend to use the same routines for take-over auditions.

**Suitable clothing** You must wear suitable clothing for the kind of movement or dance required. Basically, the freer the movement form, the more 'flexible' your clothing needs to be. Short of being naked, leotard and tights are the only clothes that give your body full freedom to express itself. It is also well worth being neat and stylish in your appearance to help the impact of your presentation.

**Be ready on time** Come suitably dressed or arrive early enough to give yourself time to change (and, if necessary, for a warm-up) before your appointment. The choreographer will probably be teaching a routine to anything between ten and twenty people — and sometimes more. The schedule will be very tight because so many people are being seen. So each session must start as close to time as possible. If you are late because you've been changing, you are holding up not only the others in your group, but also the director, the MD and the rest of the day's hundred or so auditionees.

**Warm-ups** If it's a 'considerate musical audition' the choreographer will probably do a quick warm-up, with everybody, before teaching the routine. If it's a 'cattle-market' you'll have to get there in sufficient time to do your own.

**All those other people** Don't feel insulted by the fact that there are lots of other people, and don't be put off by the specialist dancer with hankerings to act who seems to pick up the routine in thirty seconds flat. Don't get angry with yourself when you just can't quite get it together. That dancer is probably not nearly the actor or singer that you are, and any anger sours the atmosphere for everybody else. Nobody will employ an actor who might waste time in rehearsals through self-defeating anger and frustration.

**Can you see?** Make sure you are standing in a good position where you can see the steps being demonstrated and hear the choreographer.

This is your responsibility. Don't ask the choreographer to ask the person who is masking your view to move. Sort it out yourself.

You can ask the choreographer to go back over steps you've not quite grasped. However, if you keep on asking — especially if you've not placed yourself properly — you won't get the job. A remarkable number of people don't seem to be able to get themselves organised in this simple fashion.

**Time** There should be enough time to go through the steps and run the routine two or three times before the choreographer sits back and watches everybody go through it to make his or her assessments. You may feel you've not had enough time to learn that routine, but that you could get there given time. Well, I'm sorry; there's limited time in rehearsals, as well.

**Continuous assessment** Don't think that this final go is the be-all and end-all. Yes, it is your chance to put everything together into a performance on which judgements are based, but the choreographer will also have been watching each person through the teaching of the routine — and so will the MD and director. After all, they don't just want good performers. They want to be sure that you would be good to work with. Dance may seem cut and dried to the non-specialist, but most musicals require performers who can give and invent as well as receive instruction.

**Sell yourself!** Having learnt the routine, perform it. Don't just mindlessly go through the steps you've been taught; that's almost like just reading the words out loud with no inflection in a reading. There is nothing more dull on stage than dancers just going through a series of steps with nothing behind the eyes. You may be in that majority of actors who've only done a basic dance training and have to concentrate extremely hard on what your limbs are doing. If this is so, you will enhance your chances if you perform the routine with style — and, if you go wrong, go wrong with style. Everybody is looking to see if you'd look good on stage. Have a positive purpose behind what you do. Sell yourself!

## Final notes

**Know your own capabilities** You have to know your own strengths. You have to find ways of overcoming your weaknesses. If they are going to be a serious problem in that particular part, then be honest about it.

**Injury** Find out if it will be all right to go or not if you have some physical injury which will prohibit the demonstration of either skill. You could be wasting your interviewers' time.

**'On a good day'** My experience of singing and dancing auditions has been fraught with auditionees claiming things that they can't do there and then but could do on a 'good day' or with 'a bit of practice'. Is every performance going to be on a 'good day'? And why wasn't that 'bit of practice' done in preparation for the audition? Don't claim anything unless you are prepared to do it there and then.

**Covering up your deficiencies** There is no point in suggesting that you could stand at the back of the chorus line or that the radio mike could be turned up to help the lack of volume on your top notes. Even 'the back of the chorus line' will be seen from somewhere in the auditorium, and if the radio mike is 'turned up' the audience will also hear lots of other extraneous noises and may well be assaulted by a dreadful whining feedback.

Be honest and straightforward about your singing and dancing abilities. Even if one skill is not so strong, remember that in this country there are very, very few individuals who are brilliant in all three. Much casting is done on the basis of expertise in one or two of these skills and only competence elsewhere.

# Chapter Sixteen

# *Television, Commercials and Films*

The fundamental difference between these and the theatre is their far greater emphasis on the visuals — which are two-dimensional. and the stress is on making everything appear as realistic as possible. There are occasional courageous experiments that use non-naturalistic settings, but these are, regrettably, few and far between — so how you appear can play a large part in your chances. You have to be able not only to fit inside the appropriate screen but also 'project' from it. For the interview you must be aware of the production's specific requirements as many directors don't seem to be able to visualise very far beyond what they see in front of them. They tend not to understand that it's an actor's job to become someone completely different. This is not to imply that they are unpleasant in interview — in fact the opposite seems to be generally the case — simply that many lack a basic understanding of acting. There are some notable exceptions, but they are generally those who started out in theatre.

## Showreels

A showreel is a short collection of your screen appearances supplied on video, CD or DVD — and uploadable to the Internet for everyone to view.

**Getting one made** There are numerous companies listed in *Contacts* and who advertise in *The Stage*, who will not only put one together for you, but will also advise on content. You should use many of the same parameters I suggest in the 'Getting good photographs' section (page 78) to find the one for you. These might be summarised thus: ask around for recommendations, ask to see samples of a company's previous work and don't be beguiled by a friend's spanking new digital video camera and multi-megahertz computer. It is essential the finished product is professional-looking and of broadcast quality, which takes a lot of skill.

**Length** There's much debate about this. Some people maintain that you should go for as much as ten minutes; my feeling (shared by a number of people whom I've talked to) is that 3 or 4 minutes is sufficient — that is slightly longer than an audition speech.

**Content** It is much, much better when it contains snippets of actual broadcast work — preferably showing a range of performances. Some specialist companies will offer scripts and the facilities to record them; you could also write your own. (Don't use sections from stage plays — writing for the flat screen is very different from that for the theatre.) However, I've never seen one of one of these invented pieces that showed the actor(s) in a good light — although I have been told of the occasional good example. The other problem is that it can take a long time to rehearse and record an 'invented piece' properly, and studios currently charge at least £100 an hour.

**Copyright** It is likely that some (or all) of the material that you are using is somebody else's copyright. Although the fees involved will probably be quite small (sometimes waived) it is essential that you have the appropriate permissions before you start creating your showreel. It can take some time. Some showreel companies will help with this, and it's worth going to one who will as copyright can be a highly complex issue.

**'Do I actually need a Showreel?'** You can easily spend several hundred pounds getting one made, let alone the cost of extra copies. There's no question that a good one can tip the balance in your favour, but an indifferent (or worse) one can be deeply damaging. Effectively, you are doing an audition without actually meeting the auditioners. Ask yourself (and others) if you really are exposing yourself in the best light? A showreel might show how you appear on screen, but a good letter, CV and photograph, and actually seeing you in the flesh is far more important.

Unlike CVs and photographs, showreels are not yet the 'norm'. They take more time and more filing space than their paper counterparts. However, I suspect that when broadcast-quality video becomes widely available on the Internet, they will become more acceptable.

## Television interviews
Essentially you should follow what you need from the guidelines outlined in chapters 12 and 14. The crucial differences from a theatre interview are the following.

**'Where is the interview?'** You might find yourself in a vast building with a receptionist and a veritable Minotaur's labyrinth of corridors. Allow time to find the appropriate room when called to the BBC, for instance — and make sure you have got the right bit of it! Also allow time to find the exact location of one of the growing number of independent production companies. There are many of these in central London; often hidden behind vast anonymous facades, with only the smallest of labels to identify them. On the other hand, you might find yourself in a far-flung suburb looking for the tiny offices of a small independent production company. It is essential to estimate not only your travelling-time but also the time you will need to complete the initiative test of finding the interview-room.

**A script** You will almost always go to a television interview equipped with only the briefest of character descriptions because it's usually original material. Occasionally, established plays are squashed on to the small screen and, more often, adaptations of books are given similar treatment. In these circumstances it is essential that you have a working knowledge of the original play or book, but be prepared for a featured character in the original to be reduced to two lines in the television script.

It is worth arriving reasonably early because there might be a script available for you to look through.

**More than one interviewer** There will probably be more than one interviewer. A director, producer and casting director (and, possibly, the writer) is quite a common line-up.

Not every interview is held in private office — there could be a lot going on in the background.

**Your presentation** How you present yourself — both visually and verbally — is crucial. Of course there are limits as to how far you can adapt yourself to suit each occasion, and you wouldn't be there if you didn't already seem something like what they are after, but you will get less of the benefit of the doubt than you would in a theatre interview.

However, the director may not be able to find the physiognomy that is in his or her head; you could be a compromise or might even fit another part. Your own personality may do the trick. A friend, with a naturally outgoing and bubbly personality, went for a small part of similar temperament in a major series. He dressed casually, the interview was funny and fine, and my friend left feeling reasonably optimistic. On the off-chance he sent a copy of his showreel to the director. This contained a whole range of performances from the 'classical serious' to the outrageously silly. A few days later he was offered a much better and more serious part. Eventually he discovered that the showreel had swung the better part his way. Pleased but curious, he gently asked the director: 'Why didn't you discuss the "serious" part at the interview?' 'I hadn't really got time,' came the limp reply. My friend was lucky that the director happened to have a few minutes to look at the showreel.

There is a distinction between 'dressing appropriately' for the part and 'dressing as' the part. Television directors, however much many of them lack the understanding of an actor's ability to play a whole range of parts, will be very annoyed if you do the latter because it will seem that you have no respect for their powers of judgement.

**Level** The tone of the interview will almost always be pleasant but low-key, probably because television requires low-key, intimate acting, but be careful that you don't get so low-key that you start to disappear. Television acting is larger than life in spite of being on a small screen. It needs to be contained, but not bottled up. It is smaller in scale than stage-acting, more compact and economical physically — especially facially and obviously vocally but you should still aim to shine through the small screen.

(NB In your 'containment', be careful that you don't drop too many consonants — an all to frequent failing.)

The crucial thing to remember is that you may not even be asked to read, so your interview 'performance' will be a large part of the judgement made on you.

**The structure of the interview** You may be asked something about yourself or the interviewer may simply rely on your CV and plough straight into telling you what the script is about — which can take time. Compose yourself, try to sit reasonably still without concentrating so hard on that that you cannot 'listen and receive' properly. (See 'Listening and receiving', page 114.) Then you might be asked to read, and that could well be that. What about the whole 'getting to know you' process? It often won't appear to happen — another consequence of that lack of understanding of acting.

**A reading?** If you are asked to read, follow what's right for you in chapter 14 but bear in mind that you should aim as far as possible for a 'performance' and bear in mind the scale necessary. You need to demonstrate that you can be physically and vocally contained but still perform.

### Your first 'telly'

You will probably get very little rehearsal and may well not even do a read-through — discussions on character and motivation will often be non-existent. The rehearsal-time will often be concentrated on where you are to stand and move. When it gets to recording (probably not in scene order) you will be expected to know jargon like 'MS' (medium shot — your top half), 'CU' (close-up), and so on.

Many directors will all but ignore you and concentrate on the technical side, and any instruction you get will come via an assistant with a headset. Whoever the director, there is a general sense of relying on you knowing how to do your job however inexperienced you are.

If you are still learning, then talk to the person behind the camera about how big you are in the frame and how you are coming over. I have heard numerous stories from actors new to television being rescued by one of this marvellous breed. The other crucial thing to remember is that you'll probably do a lot of waiting around whilst technicalities are sorted out. ('They pay me for the waiting. I do the acting for free.' Burt Lancaster.) In spite of the amount of waiting around you have to do there is very little time to do anything. Any hold-up or going back on a scene will cost the time of at least a dozen people and probably a lot more, and time costs a lot of money in television. It is also essential that you never let your concentration, energy and 'believability' slip with repetition. The take they choose will be the one where the action — not your acting — looks best.

## Commercials

Auditions for these are usually called 'castings' and are often akin to the 'cattle-market' musical audition in apparent insensitivity towards the craft of acting. Only a 'casting' is probably more like a sheep-dip where each person is processed to see if they fit the interviewers' requirements with no interest in 'potential'.

If it seems as though your face might fit you could well have to go through hundreds of 'castings' before getting a commercial. As time goes on and you get some 'pencils' (come in for definite consideration but don't actually get it), casting directors will know better when to call you in and your 'strike' rate could become higher, but not necessarily. However experienced you are, you will still have to go through this 'sheep-dip' in order to get each one.

Most commercials shown on UK television are extremely clever and well made. They should be. Teams of creative people spend hours/weeks/months dreaming up ideas and developing the scenario, layout and visual ideas to be presented to the client company. When the script has been approved and finalised a production company will be given the job of filming it and they will look for actors to fill the very specific scenario.

**Presentation** 'If an advert was casting for Roy Rogers, then the person who came in fully dressed as a cowboy will stand much more chance of getting the job.' No, this remark is not from a cynical embittered actor, but from a realist who gets commercials periodically. There is a sense in which they are not looking for an actor to fill the role but that the real person, as defined on paper, should walk in through the door. So make every effort to 'look right' for the part. Don't go over the top — the 'Roy Rogers' analogy above is an exaggeration — be subtle about it. (See 'Your presentation', page 168.)

You should be told what the part is beforehand, but beware: details can get altered in the 'Chinese whisper' chain of communication between director, casting director, your agent and you. A friend, who has a good 'strike rate', was told she was to appear as a dowdy character. She did so. The basics were gone through, and it emerged that the opposite was

required. She explained that she'd been misinformed, but the director still asked: 'Have you got any other clothes?' That is a classic example of some directors' level of imagination as far as actors are concerned.
NB Commercial castings are often carried out at short notice, so you need a good choice of outfits always readily available.

**Arrive early** It is definitely worth arriving early. At least you'll get a chance to look at the script, learn it reasonably well — taking in the stage directions — and begin to get ideas on how to tackle the reading. There won't be time for study once you are in there. The 'script' will probably be no longer than two pages and could be entirely stage directions — occasionally with only one line that involves you.

**The committee** The room will usually be dark with a brightly lit acting area. There will usually be a 'committee' of people in there, most sitting in semi-darkness. The session might be run by the casting director (sometimes the director won't even be there) and there will probably be several other people sitting in the background — often from the client company. The latter won't speak, but don't ignore them. You probably won't be introduced to them, they will know virtually nothing about actors and acting, and they will appear catatonic. If you can make them laugh easily in what follows, it can enhance your chances.

**Passport control** You may well have to fill in a form (or forms) asking basic details like height, age and agent. They may well take a Polaroid of you 'just for the records'. Then you may be led to a chair and plonked in front of a camera.

**'Ident.'** You may be asked to 'Ident. for camera.' (Sometimes, simply 'ID'.) They want you to give your basic details (usually name and agent) to mark the beginning of your section of the video-tape. You may then go straight on to the reading.

**The interview** As someone put it to me, 'You go in there as though you had no CV at all.' What matters is how closely you fit the scenario. You might be asked a few questions about yourself. The interviewer might look at you, but often will be looking into the monitor connected to the camera to see how you are coming across on it. He or she is almost certainly not thinking: 'How well could we work together?'
    You have to try to find out what they want and conform to it. Their imaginations are tied by what's on their pieces of paper. You should aim to be individual but don't go over the top. Be aware that you are probably being videoed from the moment you are plonked into that chair and possibly from when you walk through the door. Be happy about all this and be warm to this apparent wall of indifference.

NB You may well be asked if you've done any other recent commercials in the same country (many foreign commercials are made in the UK) — the client won't want the same person endorsing another product.

**The reading** What you have to do will probably be over-explained to you. Take what you need and ignore the rest, and hold on to what you've worked out unless a new unscripted factor is introduced.

Your main objective is to present them with a performance.

1 You have to avoid looking at the script as much as possible — they'll want to see your eyes. It is useless to be constantly looking down at the page whilst on camera. You have to be a quick study.

2 You will be expected to perform there and then, conforming to all the stage directions and mime props when necessary. Be neat and clear with the mime; never do it tokenly as you might when in the early stages of rehearsing a play.

3 Sometimes you will be asked to do an accent. Make sure that you can do what you say you can do off the top of your head. It is a good idea to have key phrases for each accent that contain enough of the pertinent idiosyncratic sounds, inflection and rhythm to set you off on the right foot.

4 There may be another actor reading with you, or the casting director will 'fill in' and you may have to react to badly given feed-lines.

5 You might be asked to do it again with a simple note in mind — 'slower', 'faster', 'bigger', 'smaller'... Go with what you're asked to do; this is not the moment for discussion, whatever you feel about that note. Have an open mind about what they want.

6 Occasionally you might be told to 'Forget the script as it's being rewritten', and 'Just improvise'.

It is instant acting and it's very silly, but you shouldn't feel silly. In fact you should take it very seriously. Use all your instinct and experience and do whatever comes off the top of your head without resorting to caricature unless that is specifically required.

**Your whole body** It's not just how you bring the words off the page that's important. You should be aware of what each and every bit of your body is doing and incorporate it into your performance. That's what you have to do: perform with no rehearsal and no real direction. You may be given specific directions about how, when and where to move — all at precisely defined moments and to precisely defined positions. Don't let your performance be reduced to just a set of mechanics — there has to be a real person carrying out these otherwise robotic motions.

It is important that your hands are in good condition. They may be used in close-up, and a Polaroid may be taken of them.

**Stanislavski** In performing don't dismiss the reality of character but do aim to concertina real reactions — a kind of subtle mugging.

Sometimes you'll feel that you're being asked to exaggerate badly, even be blatantly 'off the wall' — you should still bring that inner core of 'truth' to your performance.

**The camera** Through all this you should make the technology your friend. Unlike most television drama you may have to look directly into the lens. As with a static photograph, it will show graphically if you are 'camera-shy' or nervous. Treat the camera as another actor who could respond to anything you present to it. This simple device of the imagination can easily overcome any camera inhibitions you may have. You may be reading with someone else or concentrating on a prop and not talking directly to the camera. In this circumstance the camera is the 'fourth wall' of a theatre, and you have to ensure that everything necessary can be seen by 'cheating out' in that direction and that you are 'thinking' everything out to the audience.

**Finally** Somebody once described commercial castings to me as 'in — grin — out'. Think fast and concentrate on the camera. It will probably all be over in a few minutes. A friend once described acting as 'committed pretending' — I think that's a very good concept to carry into a commercial casting.

## Films

Most of the parameters that apply to television interviews apply to those for a film. The extra elements are that there may well be an American involved, and they find it peculiar that we don't 'hustle' like our transatlantic counterparts, and that the film could be for both the big screen and the small one. As in television, you will find some directors who do know how to conduct an interview and have an understanding of actors' methodologies, and those who patently don't. Interviews for this medium seem to range over the whole spectrum.

If you are lucky enough to get an interview and reading for a film, remember that the acting required is on the most intimate scale because your image will be blown up on to a giant screen where the merest flick of an eyelid in close-up can create waves round an auditorium.

**Processes** Film interviews are largely like those for television, sometimes veering towards those for commercials. They do, however, sometimes seem to provoke the most extreme forms of behaviour.

*The meat market* The late, great Alfred Hitchcock walked along a line of nervous actresses. He inspected each one closely, then grunted some thing at an assistant and walked off. The assistant did at least say, 'Thank you' before they were ushered off the set.

*Be prepared for anything* These film-interviews were 'conducted' by a famous actor/director/writer.

An actor was led in by a PA. The star was crouching down and holding the radiator and never looked at him. The actor was supposed to be reading; the accent was South African, which, in the circumstances, just would not come out right. So he stopped and started himself again and then finally gave up and said, 'I'm terribly sorry,' and the PA said, 'Well, we are so pleased to have met you and we'll let you know,' and escorted him out.

Another actor was ushered in to find the star sitting at the desk. Halfway through the interview — without saying anything about it — he quietly tore up the actor's photograph.

Yet another actor found him sitting cross-legged below the desk and he spent the whole interview making additions to the actor's photograph with a felt-tipped pen.

*Falling off a log* One friend fell on his feet at his first film interview straight out of drama school.

The very first audition I ever went to was for a film called *North Sea Hijack* and it was being held by Alan Foenander at the Park Lane Hotel. I walked in to find a couple of well-known actors laughing easily over coffee and tales of agents. Alan comes out and tells me that, instead of the civil servant I was up for, would I like to read for Roger Moore's right-hand man, Harris, an all-action scuba-diving killer in command of Rog's private army? I said I'd think about it. Well, at least I didn't let the drool show.

I walked in; the director's Andrew V. McLaglen — more used to working with the 'Duke' and with a disturbing tendency to stand on your toes in order apparently simply to see what you'll do. I'm six foot three; he was more like six foot six. I say: 'God you're even bigger than I am!'

There is a pause.

Then he says: 'I like it. Siddown, kid.'

I knew I'd hit Hollywood.

'OK, kid, I want you to read this scene for me. The guy's name is Harris.'

He said it as though he'd given me a great insight into this man's character.

'Do you want an accent?' I ventured.

'No accent.'

I have come to learn that this usually means do it with the accent of the person who asks you, but at that tender age, and with the words of my eccentric Austrian drama tutor — 'Don't be afraid to fall on your arse!' — ringing in my ears, I essayed a cross between Sean Connery and Vincent Price.

'Can you do Scotch?' he asked.

'Scottish accent, yes, OK, fine.' (Billy Connolly meets Miss Jean Brodie.)

'Tell me something, kid. Can you swim?'

'Er... actually, yes, I swim very well. I was captain of swimming at school. I beat the school record for the —'

'Kid, I think you just landed yourself a part.'

And so I did. I went on to have a glorious two weeks in Galway, got paid a fortune, and had a 'Ripping Yarns' type time.

**Screen tests** Somehow these are the stuff of legend and often aren't part of the casting process. After a series of interviews you may be asked to do one — on video and/or film. Like commercial castings you have to be prepared to do 'instant' acting with the script in your hand (which you should look at as little as possible). Usually it will be with another actor (also 'testing' or someone hired in for the occasion), but I've heard of actors just having to do their own lines from a piece of dialogue leaving gaps for responses.

The other thing to remember is that films are largely 'action-based'. (The actual scripted words are often less important — much to the understandable frustration of writers.) In a screen test you could easily be acting out something akin to the fantasy action games you last played at primary school with chairs representing cars and so on.

## New technologies

The '90s saw a huge increase in independent production companies of all kinds of shapes and sizes. The transition into the new millennium has seen the advent of the incredibly cheap digital video and the beginnings of film being shown on the Internet. There are also 'Interactive Movies' on CD-ROM (and DVD, and the Internet) where the user makes decisions that change the way the plot unfolds. Then there are Internet adverts and games using actors... and who knows what else will grow out of the new technologies? The flat screen world is certainly expanding fast and I hope that this is going to lead to more work for actors. The interview and audition processes in these new areas are much as described above — tending more towards the style of those for commercials.

# Chapter Seventeen

# *Voice-overs and Radio*

Your voice and its working components should have been stripped down, thoroughly examined, reassembled and fine-tuned whilst at drama school. Yet it seems to be a much neglected instrument in this highly visual age. I suppose this is a reaction against the concept of the 'voice beautiful', which dates from the days when stage-lighting was so poor that the actor had to rely more on this instrument. Lighting is now an art form, and actors can be seen properly, but the ability to be able to use your voice effectively is still important. For voice-overs and radio it needn't be 'beautiful' to be exploited as a money-making asset and, as you can't be seen, there is the potential for you to play a far greater range of characters.

## Voice-overs

This market started blossoming in the 1970s and was cornered by a few well-known voices. Essentially there are two types. The personality voice that the viewer/listener thinks they know and feels confident and at home with, and the versatile voice that can assure the listener that it is telling the truth — whatever character is being assumed. The versatile voice can also change character completely but still comes from the same actor, who often looks completely different from any of the range of characters that he or she produces. (The classic example of this is the brilliant Miriam Margolyes.)

Very few people seem to listen hard enough to realise how often actors are used in this way: language tapes, narrations, commercials, talking books, promotions, CD-ROMs, dubbing, and so on.

If you have a good versatile voice with a strong natural timbre that can transcend the technology of recording, the world of voice-overs can be lucrative. However, getting voice-over work is an extremely competitive business, and the investment in time and money trying to get into it can be considerable — with no guarantee of success.

**Getting into voice-overs** The conventional way of doing this is to start by making a 'demo' (demonstration) tape for circulation to specialist voice-over agents — these are listed in *Contacts*. Once you are on their books they will get the work for you and you won't normally have to go through endless interviews. However, check which voice-over agents will actually listen to your tape — many won't — before sending out hundreds. (Remember to use your voice well when phoning to inquire.)

Voice-over agents tend not to have such a personal relationship with their clients. I don't mean that they are unfriendly, it's simply that they operate more like shops, with a collection of 'demo'-tapes as their wares.

**Other ways of getting voice-over work** A few 'conventional' agents also have voice-over sections, and a small proportion of this work comes through conventional agents who don't have separate 'voice-over sections'. (Once, a friend's 'conventional' agent phoned to ask her to find something to read (in a particular accent) for an audition over the phone — in an hour's time. She got the job and earned £1000 for fifteen minutes work.)

There is also work available by hunting around for yourself — although, it's usually not as well paid. For instance, independent local radio stations (outside London) have a lot of local commercials and probably can't afford to get them done in London. Provided you can command the essential skills, this work can earn you a reasonable amount of pocket money. You could also target television and video production companies, sound-recording companies, talking book publishers, and so on — anywhere that needs recorded voices. You can find many such organisations listed in *Contacts* and searches through appropriate sections in *Yellow Pages* can sometimes yield results. The important thing, with any potential employer, is to discover whether they will accept your 'demo' in the first place and to get a name for the person to whom it should be sent.

**Classes** There is now quite a lot of specialist tuition in this area — at the Actors' Centres round the country, for instance. There are also individuals and companies who offer both tuition and creation of your demo-tape (see 'Shop around', page 180).

**Availability** Voice-overs tend to have the shortest 'lead' times of any form of acting. It is therefore imperative that you are easily contactable at all times — see 'Contacting you', page 82.

## The 'demo' tape

You must get this right first time. If you don't, the listeners will not be inclined to bother with the next one you send, unless enough time has elapsed for your failure to be erased from their memories.

The quality of a 'demo' tape is just as important as the quality of a photograph and showreel. It is no good doing one on domestic equipment — however good the material, the 'product' will sound at best adequate. You will have to get it done in a proper studio with a good sound engineer who really knows what he or she is doing. All the flash gear in the world is useless if the tape is not recorded, mixed and edited properly

Acoustics has always been an inexact science and has taken on the status of an art form. That is because each set of equipment has to be specially tuned to each individual voice — no domestic audio system is equipped to do this. Such professional equipment takes great skill to operate so that it will bring out the best from you. A recording session — let alone the copies of your final 'demo' — could cost several hundred pounds.

**Length** Three minutes is the most any busy agent will have time to listen to. He or she can tell very quickly whether you have or haven't that distinctive 'hook' in your voice that can be sold.

**Formats** It is now just as easy to put your demo onto CD-ROM and out on the Internet — and there will be other widely acceptable formats as the digital explosion continues. It is important to discover which format will be acceptable before sending one off. It is quite remarkable how resistant some people are to change. I shall refer only to 'tape', in what follows, for simplicity.

**Your voice** Analyse your voice. What are its strong points? I'm not just talking about a facility with accents, for instance. Think about all the aspects that make it special to you the actor, such as its timbre. You should listen for those special strengths that you can bring to a character expressed only through the voice with no visual support. Find your own voice 'presence' and find what characters it suits.

**A kaleidoscope and a commentary** One side of your tape should contain a variety of snippets of material — a 'kaleidoscope' of about half-a-dozen voice 'images' rather than a detailed 'picture'. A voice agent won't really listen to the details of the actual words; more to the quality of your voice and what it is capable of. However, don't make it so 'kaleidoscopic' that it becomes confusing. Also, don't go mad and try to do lots of different accents and funny voices unless you are really very good at them. That market has been cornered by a very select few. (One was nearly sued by a Hollywood megastar for his very accurate impersonation of that star's voice on a television commercial.) Keep the whole thing simple and within your vocal range.

The other side of the tape should have a short commentary of some kind — a passage from a novel or some other descriptive passage, for instance.

NB If you have a genuine (and saleable) native accent, it is important to include an example of this.

**What voices?** Listen to voice-overs on commercial radio and television to get ideas of how to approach yours. Listen to the style, the attack (or lack of it) of each professional voice and find aspects that are useful to you.

Some voices agencies have samples of their artists' work on the Internet. It can be very useful to check these to get ideas for yourself. Don't try to copy them, however! The world of voice-overs is a very small one, and virtually everybody knows (or knows of) virtually everybody else.

**Content** Before you even think about detailed content consider which area your voice could be most suited to — commercials or narrations, for instance — and tailor your 'demo' with a specific area in mind: brief clips for the former or longer sections for the latter. Once you've broken in to one area you might move on to others.

- You could pay somebody to write your script for you. Obviously that will add further to the cost, and it will be hard to find somebody good and understanding enough to fulfil your particular needs. I've known people successfully write their own, but you have to find a way of assessing whether you can really do that well.
- You should keep it simple and with a light/comic bias. If you've got a brilliant idea for links between your pieces of material that really adds something, then do it — briefly. For example, a friend preceded his name with 'Prince of pronunciation. The acme of accents. Mr Voice-Over Himself!' and similar slogans in his 'demo'. (Don't be tempted to copy that!) It is not essential to incorporate links and/or have a story-line, but it might make that final difference if you can do it — the cherry on the cake.
- If you feel you cannot write your own material, you could copy commercials from television and radio, but aim to do them in your own way.
- Don't be cheap by telling a series of jokes or mocking familiar advertising. The key to any piece of advertising is its apparent integrity. Overall, the more original the material without being downright quirky the better your chances.
- It is a good idea to aim to make the contents, and their presentation, appear like excerpts from material you could have already broadcast, so that the listener might believe that you are already experienced in this field.
- Try out your ideas at home and, as with a photograph, get other people's opinions. It is worth working at the contents of your tape as well as at the performance of it for a considerable time before you commit yourself to the recording studio, where time is money.

**Your script** Type your script with plenty of space between lines and lay it out neatly and clearly. And take at least two copies with you — the engineer has to know what you are reading. If you go in professionally organised, you will save time and money, and you may get some good suggestions — at no extra charge.

**Shop around** You'll find advertisements in *Contacts* and *The Stage* for companies specialising in making 'demos' — many of whom will offer help with scripts, background jingles, and so on. As with photographs and showreels, get recommendations and ask about the extent of each company's services and charges. Ask if it's possible to listen to some of the organisation's previous work. Shopping around for what is best for you is crucial to the success of the final product. A large proportion of that product is down to them. Also check whether the fee includes copies of your tape from the 'master'.

Don't think it will only take a few minutes to record a three-minute tape. Even if you are completely rehearsed and prepared, it could easily take an hour or two to record properly.

## Recording your 'demo' tape

Recording is a highly technical world, and knowledge of simple techniques and technical terms can save valuable time when making the 'demo'.

**Where to stand** A good microphone will have a diagram indicating its 'directional characteristics' marked on it: the areas where it can pick you up properly and those where you are 'dead' to it. Usually you should stand within two or three feet of the microphone but this can vary if there is any shouting or whispering involved. There are several different types of microphone with different 'directional characteristics', so look out for those diagrams.

**A voice-for-level** The equipment needs to be adjusted to your voice and its level before doing anything else. People waste time when asked to do this by not using their performance-level. This may only be marginally different from your speaking voice, but that difference could make a considerable difference to the settings on that sensitive equipment. This is not something that can be done automatically; it requires skill, a good 'ear' and patience from the engineer. The important thing is that you give the person behind the glass what you will be giving in performance.

**When to start** You might get a simple visual or verbal cue from the engineer or there might be red and green lights. The red light means 'recording'; the green light turning on means 'go'. Don't wait until the latter turns off or you'll be there for ever.

**Page-turning** Find your own way of turning the pages silently without disturbing your flow. Many people like to gesticulate whilst reading. If you are one of these, then ensure a gesture doesn't collide with the script. (A radio actor's joke: 'You can always tell if you've got radio actors in the car with you: with the traffic lights at red you can't hear them turn their newspapers, and they only start chatting when the lights are green.')

**Fluffing** Even the most experienced people fluff (listen to news-readers), and of course, a simple edit will solve the problem. After a brief pause go back to a convenient point, such as the beginning of the sentence you were on (the engineer may well advise you), and start again. Don't try to go back further than suggested in order to 'get back into character'. It takes longer to find the edit-point — more expensive time-wasting.

Before restarting, the engineer might say, 'We'll rock 'n' roll on this, OK?' and he or she will rewind, tell you where to 'drop in', then hit the 'record' button and you carry on. (Sound engineers have their own jargon.)

Once you've recorded your 'master' tape, the engineer will make the copies to send out. You will need to work out how many you need and organise professional-looking labels for them. It is the ultimate folly to produce a high-quality demo with a tacky-looking label.

## Doing voice-overs

If you start getting the work, there are various things to bear in mind before you do your first voice-over. You can still fall out of the race at the first hurdle. With such considerable money at stake, time-wasting in the form of fluffing too much, or needing to have technical details explained to you (like where to stand and when to start) can put you out of favour for a long time to come. As in the visual recorded media, you will be expected to know how to do your job even if it's your first time.

You almost certainly won't get the script until the last minute. Indeed, I've heard of one producer who writes his whilst the actors are chatting before recording starts. You have to develop a real instinct for instantly picking up a character straight from the page. You probably will get no help from the producer and if what you come out with is not to the advertiser's (or whoever's) liking, then that's you out with the waste paper. Sometimes you will get asked to do it 'differently' with no specific suggestions as to how — you have to invent quickly and cleverly; at others you will be told to do it in a certain way; you will have to go along with that without any discussion. There isn't time.

In order to succeed you have to have an excellent 'ear', be able to bring character (without it being cliché) to the printed words and have the facility of saying all those words clearly within a tightly specified time at the first few attempts. The art of voice-over acting requires a great deal of instant imagination; the craft requires a high degree of technical expertise — a fraction of a second can matter. Nobody else, apart from your fellow actors, is interested in your motivation, your comments on the writing, and so on.

The ease with which the best 'voice-over actors' seem to come over is based on a deep understanding of the technical aspects of acting. It is not nearly enough to have a 'nice' voice and simply read words off a page with a little bit of enthusiasm. It is not easy.

NB Just because there will probably be very little appreciation of the art of acting, you should be pleasant with everyone — someone who does a good job and is good to work with will almost certainly be employed again. Also, it's a good idea to go reasonably dressed as the client(s) may be there — it's important to look 'professional' in spite of the fact that you won't be seen in the final result.

**Finally** Men get much more of the lucrative commercials work than women. That is the nature of our society at present: the advertisers still tend to think that a male voice inspires more trust than a female one.

## Radio

**BBC** The BBC transmits some 500 plays every year plus the classic serials — and it uses actors to read poetry, narrations and stories. There is a small core of London-based actors known as the Radio Drama Company (the 'Rep') — this used to be made up of several dozen actors, but nowadays it's only a handful because a good proportion of drama broadcast by the BBC is made by independent production companies. (The names of these are given at the end of each broadcast and you can find addresses in *Contacts*.) The BBC periodically holds workshop auditions to select new people for the 'Rep' and for recommendation to its directors for freelance work. You can write to be considered for a workshop, but most auditionees are recommended by a panel of directors who go to see theatre productions in search of potential radio talent. Some people also send tapes (a piece of Shakespeare, a poem and a modern piece, for instance), but not every producer will listen to them. What is important to them is a good theatre CV.

If you live near one of the other regional drama-production centres — Bristol, Birmingham, Manchester, Glasgow or Belfast (non-local actors are rarely used to keep expenses down) — you should contact them to find out what their procedures are and whom to write to.

It is essential that you have some good professional experience playing all kinds of different parts before you apply. Listen to radio drama and become aware of its methods. In general terms, radio acting is slightly bigger than that for television and slightly less than that necessary for a small studio theatre. In a sense you need to 'colour' your voice so that it does the visuals for you and bear in mind that you may well have an assistant floor manager making sound effects standing right next to you.

**Independent radio** Some of the commercial stations use actors for more than just commercials. It could be worth contacting your local commercial station to find out what opportunities they have.

# Chapter Eighteen

# *The Actor in the World of Business*

It is a fairly well established legend that Margaret Thatcher was given voice lessons to make her more acceptable to the public in the run-up to her first election victory. People began to realise that actors had other uses. Effective public-speaking courses for business-people (for instance) had been around for a while (even longer in the US), but the 1980s saw a growth in the wider use of theatrical techniques in business, and a few entrepreneurial actors started to exploit this potentially vast market. (At the same time arts organisations were constantly told by central government to be more 'business-like' in their operations.)

## Fields of work

Because this is a very complex (and growing) area, it is only possible to give a rough sketch of areas of work and access to them. There are no fixed rates of pay and no standard contracts, just a new and exciting relationship between two very different 'cultures'.

**Selling and demonstrating products** For years actors have been selling products and services over the phone and in department stores. The advantages of actors to employers are clear; they should be able to communicate to potential customers well and with conviction, and able to repeat the same (sometimes turgid) 'script' over and over again with energy and conviction — whatever they may really think of that product or service. Jobs of this kind are often advertised in *The Stage*, and there are numerous temporary agencies that cover them. It is very hard work but a useful way of earning money in between legitimate acting jobs.

**Training films, educational and corporate videos** The former are for a company's internal use to train staff (and are often, in fact, on video) and the latter are for business promotional purposes — commercials for trade use only. These usually use casting directors, but I've heard of occasions when actors have been all but dragged off the streets — a friend was offered such a job by a secretary (an old school friend) and asked if he 'knew any other actors'.

To get work in these you need to be known to casting directors and/or to contact companies direct. Some production companies specialising in these areas are happy to receive unsolicited letters — even videos and showreels — but, once again, it is worth checking which ones will accept any or all of these before spending money. (Look in the 'Film, Radio, Television and Video Production Companies' section in *Contacts* for names and addresses, and in *Yellow Pages* under headings like 'Audio-Visual' and 'Video Services'; these headings don't just contain firms who hire out equipment.)

Interviews tend to range from the highly civilised to the 'in — grin — out' variety mentioned on page 173. You have to be prepared for the worst and you may be pleasantly surprised. A new hurdle you might have to jump is the trade jargon. You could well be presented with a script full of it and no time to absorb complex explanations. The other thing to bear in mind is that the script may have been written by a business-person with a practical idea to convey — the dialogue may be very 'wooden'. You have to provide your own characterisation.

This is another fast-expanding market — in which there are many potential employers not known to agents. You can help yourself by trying to make your own contacts, but if you have an agent liaise closely with him or her.

**Role-playing** This is the art of taking on a character — without a script, just a detailed brief — and then 'being' that character in a prescribed situation. Medical students, for instance, have long done practice consultations on each other before encountering real patients. However, they (and the many other professions that use this technique as part of training) generally haven't the skill to be fully convincing in what is essentially an 'unreal' situation — especially in extreme circumstances, like 'being' a rape victim, for instance. The actor can bring that indispensable 'reality' and control it as necessary, or as prescribed by the requirements of the training objectives. Not only that, but actors know the art of accurate repetition. There is an incredibly wide range of role-play opportunities.

Actors are also being used to role-play characters at social occasions — historical banquets and so on. And on 'murder-mystery weekends' where a 'murder' takes place and the actors spend the whole weekend in role whilst the guests try to solve the crime. There is no script, just a carefully worked out scenario. It's very hard work — for the actors.

**Presenting at trade shows and business conferences** Any product has to be marketed, not only to the public at large, but also to the retailers who are the front line to that public — at trade shows and business conferences. Industries are beginning to use actors to help their salesmanship within the trade to give such events more impact. Sometimes actors are simply used as presenters linking various speakers and visual material. At other times miniature pieces of theatre are presented to help in the company's sales-pitch — often scripted by the actors themselves. Actors are setting themselves up in companies specifically to provide such a service. They entertain but also aim to get a message across using theatrical techniques.

Look in *Yellow Pages* under such headings as 'Business Entertainment', 'Conference Organisers', 'Management and Business Consultants', 'Marketing and Advertising Consultants', and in amongst the puppet-shows and debt-collectors are companies that use phrases like 'Creative Business Marketing' or 'Business Developments', 'Leisure and Entertainment Consultants', 'Promotions and Entertainment'. It is also worth looking in the *Business Resources Directories* in your local library.

**Enhancing the business-person's presentation and communication skills** The actor can teach business-people the use of acting techniques to enhance personal impact. This ranges from basic voice lessons to helping managers with essential communication skills in the workplace, using the actor's whole armoury from basic skills, through the fundamental ability to communicate, to the role of amateur psychiatrist.

*Presentation* Ask a business-person how many speeches and speakers he or she can remember from trade-shows and conferences. Too many exhortations to buy are presented in boring, pedantic detail that requires a supreme effort of will on the part of the listener. (Knowing is one thing; showing is very much another.) The trade audience will often go to such jamborees just for the social life — anticipating that the speakers will be boring.

Ask most people if they'd be happy to stand up in front of a crowd and speak on a subject of their own choosing and they'd 'freeze up'. How many times have you listened to someone talk on a subject and been deeply bored — in spite of how interested you were in the subject? The fact is that most people have no idea how to 'present' themselves, however expert in their subject they may be. Sometimes it is through lack of a good script. More often it is a body-tension, a vocal tension, boredom through repetition and/or a basic lack of self-confidence. Acting has techniques to solve all of these problems. Not only that, but in every actor's heart is the 'need' to work and the excitement of working. That 'excitement' is what fundamentally communicates to an audience.

Actors are becoming acting teachers to managers to help in these essential presentation skills. You may not get excited about roofing tiles, for instance, but the person in charge of the company who makes them knows them inside out and could bore you to death for hours on the subject. The actor's job is to find ways of getting that person to communicate their expertise in an exciting way or 'harness the energy of their convictions'.

*Communication* Actors are teaching managers to communicate better inside their organisations through role-playing and improvisation.

Businesses are hierarchical and there is a very definite 'pecking order' of management. A stage-production also has a 'pecking order' but, when everyone is on the rehearsal-floor, the boss/workers divide often all but disappears, and first-name terms are the norm. The 'boss' — the director — becomes simply the 'professional outside eye', standing in for the audience, and the 'final arbiter' in all decision-making. Through the teamwork necessary and the creativity inherent in the job of acting wonderful new ideas can occur spontaneously — simply through working well together. Many businesses don't work like this. The use of first names is limited, orders are passed along a chain of command, and each managerial link is very wary of the higher ones. There is a persistent 'looking over the shoulder' mentality, a tendency to complicate issues for basic job preservation, and so on. Crucially, teamwork and creativity are restricted by the heavy chain of command. Actors, using the working practices of theatre, are teaching businesses to improve their creativity (and productivity) through better communication.

## Getting work in these fields

So how do you get in on these particular acts? First you have to assess your own skills. (Do you have the ability to pass on those voice lessons you had at drama school? It's one thing to be able to do it yourself; entirely another to teach it to someone else.) Once you've worked out what you could actually do, try writing to selected local businesses — perhaps select firms that manufacture something you know a little about already. A lot of the tips in chapter 9 on writing letters will apply, but remember the modus operandi of the commercial world is slightly more formal. For instance, you should address business contacts by their title and not use first names until invited to do so. Also, when you do make contact remember that they are probably amongst the many who don't understand actors and acting.

It is certainly a good idea to get effective business-cards designed and printed, and a promotional package (brochure, website, and so on) of what you can offer makes you look as though you really know what you are talking about. (This needs a lot of time for thought and a fair outlay of capital.) Make sure that you really do know what you are proposing and what you are going to charge for it. Also be wary of acting jargon. For example, most outside our profession don't know what 'upstage' and 'downstage' mean.

Business is a conservative world; acting is a fairly liberal one. An actor can take advice or being sent up far more easily than most people. Business-people who feel threatened by too much inside knowledge or insulted by their product not being taken seriously will switch off very quickly. Tread carefully and respect their ways. Show them that you can give them what they need and want, not what you think they should have or might be fun. And remember, business-people talk to each other as much as actors do.

If you wish to tap this market, you need to be 'business-like'.

## Role-play companies and agencies

These seem to be growing, however they are quite hard to find and tend to have fairly fixed stables of actors, whom they call in as needed. You can find some of them by searches through *Yellow Pages* and on the Internet (try 'Management Consultants', 'Conference Organisers', and the like) and they do periodically take on new people — generally actors with good experience. All the ones that I know were started up by small groups of actors looking to supplement their incomes.

**As an actor you should know how to:**
- work well in a team or 'interact';
- communicate effectively and convincingly even with repetition;
- present yourself well;
- be self-motivated;
- utilise creative instincts;
- respond well to others;
- convey that 'excitement', that 'need', that made you become an actor in the first place;
- have at your beck and call all the potent power and influence of drama.

**You may also be able to:**
- teach acting techniques and skills;
- motivate others;
- transform technical ideas and concepts into potent theatrical form.

# Chapter Nineteen

# *The Business Side of Being an Actor*

Acting can be an instant business. One day nothing happens and then a few minutes/days/months later it can all be happening. You must always be ready but not constantly on tenterhooks. You have to be personally organised or you could significantly harm your employment prospects.

As an actor you are your own business. You are not only your own work-force but also your publicity and public relations office, accountancy division, IT department, transport manager and, above all, managing director. You may well have an agent, an accountant and a friend with a computer, but none of these people can do anything unless you give them clear direction. You are finally responsible for the success or failure of the business.

## Organisation of Interviews

Lead times for interviews, auditions and castings — even offers of work — seem to be getting shorter as the technology-driven world gets faster. There are a number of aspects you should consider.

**Secretaries and personal assistants** A lot of the business side of being an actor revolves round these individuals; they are the link to the busy director, agent, casting director and so on. A good one can answer all your basic questions. It is she (rarely he) who will deal with practical arrangements. You will usually not meet her or, if you do, you may well not realise it was she with whom you spoke on the phone. She, on the other hand, will almost certainly remember you — especially if there was anything 'out of the ordinary' in your conversation. She is efficient — I've yet to meet one who isn't — and overworked. She doesn't just arrange interviews; she also takes dictation, makes tea, types illegibly written reports and fields phone calls to the boss and to other senior members of staff. It is very important not to make her life any more difficult than it is already as she will have the boss's 'ear'. Her opinions can count. The secretary/PA is an often unconsidered, but not inconsiderable, link in the business of being an actor.

**The details of an interview** You must always be ready to take down full details of any interview when the phone rings. Make sure there are writing materials (and your diary) constantly close by, so you can take down the details of time, exact location, who will be there, basic details of the part and the play (or whatever) and what will be required of you — all as swiftly as possible. If you are bad at remembering all the questions you need to ask, then devise a check list which you can fill in. You will probably be offered a specific time — be ready to say 'Yes' or 'I'll phone you back' with the briefest of pauses for thought. If you can't make the time offered, be ready to suggest an alternative. If that's not possible off the top of your head, don't worry. Phone back when you've had time to think. Whatever you do, don't mess about! Remember, that secretary has probably had to make thirty similar phone calls that afternoon. She has probably never been to the interview-room itself and cannot be more specific than the postal address. Also, she probably knows no more details about the part and the production beyond the brief character-breakdown she typed earlier.

**Phoning back** If it happens that you have to change your time (or cancel), phone back as soon as possible and make sure that you have your original time and date to hand so that the secretary/PA doesn't have to waste time searching.

You may need other information, but don't keep on phoning back time after time because you've thought of yet something else. Think before you phone again. Is there anything further you should be asking about?

Don't be put off a legitimate enquiry by a brusque response. There may be five other people breathing down her neck at the same time she's on the phone to you.

Finally, bear in mind that a recall won't necessarily take place in the same venue as the original interview; it may be in the same building but not in the same room, or in a completely different place altogether.

**An interview whilst you are working** If you are supposed to be working elsewhere at the time of a proposed interview, make sure with your current employer that it will be all right to get away before you accept the appointment. Even if it's only a job to pay the rent, don't think of just 'bunking off'. Don't add to actors' generally untrue image of unreliability.

The best solution is to find a non-acting job that can be flexible and where the employer is sympathetic to some mornings or afternoons being taken off on an irregular basis and at short notice, and to whole weeks or months off whilst you're acting. Or you can sign up with a 'temp' agency. They seem to cover most jobs these days.

If you are working as an actor, most directors are sympathetic and will let you go if at all possible. But don't put him or her in the embarrassing situation of having to say 'No' because you've asked for an obviously busy time — like a production week. However small a part you've got, your absence will affect too many other people adversely. Except in dire emergency, don't make non-urgent doctor's or dentist's appointments unless you are sure you won't be required for rehearsal at that time. Generally, you should make a request to be absent at least three days in advance — if not more.

**Devious tricks** You may hear that 'so-and-so' is interviewing, so you phone up and you are politely told that 'the lists are full'. This might well be true, but it may be worth leaving your name or, much better, writing immediately with all your details — don't rely on your previous submission being found. Don't resort to pleadings or plain deviousness. Someone phoned my dear friend Barbara — now retired, but in her heyday known over the phone to countless agents and actors for her untiring patience and interview-list compiling. The caller asked: 'Where are the auditions next week? Only I have to meet a friend there.' Why couldn't she ask her friend? Yes, it can be worth gate-crashing, but she diminished her chances by trying to pull the wool over Barbara's eyes.

**Always be contactable** If you are moving, make sure that someone will forward letters and pass on new telephone numbers. It is probably better to have some kind of safe house (family, drama school, or the like) who will always do this for you. In fact not all interviews are arranged by phone. For instance, some people prefer to put all the details in writing — saving endless phone calls. (See 'Contact details', page 68.)

If you change agents, don't rely on your former agent passing on the name of your present one. The majority will gladly pass on the inform-ation, but I have been met several times with a dark 'Sorry, we can't help.'

You should keep The Spotlight's Records Department up to date with your 'primary contact number' and agent as they are the final recourse in the search for an untraceable actor. (Equity will not pass on private addresses or phone numbers; they will only forward letters.)

Don't rely on a filing system to match your change-of-address letter with your original letter. Some organisations completely gut their filing systems more often than you might think.

Fundamentally, it is vital that you are always able to receive a message within a few hours. An interview can crop up at any time. You can easily be subject to very short notice — for all kinds of reasons. Always be on standby, but not on tenterhooks. Being an actor is a bit like being a fireman — without the regular salary.

**Recorded messages** So much 'professional' communication is done by phone that these are very important. You should be clear, have a positive attitude and ensure that you can easily be identified — that is, with your full professional name and 'primary contact number'.

*'Whacky' outgoing messages* Most of these are facile and off-putting to a 'professional' caller. I know that the 'child' in you is an essential

part of your actor's make-up, but this kind of message can make you sound irresponsible — the last thing an actor can be.

*Leaving messages* You should ensure that any message you leave is easy for the recipient to write down. Remember, we think faster than we can talk and talk faster than we can write (except those good at shorthand) — think of your voice-teachers as you speak. It can also be an idea to repeat your telephone number. Don't leave messages that are too complicated with numerous different contact numbers and times. You're life may be complicated, but don't make it hard for someone else to follow.

*Checking for messages* You should check at least every day, if not twice. And be prepared for a frustrating nothing.

**Responding to messages** When responding to a message don't presume that the person who left it will remember all about you the instant you give your name on the return call. He or she could easily be awaiting several responses and could now be preoccupied with something completely different.

**Mobile phones** These seem like the perfect answer to the problem of 'always being contactable'. However, quality and reliability of reception is very variable except with the most expensive phones and connection services. Also they are too easily stolen and you can be caught in situations where it's difficult to write down complicated details. Yes, they can be useful for urgent communications, but I suggest that it is much better to have a secure conventional telephone with an answerphone (or a 'Pager' or use a message service).

**The dreaded phone** Some people have a phobia about making phone-calls to people they don't know. There is only one solution: you have to 'act' your way out of it. Try making brief notes about what you need to ask or say. I know someone who suffers from a terrible phone-phobia so he phones a friend first as a warm-up in preparation for a 'professional' call.

It's a good idea to be warm with your 'Hello', or whatever your opening gambit is, when answering the phone. This can ease the way into the conversation, and you might get more from it because you've set yourself up as a friendly sort of person. There is nothing more offputting than a dull, bored voice answering my well-intentioned call.

*Tip* If you're sitting right next to the phone when it rings, don't immediately answer it. Give yourself at least a couple of rings to collect yourself first. Similarly, if you're running for the phone, catch your breath before you pick it up.

**Always confirm** Confirm an appointment if you haven't got an agent and got the details from your flatmate, for example. It is always wise to check those details if they've been passed on verbally unless you feel you can utterly rely on the communicator. Most people not in this profession have no comprehension of how it works and don't realise the importance of taking accurate details.

If the invitation is in writing, it is still essential that you confirm. Just because you know, it doesn't mean that they know that you know. And there are plenty of other people lining up to take your place if you cannot attend. If you can't, say so as soon as possible. It is an act of ultimate selfishness not to do so; too many actors are guilty of this.

**The irrelevant interview** If at the last minute you can't get to an interview or you've got another job which makes it irrelevant, you must communicate that information at once so that there is the possibility that your space can be given to somebody else. Employment-brokers may have short memories in many ways, but they tend to remember people who waste their precious time by simply not turning up.

**But perhaps not so irrelevant** It can be worth going to an interview/ audition even if you can't for domestic reasons work that far from home, say. The director will be doing other productions and a future one might be closer to your home. But tread warily, you may even get an offer. (See 'Turning down an offer', page 99.)

Even if you are committed to another acting job that clashes, it is often a good idea to ask if you can still go along to meet someone you've never met before — you never know what the future may hold — provided he or she is still happy to take time with you.

The crucial thing is to be sure you are not seen to be wasting people's time. Don't go for a musical if you patently cannot sing or if you have two left feet. You have to work out whether you can safely hide unavailability or inability. Be careful!

It is worth going if you've got just a couple of days' filming, for example, that clash — providing it's not at a crucial time during rehearsals. Your having time out can be made a condition of contract. Given sufficient notice, the director might be able to plan things so as to work without you on those days.

**Do your homework!** Much of the preparation work that I've discussed throughout this book could be summarised under this heading. Sufficient 'homework' is an essential part of success in the work-getting jungle. However, don't get paranoid about it and don't find yourself so encumbered with information that you cannot relax and enjoy.

## Casting information

The simple fact is that, with the exception of major musicals, some Fringe productions, most TIE companies and certain specialist casting, managements do not advertise their requirements to the profession as a whole. They'd be swamped if they did.

Not every actor has an agent and no agent is privy to the details of every new project being mounted. You can create opportunities for yourself by hunting out what's in the pipeline and writing in advance of others.

**Getting reliable information** The only way to get reliable casting information is to phone managements directly about future plans. Some will give you short shrift; others will be more helpful. However, if the response is along the lines of 'We don't know yet', don't try to ask for hints of possibilities. It can be very irritating for the person at the other end of the phone because any hold-up in the decision making is holding up almost everybody else in the organisation, and if you are too persistent you will be rubbing salt into the wound. Of course the 'powers that be' have some ideas of what they might or would like to do, but there can be all kinds of hiccups preventing the formal announcement.

**Casting information services** A less time-consuming method is to resort to the various casting information services that advertise in *The Stage*. However, these cost and there are limits to their usefulness — information is sometimes inaccurate, out of date and even occasionally not true.

Very few paying managements actually use these 'casting services' to advertise for actors. In general, it is leaks from 'casting breakdowns', combined with judicious phone calls and combing of forthcoming productions announced, that go into their listings. Essentially their information is of a 'second-hand' nature and is not essentially accurate or still relevant. Writing to try to promote yourself on the basis of what turns out to be 'misinformation' will immediately consign your efforts to the bin, so its well worth checking before committing yet another submission to the post.

For instance, I was inundated with letters from young women (and agents suggesting same) to play a character called Jan in an Agatha Christie play. In their various ways they claimed they could brilliantly convey Jan's 'strange innocence and sweetness of manner'. If they'd read the play or even just the relevant stage directions, and not relied totally on the 'service' concerned, they could easily have discovered that the Jan in question is male.

I'm not saying that all such 'services' are inaccurate — some are very useful, doing their best to ensure the efficacy of their information — but there are ones who seem simply out to exploit actors' hunger for any information at all. Check carefully before you commit your meagre funds. It can be an idea to subscribe to one (or more) in groups to cut down the cost. (Also see 'Internet casting information services', page 92.)

## You!

**Your budget** Somehow accountancy and acting don't quite fit together. It may be that like so many people (not just actors) your grasp of basic mathematics is not good and you wouldn't know a 'cash-flow crisis' until you were drowning in it. The fact is that as an actor you will have an irregular income so you will have to work out some way of organising your funds so that money worries don't take over your life and severely affect your ability to sell yourself — let alone work.

**Your tax and benefits** The actor's tax status has always been a grey area. In the late 1980s the Inland Revenue argued that actors working in theatre should have income tax deducted at source under 'PAYE' ('Pay As You Earn', otherwise known as 'Schedule E'). On 6th April 1990 newcomers lost their 'Schedule D' (self-employed) status for theatre work — this also meant they couldn't offset nearly as many professional expenses against tax. (Under 'Schedule D' you are allowed to offset expenses that are 'wholly and necessarily' incurred; under 'PAYE' expenses have to be 'wholly, exclusively and necessarily' incurred.) In practice this meant that many essential expenses, like photographs, were disallowed. Equity and the managers fought this decision through a test case involving the actors Alec McCowan and Sam West — and won. In 1996, 'Schedule D' for everybody's theatre-earnings was restored. 'Self-Assessment' arrived in 1997 and who knows what the future may hold.

The important thing to do is to keep careful records of your professional expenditure and income (remember, employers have to declare what they've paid you to the Inland Revenue) and be prompt with your tax returns. If you find the annual sorting of all your receipts extremely disagreeable, keep weekly record-sheets. That will lessen the overall strain at the end of the financial year. If in doubt get an accountant who is expert in the ways of the entertainment industry.

The whole question of state benefits for actors changes all the time. Equity rises to every change of legislation and its interpretation. Not only do they have a very good Legal and Welfare department, but they also publish an *Advice and Rights Guide* (free to members) which gives good advice on tax and National Insurance contributions.

**Your body** Do your teeth look OK (especially for television)? Are your hands and fingernails in reasonable condition? Is your body fit and ready for any part? Do you have access to a reasonable range of clothes to cover the many and varied interviews you will attend? Do you have footwear that will not only co-ordinate with these outfits but also leave you with dry feet through the monsoon that suddenly hits on the afternoon of your interview? Think about all aspects of the physical side of your presentation. It is worth investing in clothes, hairdressing and so on, and they are tax-deductible — as is cosmetic dentistry if you can prove your case.

**Your mentality** You should be organised, by keeping notes on every letter written, contact made and so on, but don't make so much of it that you develop a 'filing-cabinet' mentality. I've known actors for whom self-management has become seriously obsessional and has all but killed off the essential free spirit that is fundamental to an actor's emotional equipment. Your imagination and your instinct can be squashed by excessive devotion to your own organisation. It is not only detailed filing that can do this.

**Your psyche** You may have left drama school, but you can (and should) keep on learning. Go to classes — there are now several Actors' Centres round the country (see *Contacts* for addresses). Learn new skills — or revive dormant ones that might improve your work prospects. Take a youth drama group. Go to see plays, read plays, arrange play-readings with friends and perhaps rehearse a few scenes and/or audition speeches. Never sit around moaning — if you've got a legitimate complaint (about your agent, for instance) then do something about it. Never let your activity-level drop below the point where you can no longer act. Very few are able to rise instantly out of a slough of television, cigarettes and alcohol to get work — in spite of what some may claim. You should honestly be able to respond to 'Any work?' with 'No, but I'm very busy.' And, remember employment-brokers can 'smell' desperation.

**Your other job** Make sure that the other job(s) that you do when out of acting work give you sufficient stimulus. It's possible that nothing can replace acting for you, but when your not earning from it you need to have paid work that will not deaden those essential creative juices. Often a positive attitude to a seemingly mechanical job can do the trick. It is important to have a foot in the 'real' world — don't just live in a world of acting.

**Getting stuck** It is true that if you keep on working in the same places or media you may not be considered for others. The director of a straight play can be deeply suspicious of someone who has only done musicals for several years, for instance. As a general rule it is better to aim to move around at least to some extent. Some such prejudices are irrational and unfounded, but there is a general truth lurking in the background. Acting is about what you can do with your instincts, energies and imagination as well as with your technical skills. The former (and possibly the latter) will always fossilise somewhat if you work in the same area for too long. The same is true of being stuck out of work.

**Typecasting** It is possible to become stuck in a type of part — 'typecast'. Too many people complain too much about this. If your 'type' is consistently getting you work — stick to it. Changing your image (unless you reach a very high level) will put you many rungs down that casting ladder.

## 'Professional' public relations

Apart from the letter-writing and interview-round you will always be on the lookout for a 'chance encounter' with someone of influence. Employment-brokers of all kinds, and in all media, can seem elusive — there is too much else to be doing, as I hope is patently clear from the earlier chapters — so think carefully about your social intercourse with them outside the interview-room.

**Fool's gold** It can happen that you phone an organisation, expecting the secretary, but by chance you get straight through to someone with 'casting clout'. Don't think you've struck gold and try to keep them talking to draw attention to yourself unless they really seem happy to chat. You should measure this situation as you would measure an interview and exploit it carefully. It is an insensitive individual who can just slam the phone down on somebody who hasn't finished a conversation. Concentrate briefly on the purpose of your call and don't be a limpet! Bad behaviour in this area is likely to be remembered and count against you in the future.

**'How did I do?'** It can be useful to find out how an interview or audition went. Some directors are willing to discuss this but almost never directly with the interviewee. The only way to get this kind of feedback is via your agent. Don't phone the director concerned yourself; you could cause great embarrassment even if you did come over well.

**'They left in the interval'** This is one of the commonest complaints I hear from actors about agents and casting directors who've come to see them in a production. It doesn't necessarily mean that they hated you. Such people see a lot of plays, have been working all day and will probably have to work all day tomorrow. And they can often learn all they need to know in one brief appearance.

It has been suggested to me that when inviting you could add, 'I don't mind if you leave in the interval.' I'm not so sure if this is a good idea; it sounds a bit pathetic to me. Much better simply to face up to the possibility and accept gracefully any subsequent apology.

**'They didn't even come!'** It's a simple fact that there are far too many productions for agents and casting directors to cover — and do the rest of their work. You simply have to persist and be inventive with your invitations.

**'What did you think?'** If you do meet them in the bar afterwards, don't put someone of influence in an embarrassing situation by asking this. I know it can be good to 'cut through the crap' and maybe get some constructive notes, but it's hard work giving constructive criticism, you may get more than you bargained for and you don't know who that person knows. Discretion is the better part of getting work.

**Adrenaline** After a live performance you will be more 'adrenalised' than members of your audience — which may contain somebody of 'influence'. Should you encounter such a person in the bar afterwards don't 'splurge' all over them.

**Turning up on spec** Don't turn up on spec at the office of someone with casting clout, hoping to meet the incumbent. It is a hard-hearted individual who says 'No!' when you are on the doorstep, and you will put the secretary/PA into an awkward position. I know this kind of 'hustling' happens elsewhere, but that's not the way we like to do things in the UK.

**The chance encounter** You may be seeing a production that a friend is in and be introduced to the director in the bar afterwards. Don't try to monopolise him or her. Write the next day. The same is true with somebody else's agent, a casting director whom somebody else has invited, and so on.

Similarly, you might meet such a person at a party. The same rules apply. Let them have the night off and have a good time! That's what parties are for. They will be aware that you regard them as a potential employer. If you can temporarily make that seem irrelevant, you've scored a lot of points. I introduced myself to an actor whose performance I'd very much enjoyed and told him so. He knew that I was a director and was very appreciative, but quickly and easily changed the subject. It became a delightful chat between two people on mutual interests and concerns. Very shortly afterwards a suitable part came up and I offered it to him. In a sense he'd done an audition speech/reading (the performance) and an interview (our chat). What more did I need to know?

The opposite is also true. I have known actors walk deliberately away — as if I had leprosy — in order not to put me in a quasi-interview situation. That is equally alienating.

**Another time, another place** If you've already met a director, casting director or an agent, don't be unduly perturbed if they don't remember you immediately when you meet in a different context. It's not necessarily a reflection on their attitude towards you. Once, after a long day of auditions, I bumped into an actor I'd interviewed and liked only about an hour earlier. He said 'Hello,' but for what must have been a good thirty seconds I didn't know who the hell he was. He was most offended, but as I pointed out he now had a hat on, we were meeting again in a totally different context and I'd met thirty other actors that day.

**Being seen around** It is true that being seen in the 'right' places at the 'right' times can create work opportunities. There are restaurants and clubs that are fashionable for the casting Mafiosi. And it is possible that a chance sighting by one of them could set up the chain of events that lead to work. However, this gambit is rarely successful. Persistent wining and dining can be very expensive, and all fashions have a nasty habit of changing. Only a good agent, with a very good knowledge of what's going on, can guide you in this respect.

Going to productions and other related events can make you contacts. But go with the idea of being involved in the main purpose, let the chance of 'being seen' remain a possibility at the back of your mind. If this kind of 'possibility' dominates the proceedings for you, you will almost certainly alienate the person you seek to impress. (There are certain actors' haunts where I have so often observed people sitting, pretending to read and eking out cups of coffee, but with eyes flicking this way and that. Once, I swear, I saw someone seated in the same place for the eight hours I was working in that building.) Be aware of chance! It is extremely difficult to create; you can only be aware of circumstances in which it might happen.

**'Keep in touch'** Take this statement at face value. It can occur in all kinds of circumstance — after a close-run rejection, for instance. It may take years to evolve into an actual job, but it is well worth writing periodically with an update of your recent doings. That original statement was made because the speaker cared about you and your work. You should reciprocate without trying to embarrass him or her into employing you. This could pay dividends in years to come.

## Public relations whilst working
It is not just communications with influential professionals that you need to consider carefully. When in work there are other people to bear in mind.

**Learn names!** A well run organisation will send you a list of names before starting a job — cast, crew and sometimes permanent staff. Try learning them beforehand and aim to establish contact with as many as possible as early as is feasible — without wasting anybody's time. Of course this will be more difficult in the larger organisations; in fact you many never finally succeed in meeting everyone — but word of your positive efforts will get around and stand you in good stead.

**Technical staff** 'A lot of hard, and sometimes dirty work, and very little of the glory' is the lot of the technical team. An actor's response might be 'We take the criticisms.' Yes, actors are the front-line troops, but a 'front line' is useless without reliable back-up. You will get better support if you work 'with them' instead of treating them as servants, and backstage misbehaviour travels easily to front-of-house. Always aim to get to know and work well with everyone involved. The most surprising people can have good ideas to help you. And a few of them will rise to positions where they could employ you — directors (and other employment-brokers) have got to start somewhere. Some actors like to give dressers, cleaners and stage-doorkeepers tips or presents at the end of a run. This can be a pleasant gesture to the apparently 'lowliest of the low', but not everybody can afford it and some regard it as patronising. Whatever you feel and whatever your financial situation, they are part of the 'bricks and mortar' of the profession and need just as much care and attention as you do. (In television the equivalents are dressers and make-up artists.)

Always take care of your costumes, leave your dressing-room tidy and clear it out properly when the production is over.

**Other members of staff** Don't ignore, or be offhand with, members of staff not connected directly to the production side — the box-office, for instance. A theatre, for example, is a tight-knit community; word will get around. Especially, don't get into the traditional slagging off of the administrator and the publicity department. I know that some are less efficient than they should be, but it is unwise to think that an idle barb shot in their direction will do you no harm. These are the kind of people who are close to the director's everyday thinking and might well be asked their opinion of an actor or for a suggestion for casting. Administrative staff work totally different hours from actors, and what they put into their work is often badly misunderstood. (And vice versa.) If you feel you have a legitimate complaint or even a positive suggestion, make sure you place it in the appropriate ear and don't shout it round the bar or backstage.

## Essential professionalism

Being an actor carries as much responsibility towards other profes-sionals as being a parent does for a child.

**A call** A 'call' means ready to start at that time, not the time for you to grab a cup of tea. The actor may be last in the organisational chain of command, but that doesn't mean that you can be lax about being 'ready to start'. I know that calls rarely start on time, but there is usually a good reason. Whatever that 'reason', there should be no reason for you also to be late. As you are last in the 'chain' you have the potential to hold up all those people ahead of you. If you are just five minutes late and have kept a dozen people waiting, you have wasted the equivalent of one 'man-hour' of working-time.

**Waiting** This invariably happens whilst everything technical is sorted out (especially in film and television) — the time this takes can be as long as the proverbial 'piece of string'. Your call includes that inevitable wait and you must be prepared for it. You absolutely cannot be late — keeping the technical crew waiting, even for a few minutes, can cost a disproportionate amount of money.

**Responsibility for yourself** Acting is not something you can do 'under par'. If you persistently put yourself at risk by indulging in such potentially dangerous sports as hang-gliding, heavy drinking and trusting that the train company will get you there 'just on time', you could endanger your ability to work well and could waste other people's time. Once again the public image of the chaotic, dizzy actor cannot be part of your working life.

Even when you are not working as an actor, such risk-taking can cost you dear if it becomes well known.

**Personal problems** Part of the professionalism of acting is not to bring your personal problems into the production. In extreme circumstances, directors are generally very sympathetic and realise that there is a limit to this aspect of professionalism. An actor with real emotional worries on their mind will probably not be able to work well and can waste working-time. For the sake of the production it is better to give someone in this situation time, within limits, to sort things out. A friend was given a whole day out of a tight filming schedule when her father died suddenly and unexpectedly; she only went when the director insisted.

**Private information** As I've said before, rehearsing is probably 'one of the most intimate shared human activities'. You will discover a lot about the private parts — in a general sense — of your compatriots. Keep that information to yourself for your own good as well as theirs. The whiplash of gossip can rebound on you.

**Your address book** Apart from basic tittle-tattle, keep written information like your address book to yourself. You may be given the private addresses and telephone numbers of famous and/or influential people whom you work with. These will often be ex-directory for a good reason. Giving out such information is a betrayal of that trust inherent in, and so necessary to, our profession. Also, keep your address book in a secure place.

## Final notes

Be straightforward and efficient. Don't faff around. If you do you are wasting busy people's time; such irritating behaviour will almost certainly be remembered and count against you for a long time to come. You never know who or what could have an influence on the casting process. In fact anybody outside the profession — someone you work for or socialise with — could be an influence on your getting work in the future. I know someone who got a business presentation job which earned her over £2000 in a week via someone for whom she had cleaned seventeen years earlier and hadn't seen since.

Remember that 'bad news' travels very fast in this profession. Be careful about running somebody down; you never know who might know who, who might know... The grapevine is very strong and can exaggerate remarkably quickly. The tiniest misbehaviour can damn you for some time to come.

Finally, if you've enjoyed doing a particular job, it is well worth dropping a 'thank you' note to the director or whoever is appropriate — without being creepy about it. It doesn't cost much and can earn you a lot of goodwill.

# Coda

What follow are some of the underlying ideas that guide my working life, which I hope you might find useful as you battle on through your career.

## Two theories

**Energies** Much of what I've written can be summed up by saying 'assess and respond to the energy of the situation'. For example, some directors like to be laid-back; that doesn't necessarily mean they are not working well, and we all know people who operate at such intensity that it can be difficult to get a word in edgeways. Some brilliant work can be achieved by the intense director communicating so well with the actors and technicians that they in turn communicate to the audience with such success that it glosses over the cracks in the production. The same can be true of the laid-back approach where the director acts, overtly, as an observer rather than as a motivator. The actors and technicians seem to do all the work themselves, but subtly the director may well be drawing very good work out of those people. Most are somewhere in between or may adjust to each circumstance. Whatever the approach, try to respond to it and try not to dissipate the overall energy of an interview, for instance through over-apologising or talking too much. Aim to keep your energy going, look for a way to exchange energies with your interviewer and make sure that the overall energy of the situation doesn't get so low that the whole thing fizzles out or so high that it explodes out of control.

**Absolutes** There is no such thing as an absolute. I know that is an 'absolute' statement, but in order to exist we have to have faith that certain things (like that there is solid ground beneath us) are absolutely true in order to stay sane. Quantum theory says that measurements of physical objects (position, speed, and so on) are only true to a certain degree of certainty, or tolerance, however good our measuring instruments are; even the simple act of observation disturbs the observed object. This makes no perceptible difference with everyday objects. It only really matters when observing extremes. (This is not a fanciful abstract idea. The microchip is just one example of its practical application.)

   Much of what I have discussed in this book is, I believe, a manifestation of the equivalent in human interactions: for example, the speech that works well for one director but dies a death for another one — sometimes for no apparent reason. If this is the case, and you have faith in your speech and the way you do it, then stick to it. It is your 'absolute' (until some improvement hits you), all the time recognising that its reception is finally beyond your power. In other words, develop a feel for probability to help you through, which is always open to receive a chance bonus or cope with an unforeseen knock.

Some people find this non-deterministic, non-causal concept of life very disturbing. I find it very comforting. It means that we've got very little to lose and a lot to gain — especially in the profession of acting where there are too many variables to comprehend fully. And good acting is finally about what you can do beyond the apparent confines of mortal mind and body.

## Some other thoughts

**'But habit is a great deadener'** So says Vladimir in Samuel Beckett's brilliant tragi-comedy *Waiting for Godot*. You might like to respond with Estragon's line, earlier in the play: 'We are all born mad. Some remain so.' I am simply using it as a headline because it has a certain ring to it which illustrates my next point. As an actor you have to be continually exploring your art. Sticking only to what you know, especially in your first few years, can deaden those essential instincts that are fundamental to acting. Of course, you will need to fall back on 'what you know' in certain circumstances, but you must always be prepared for that flash of inspiration that can move you on another quantum leap. The need to learn and explore should stay with you, without your becoming obsessive about it. Excessive internal examination is just one route to despair.

**Despair** As an actor you will often be disappointed, therefore despair is a potential part of the actor's condition but it cannot become part of your professional persona. Despair is a cancer that drains essential energies out of not only you but also those around you — and other actors, like relatives, are especially vulnerable. Nobody wants to employ an actor who threatens, however unconsciously, to depress the rest of the company.

I have, on several occasions, been asked to consider someone who 'has been through a bad time'. I will consider him or her if appropriate, but not on the grounds of charity. I am sympathetic, but it is not an area in which I am prepared to take risks. It has been suggested to me that by giving such people a job I might help in their rehabilitation. This may be true, but I am only an amateur psychiatrist, which could be dangerous, and is there really the time available? Those people and their nearest and dearest have to solve the essential problems. Any work can only be seen as the final stage of the rehabilitation process. Despair is not something that you can 'act' your way out of; only patient effort can destroy it.

Clinical depression requires professional help, but you can help yourself to avoid it overwhelming you by consistently looking for ways to keep yourself buoyant.

**Keep buoyant** You have to believe that somehow, somewhere there is acting work for you. You cannot sit back and wait for it; you have to work at getting it, but don't dedicate all your waking hours to this task. Have other things to do and keep in touch with other people, not just with other actors. The everyday events in the local newsagents can provide not only light relief but also valuable character-studies. Build yourself a set of activities to cope with the inevitable waiting-periods — for an offer (or not), even for an interview. Find a temporary job which gives you contact with other people. Don't feel you are no longer an actor if you are having to spend your evenings serving behind a bar instead of treading the boards.

Waiting can be the principal contribution to an actor's psyche breaking down and with it his or her ability to function at all. Keep your despair for your lover/mother/cat/budgie/pillow. Learn to handle waiting well; don't allow it to get you down constantly. You have to keep up your survival and fighting energies or you will sink without trace. I have seen this happen too often. Keep buoyant.

**Determination** The extraordinary example of Nelson Mandela who, after 27 years in prison, emerged almost as if he'd never been incarcerated at all is an object lesson for us all. I do not exaggerate when I say that you, the actor, will often need to be similarly determined in your quest for work. I've known a number of now well-known actors whilst they struggled up the greasy pole of success. Some found it within a few years, but it took at least one twenty-five years of determined effort — keeping going in spite of persistent rejections. That determination is not blind; it is also allied with a little cunning.

'The point is to keep going; not to get rotten.'
Henri Cartier-Bresson

**Finally** Find your own way of using all this advice. Think of this as a set of guidelines to make your life easier. If you use it slavishly, denying your actor's imagination and instinct, I certainly won't employ you. If you can't find something you wholeheartedly disagree with, then give up now. I am not saying that I don't believe in everything I've written and am trying to cover myself. The greatest exponents of any art (or science) are those who know and understand the rules and then go beyond them. 'Logic controls the excesses of my imagination' was how a man — the nearest to 'genius' I've ever met — put it. The most interesting actors are the ones who cleverly break rules and appear dangerous.

# Postscript

After decades of decline things are beginning to look up on the UK theatre funding front and we have promises of more original drama for television. Combine these with the rise of the Internet and I can foresee an increase in the amount of acting work available — with the latter also empowering actors through the enormous opportunities for easy exchange of information it provides. However, we must be vigilant and continue to resist the attempts of commerce to rule and erode 'quality' work. ('Whenever I did anything just because I thought it was going to be commercial it was a failure. And whenever I did something because I thought it was good it turned out to be commercial.' Jean-Louis Barrault.)

'Anybody who thinks he's written the definitive book is a fool.' I caught this statement on Radio 4. I don't know who the speaker was, but I certainly agree. New thoughts and ideas come to me every time I reread this. Others come from friends and from working with actors and students — an ever bubbling stream of qualifications, clarifications and illumination. However, there comes the moment when commitment to print is necessary. This will not stop me from continuing to collect material — I will go on enquiring, listening observing and experimenting. The Internet has given me the marvellous opportunity to publish periodically any changes, new thoughts and experiences. You will find all these on my website <www.simon.dunmore.btinternet.co.uk>. Meanwhile I will continue to receive all comments and criticisms gratefully.

Finally, this book cannot create more work, but I hope that it might make whole process of getting it a little fairer.

'If we need a new world we are certain, finally to invent it.'
(From *White Rose* by Peter Arnott.)

# Bibliography

## Books for aspiring, student and young actors
Peter Barkworth, *The Complete About Acting* (Methuen, 1991). Another very good book about acting and getting work.

Simon Dunmore, *Alternative Shakespeare Auditions for Women* (A & C Black, 1997). My first collection of fifty less well-known speeches for women.

Simon Dunmore, *MORE Alternative Shakespeare Auditions for Women* (A & C Black, 1999). My second collection of fifty less well-known speeches for women.

Simon Dunmore, *Alternative Shakespeare Auditions for Men* (A & C Black, 1997). My collection of fifty less well-known speeches for men.

Ellis Jones, *Teach Yourself Acting* (Hodder & Stoughton Ltd., 1998). A good overview of acting and the profession.

Anna Scher, *Desperate to Act* (Lions, 1988). Brilliant, basic advice for those so 'desperate' from a lady who should know.

William Shakespeare, *Hamlet, Prince of Denmark*. Especially Hamlet's advice to the players (Act 3, scene 2), which is some of the best advice on acting ever given.

Clive Swift, *The Job of Acting* (Harrap, Revised 1984). Although some of it is out of date, this book is a wonderful read from an experienced and caring professional.

Malcolm Taylor, *The Actor and the Camera* (A & C Black, 1994). Another good 'primer' for the beginner.

## Other career advice books for actors
Ed Hooks, *The Audition Book* (3rd edition, Back Stage Books, 2000). Excellent reading if you're thinking of trying your hand in the US. It's also worth looking at Ed's website for his excellent 'Craft Notes' <www.edhooks.com>.

Peter Messaline and Miriam Newhouse, *The Actor's Survival Kit* (3rd edition, Simon & Pierre, 1999). Well worth reading if you're thinking of trying your hand in Canada.

## Books for any actor
Stephen Aaron, *Stage Fright: It's Role in Acting* (University of Chicago Press, 1986). Fascinating book, written by a psychotherapist who is also an experienced director and teacher.

Brian Bates, *The Way of the Actor* (Century Hutchinson, 1986). Very interesting insights into the inner workings of the actor's psyche.

Peter Brook, *The Empty Space* (Penguin, 1990). Written in the 1960s, but still essential reading.

Adrian Cairns, *The Making of the Professional Actor* (Peter Owen Publishers, 1996). A fascinating study of the history, and possible future, of the art of acting.

Simon Callow, *Being an Actor* (Penguin, 1995). Autobiographical books by famous actors are generally useless in terms of practical career advice. However, this one — part autobiography and part advice — has a great deal of down-to-earth common sense. His famous 'manifesto' on directors' theatre is spot on.

Nicholas Craig, *I, an Actor* (Pavilion Books, 1988). A very funny send-up of the starry actor's autobiography. A must.

Uta Hagen, *A Challenge for the Actor* (Macmillan, 1991). The best book on acting ever written.

Richard Hornby, *The End of Acting: a radical view* (Applause Books, 1992). Revelatory insights into the processes of acting.

David Mamet, *True and False* (Faber and Faber, 1998). This book cuts through much of the mythology that surrounds acting.

Kenneth Rea, *A Better Direction* (Calouste Gulbenkian Foundation, 1989). A very thorough inquiry into directors and the need for more training opportunities.

Michael Sanderson, *From Irving to Olivier — A Social History of the Acting Profession* (Athlone Press, 1984). A very expensive, but nevertheless fascinating study of the actor's world over the last century.

Michael Shurtleff, *Audition* (Walker & Company, 1984). An American book which should be read. It contains brilliant insights and thoughts to help any actor.

# Index